AFFAIRS IN ORDER

AFFAIRS IN ORDER

A COMPLETE RESOURCE GUIDE
TO DEATH AND DYING

Patricia Anderson

MACMILLAN PUBLISHING COMPANY
New York

MAXWELL MACMILLAN CANADA
Toronto

Macmillan Publishing Company
866 Third Avenue
New York, NY 10022

Maxwell Macmillan Canada, Inc.
1200 Eglinton Avenue East, Suite 200
Don Mills, Ontario M3C 3N1

Macmillan Publishing Company is part of the
Maxwell Communication Group of Companies.

Library of Congress Cataloging-in-Publication Data
Anderson, Patricia.
Affairs in order: a complete resource guide to death and dying / Patricia
Anderson.
p.   cm.
Includes index.
ISBN 0-02-501991-0
1. Death—United States—Handbooks, manuals, etc.   2. Wills—United
States—Popular works.   I. Title.
HQ1073.5.U6A53   1991
306.9—dc20   90-43268

No village law, no law of market town,
No law of a single house is this—
Of all the world and all the worlds of Gods,
This only is the Law, that all things are impermanent.

E.A. BURTT, ed.
The Teachings of the Compassionate Buddha

Contents

vii

III: IN THE AFTERMATH

Preface

A student, enrolled in a death education class, volunteered to take part in an experiment that included a simulated dying experience. Later, when asked if the experience had been of any help to him he responded: "Definitely. It has given me a much calmer fear of death."

Peter R. Prunkl and Rebecca L. Berry, *Death Week: Exploring the Dying Process*

I am going to die. So are you. Everybody is. This truth remains in spite of the fact that most of us ignore it completely. Thus, when death enters our lives, as it absolutely, inevitably will, it often surprises, and almost always frightens us, considerably.

This wasn't always so. In fact, it very recently wasn't so. In the past, death was viewed differently than it is now—more familiarly, more a part of the natural order of things. But something happened. Things changed.

Over the last fifty years our view and experience of death have altered dramatically. As described by Philippe Ariès, a social historian who has written widely on the subject:

In our day, in approximately a third of a century, we have witnessed a brutal revolution in traditional ideas and feelings, a revolution so brutal that social observers have not failed to be struck by it. It is really an absolutely unheard-of phenomenon. Death, so omnipresent in the past that it was familiar, would be effaced, would disappear. It would become shameful and forbidden.[1]

Death moved out of the home and into the hospital, where doctors practice "death management" and death itself means failure. Science and technology proceed in efforts to transform death from an acknowledged certainty to a possibly curable disorder. In the meantime, people live longer and die out of sight; we can grow up never seeing a real person die, never knowing what death actually looks like. Today dying is different than it was before, and we are different because of it.

Our discomfort with death has been widely noted, spurring some efforts to reconsider the fact of death in our lives. New phrases in our vocabulary such as "right to die" and "death with dignity"; a growing body of books and articles; an increased interest in finding better ways to provide death care and support; the pressing requirements of new medical and legal options; scientific exploration of "near death" and "after death" states, all indicate a growing interest in the popular culture and a concern about the experience of dying.

Still, most people have little or no functional information to help them when actually confronted with death, their own or that of another. The purpose of this book is to provide that information and help you make decisions around and about dying. It answers the practical questions that will arise when you are faced with death and addresses the choices you have when considering your responsibilities toward others and toward yourself. It describes requirements and alternatives, lists resources and references, and collects in one sourcebook a variety of possibilities.

This book is offered in the hope that if we have some idea of what we can and can't do about it, we, too, will gain "a much calmer fear of death."

Acknowledgments

The material in this book has been drawn from a range of sources, including interviews, telephone conversations, letters and other printed materials, as well as all the books listed as resources, bibliographic references, or otherwise cited.

Many professionals have answered questions and provided information, giving generously of their time and attention. I am indebted to all of them.

In particular I wish to thank Elizabeth V. Smith, R.N., M.S. (hospice nurse and pain management consultant) and Fenella Rouse (executive director, Concern for Dying/Society for the Right to Die) for their knowledgeable advice and congenial assistance. I am grateful as well to the numerous friends and acquaintances who tolerated what I'm sure seemed a rather perverse curiosity on my part and were kind enough to give their time and open enough to share their personal experiences.

My undying gratitude goes to Tom Damrauer, Barbara Osborn, and Laura Green, who not only provided excellent research and editorial assistance but splendid moral support as well. Thanks also to Kevin Osborn, who helped develop portions of the text, to Robin White, who read and made suggestions on several chapters, and to

Theresa A. Czajkowska, whose expertise helped this book get into print. I would like to express my personal appreciation to my agent, Elizabeth Frost Knappman; my lawyer, Peter Matorin; and my therapist, Bob Mendelson; to my *hanai* sister Joanna Wyss, whose personal and professional advice are both invaluable; and to Peter Berg, for all these years. And last, but most especially, I want to thank my husband, Gregory Scott Shifrin, for his unqualified support and (okay, okay) *infinite* patience.

How to Use This Book

This book describes your options, tells you what you need to know to make good decisions, and lists where to go for help and what to read to find out more. It is divided into three parts—before, during, and after a death.

Part I tells you how to plan ahead. It addresses making a will, planning for disposition and commemoration, and preparing an advance directive or "living will."

Part II is about dealing with imminent death. It covers the definition of death, bioethics, euthanasia, and the uses of life-support systems; describes where you die and why it matters; and tells about hospice programs and death care.

Part III is for survivors, those dealing with the aftermath of a death. It describes how to make arrangements for disposition and for a funeral or memorial service; how to administer an estate and finalize business affairs; and how to find help in grief and bereavement.

A listing of *Resources and Support* follows each chapter, describing books, groups, organizations, and agencies offering assistance.

An *Appendix* listing books and resources for finding help facing death follows Part III.

We have made every effort to list only books that are readily available. Check with your local bookstores and your public library. If stores do not have a book in stock, ask if they will obtain it for you. Or you may wish to order directly from the publisher. (Many publishers have toll-free telephone numbers and will fill your order quickly.)

140,348 people die every single day;
140,347 of them are not ready.

Although death itself is inevitable, its consequences are not. There is a lot we can do to affect the quality of the experience both for ourselves and for others. Here's how.

Planning Ahead

I

I

Your Will

I have nothing, I owe a great deal, and the rest I leave to the poor.

Rabelais

~~~~~~~~~~~~~~~~~

Preparing a will is a smart thing to do. It's the only way to ensure that your property goes where you want it to go. More than smart, making a will is a considerate thing to do. Taking the time now to effect a clear and orderly statement of your wishes regarding money, real estate, and personal property will save your survivors a lot of problems later, when they are least able to cope. Your will helps and protects those you love after you are gone.

So if it's such a great thing, why do 70 percent of us die without one? People often assume that making a will is a complicated and confusing process. We believe lawyers are the only ones who can do it and that it will cost a lot of money. We think we don't need one, or we try not to think about it at all.

Some find it difficult to make decisions about gifts and legacies and the division of property. Indecision can cause procrastination. But the most interesting excuse is the one least admitted to—super-

3

stition. Many of us fear that preparing for death will somehow bring it about.

Don't let any of these reasons keep you from doing it. We can clear up our confusion quite easily. There are choices that minimize or eliminate costs. Decisions can be made and changed if need be. And to date there has not been one single documented case of death from will writing.

DOES EVERYONE NEED A WILL?

Sometimes people think they don't need a will because they don't have a lot of money or property. They're wrong. Just about every adult needs one, because a will helps clarify the questions that are raised at every death, regardless of the circumstances.

A will addresses a number of matters. You can forgive debts owed you at the time of your death; you can reinforce directions and wishes regarding body or organ donation; if you live with someone to whom you are not married, you can ensure that they are given the authority to carry out your wishes; and you can make specific gifts to particular friends or family members.

Beyond property is the matter of children. Anyone with minor children most definitely needs a will, because a will is the legal means by which you name a child's guardian in the event of the death of the parent(s).

In addition, sometimes people who have been financially poor during life die in a way that leaves unexpected money (i.e., a "wrongful death" lawsuit creating a substantial amount of cash to be dispensed by your estate, etc.), or you might receive an unanticipated asset before you die. If you win the lottery one day, and are killed by a bus the next, your loved ones are going to wish you had made a will.

YOUR ESTATE

In Western culture we place a high value on material objects. Property, tangibles, and currency itself are the most esteemed commodities in our society. Our habits, politics, and customs reflect this priority, as does the legal system. When we die, that system moves into action and regulates the disposition of our material belongings. In fact, as far as the state is concerned, once you're dead, your property is pretty much all that matters. Your life may be over, but your "estate" lives on.

The word *estate* simply means what you own (and what you owe). It is the legal word for the sum total of all your possessions and assets as well as debts and other claims against you. You have an estate whether you are rich or poor.

WITHOUT A WILL

When you die without a will, it is called dying "intestate." Having ignored your right to direct the division of your property, you lose that right, and the state does it for you, based on laws drawn up by the legislature.

Intestacy laws vary from state to state, but in general the formula divides property among spouse, children, or parents, or if there are none, brothers and sisters or more distant relatives. If you have no relatives with a legal right to inherit, your property goes to the state.

In some states the surviving spouse receives half and any children the balance; other states divide among spouse, children, and parents, while still others do otherwise, depending on differing circumstances and legal definitions of "child" or "next of kin," etc.

Who Is Your Next of Kin?
The definition of the phrase *next of kin* can be disputed. Most interpretations include husbands and wives, but some are limited to the nearest *blood* relation. Another long-standing issue before the law is the question of legitimacy. Does an illegitimate child share, equally and legally, in an inheritance? What about adopted children? These kinds of questions can be avoided altogether if you leave a clearly written will but can cause trouble if you die intestate.

The state looks at beneficiaries as ciphers in a formula, not as individuals who meant something to you. If you die without a will, it is unlikely that your property will be distributed as you would have wished.

Who's Minding the Kids?

If you die without a will, who gets custody of your children? The law does not view children as property. It does, however, require that minor children (under the age of eighteen) have a guardian. A surviving biological parent has priority rights as concerns guardianship, but what happens if both parents die simultaneously? Or if the natural parents are separated or divorced and the survivor is not available or suitable to take over as guardian?

In such cases, the court decides who should be the legal guardian. The person named in a parent's will is given primary consideration in any final judicial decision.

Without a will the court does not know what you would have intended. A decision then depends on many unforeseeable factors and can take a considerable amount of time. The court becomes very receptive to anyone volunteering for the responsibility of guardianship. If no one comes forth, government agencies take charge of the child. Without a will you are leaving your children open to the vagaries of the judicial system and quite possibly to considerable trauma.

Naming your choice of guardian for your child could be the single most important function of your will. Don't assume you'll survive the other parent of your children or that s/he will survive you. It is important to realize that your children could be without either parent and to provide accordingly.

Who'll Take Care of Everything?

If you have no children, are not married, and don't care how your property is distributed, you may think: Why bother? If I die tomorrow, I'll just let the state take care of it.

The problem is, the state doesn't "take care" of anything; it simply enforces the law. Someone else will have to take care of everything, and that means hiring a lawyer, petitioning the court, making sure that taxes, fees, and debts are paid, and finalizing your affairs. Dying intestate can cost a lot. Legal fees can mount, and taxes may be significantly greater than they would have been otherwise.

Someone will be compelled to handle all this and more. You can leave it to chance and the possibility of imposing a real hardship on those you leave behind, or you can name someone beforehand who agrees to take this responsibility and who will know what you wanted and why. This person is called an executor.

THE EXECUTOR

An executor* (also called an administrator or personal representative in some states) is the individual you name in your will to administer your estate. S/he is the person who will take care of things.

Your executor need not be a lawyer and usually isn't. Most people choose their mate, another trusted relative, or a close friend to serve in this capacity. The main criterion is trust. You want this person to fulfill your wishes when you are no longer there to request, advise, or beseech. When possible, choose someone who benefits under the will, as they then have a real interest in doing the job. You should name an alternative executor as well in case your original choice is not alive or capable when your will goes into effect.

Generally speaking, as legally defined, an executor's powers and responsibilities are pretty comprehensive. However, in the average case, what an executor actually does is to hire an attorney (if one is needed), sign legal papers, take care of paying the final bills and any taxes owed (with money from the estate), and make sure your property goes where you said it should go.

If you don't have a will, someone must petition the court to appoint an executor to take care of the business of your estate. This appointee may be an officer or crony of the court, not someone known to you or in any way aware of your circumstances, desires, or preferences. In addition, a court-appointed administrator or executor requires a bond and often a fee, whereas the executor named by you in your will, while legally entitled to a fee, often agrees to forgo compensation, especially if s/he is an inheritor of the estate.

Naming someone you trust as your executor gives him or her the power to ensure that your wishes are followed and, if anything has changed or affected the letter of your instructions, to decide how to follow your intentions. Someone will have to do it in any case. If you name an executor, s/he will be able to take care of your business with impunity.

If you are serving as executor for someone else, see part III, chapter 9.

---

*The terms *executrix* or *administratrix* are sometimes used to connote a female executor. Herein the term *executor* will refer to either gender.

CAN I DO IT MYSELF OR DO I NEED
A LAWYER?

Having a lawyer write your will is not a legal requirement. In fact, many people can do it themselves.

Most lawyers recommend hiring a lawyer to prepare a will, thus reinforcing a common misconception that the whole process is complicated and requires special expertise. Making a will is complicated only to the extent that your property, money, or relationships are complicated.

The preparation of a will can be compared with the preparation of a tax return. If you take the time to acquaint yourself with the requirements of the job and understand what the laws are, you can do it yourself.

However, if your holdings, your finances, or your personal life are relatively complex, if you want to take advantage of intricate procedures to avoid taxes and other costs associated with the transfer of large estates, or if, for whatever reason, you simply prefer not to do it yourself, you will choose to hire a lawyer.

Following is a list of situations in which you should seek the help of an attorney.

**You Should Work with a Lawyer to Prepare
Your Will If:**

- Your estate is worth more than the Federal Estate Tax Exemption of $600,000 and will be subject to a substantial federal tax unless you engage in tax planning.

- You have property in more than one state or county (or country).

- You want to give a gift with complex shared ownership or place controls on property to be given to beneficiaries.

- You own a part of a small business and have questions as to the rights of surviving owners, your ownership share, etc.

- You must make arrangements for long-term care of a beneficiary (e.g., a handicapped child).

- You fear someone will contest your will.

- You wish to disinherit, or substantially disinherit, your spouse.

- You are in a situation that does not comply with commonplace legal assumptions about family or the guardianship of minors (i.e., a nontraditional family such as a gay couple with children or a family that is not biologically related, etc.), or you are a single parent with custody who does not wish your child to go to the biological parent. In such cases, it is wise to work with a good lawyer who is sympathetic to your wishes and will help ensure that they will not be challenged after you are gone.

- You need to do estate planning. Developing strategies to reduce the amount of probable taxes and legal and court fees can be key to saving families and survivors significant amounts of money and time, not to mention emotional distress. This specialized work is called "estate planning" and goes beyond the basic process of making a simple will. (See more about estate planning later in this chapter.)*

If none of the above applies, you can almost certainly make your own will using any of a number of self-help books or computer software programs that serve as guides. (For examples, see listing at the end of this chapter.)

When preparing your own will, be sure to carefully follow instructions in whatever guide you select. Don't skip any steps. There are a number of pertinent formalities that, while easy to follow, can create real problems if left undone and are necessary to preparing a legally binding document.

How to Choose a Lawyer
If you do choose to work with an attorney, be sure s/he is a good one who actually knows about preparing wills. This may sound obvious, but in fact it is often assumed that any lawyer can prepare a proper will. Not true. To do a good job and save you money, a lawyer must be experienced and up-to-date in current testamentary law, and the more complex your situation, the more expert the lawyer must be.

The *Simple Will Book* by attorney Denis Clifford is a comprehen-

---

*Parts of this list are taken from Denis Clifford, *The Simple Will Book* (Berkeley, Calif.: Nolo Press, 1988).

sive do-it-yourself guide to writing a will. It also contains good advice about finding a lawyer when you need one. Clifford discusses several points to keep in mind, including being clear about what type of lawyer you need (depending on your situation); trusting your intuition; shopping around until you've found the right one; and being careful when using a bar association referral. (The main qualification for such a referral can be that the lawyer in question needs the work.) The most reliable method of finding a good lawyer is to ask a friend or associate who has worked with one they can recommend.

WHAT WILL IT COST?

If you do it yourself, a will can cost as little as the $9.95 price of a "how-to" paperback or as much as the $59.95 list price of a computer software package that lets you write your own will on your personal computer. (You can often find these programs on sale at computer stores for considerably less.)

If you hire a lawyer, the price can range from $50 per hour up to $350 per hour or more for highly specialized estate planners. The total price will depend not only on the size but also the complexity and the nature of the estate. If, for instance, your assets lie in jointly owned business interests or variable stock investments or the like, it will require an experienced planner to properly prepare a total estate package. This can wind up costing a lot, but if you are in the position of holding significant assets in the first place, you'll probably be able to afford to protect your beneficiaries. In the long run, it is money well spent.

WHAT MAKES A WILL VALID?

Whether you do it yourself or work with a lawyer, there are several basic requirements that must be met to ensure that a will is legal and valid. State laws govern wills, and yours must be written in accordance with the laws of the state in which you legally reside.

Although these laws vary from state to state, generally speaking, they are as follows:*

---

*Except in Louisiana. Louisiana law is based on the Napoleonic code, or French civil law, rather than the English tradition that is the basis for U.S. testamentary procedure. As a result, Louisiana law may vary from that of other states.

In most states you must be either eighteen or twenty-one years of
age. (A few states allow you to be younger under certain circumstances; for instance, if you are married.) To check the law in
your state, call the probate court in your county.

You must be of "sound mind." This means that you know you're
making a will and you know what a will is.

The will should be typewritten. (In some states, handwritten or
oral wills are acceptable, but only in very restricted situations.)

The will must state clearly that it is your will and must be dated
and signed by you.

The will must be witnessed by individuals who do not inherit
anything from the will. (Some states require two witnesses and
some require three.)

The will should appoint an executor.

The will must have at least one provision. In other words, it must
distribute some property or name a guardian or do *something;*
otherwise, what's the point?

There is no requirement that a will be recorded or filed with any
government agency in order to be valid.

Challenging a Will

The most common grounds for challenging a will is the famous issue
of "sound mind." If it can be proved that the testator (the person
making the will) was gaga when s/he wrote it, then the provisions
of that will can be challenged.

However, as described by attorney Clifford:

In reality, a person has to be pretty far gone before a court will rule
that s/he lacked the capacity to make a valid will. For example,
forgetfulness or even the inability to recognize friends do not by
themselves establish incapacity. Also, it's important to remember that
there's normally no affirmative burden to prove to a court that the will
writer was competent. It's presumed that the will writer was of sound
mind, unless someone challenges this in a court proceeding—which
is rarely done.[1]

Generally speaking, when wills are challenged, it is because of
misunderstanding or disagreement among family members and/or
survivors. At that point, a technical matter of validity may become
an *issue,* but it is almost never the *reason* for a challenge.

The primary impetus for meeting all of the requirements of validity is to ensure that when you die, your last will and testament will be accepted and enacted without time-consuming delays and snags and without incurring additional legal or court fees.

Other Points of Note

A will does not have to be notarized in order to be legally valid. However, if the will maker and the witnesses sign an affidavit before a notary public, it makes the will "self-proving." (Witnesses needn't know anything about what is in your will; they just need to hear you say it is your will and sign to that effect.) This step can simplify the probate process by eliminating the requirement that witnesses appear at any probate proceeding after you die. But this requirement is not uniform in all states, nor is the "self-proving" law. If you have questions about notarization check with the probate court in your county or with a lawyer. Notarization is *not* required to legalize your will.

There are a couple of things you cannot do in your will: You can't leave money for an illegal purpose or make a bequest on the condition that the beneficiary marry, divorce, or change religion (Hollywood melodramas notwithstanding); and there are state laws limiting the disinheritance of a spouse. If you are legally married to someone, even if you haven't laid eyes on him or her in years, s/he has a right to a portion of your estate (and in some states pretty much all of your estate). If you wish to disinherit someone to whom you are legally married, see a lawyer.

How to Learn the Law in Your State

As noted above, state laws govern wills; they are administered at the county level. Call your county court offices and ask which court handles wills and probate matters. You should be able to get such information as:

- Age, witness, and all other requirements for valid wills in your state
- Small or "family" estate exemption levels
- The laws of descent and distribution in your state
- Schedule of death taxes in your state

Another aid to doing your own legal research is a law library or a public library with a good law collection. (Sometimes the county courthouse has a law library open to the public, supported by tax dollars or money from legal fees.) A good book to help you do your own legal research is *Legal Research: How to Find and Understand the Law* by Stephen Elias. (See listings at the end of this chapter.)

THE BASIC WILL-MAKING PROCESS

Whether you do it yourself or work with a lawyer, knowing the basic formula for preparing a will makes the whole thing easier and can save you time and money.

The process can be divided into three steps:

1. Figuring out what you own
2. Deciding how you want it distributed
3. Choosing someone to oversee that distribution (and a guardian for minor children if appropriate)

The remaining requirements comprise the various formalities of validation (as shown above), assuring that the document is legally binding. In other words, follow the state laws validating your will.

1. *Inventory your property.* This means listing your property and assets (e.g., house, car, jewelry, bank account) and figuring their worth, minus liabilities against them (a mortgage, debts, etc.). The basic question is, what do you own that will be left to deal with after you die? If you are writing your will yourself, a good how-to book or your personal computer software program will guide you through the process. If you have decided to hire a lawyer, s/he will do so.

2. *Make your choices.* This can be the fun part. Most people enjoy giving gifts, and that is essentially what you are doing. In *The Simple Will Book,* Denis Clifford describes the satisfaction you can take from the prospect of providing for those you love or entrusting treasured property or objects to those you know will care for them.

3. *Name an executor.* The executor is the individual who administers the provisions of your will. As noted above, your executor need not be an attorney. People often choose their spouse

or an adult child to fulfill this role. If you are preparing your own will, advice on choosing an executor will be detailed in whatever how-to guide you choose. If you are working with an attorney, you might ask his or her opinion, but remember, your own knowledge and instinct about whom to trust is the key here.

These are the fundamentals. This basic process is quite standard, as is the traditional format for writing a will. Why, then, one might wonder, isn't there a standardized form we can all use to write our wills? Primarily because people haven't demanded one. No federal mandate requires uniform testamentary statutes of the states, and the legal profession has no reason to publicize the routine nature of the process. Why should they? The lack of uniformity provides lawyers with a lot of work. Although there have been periodic attempts to standardize a statutory will form, they have met with little success. In the case of wills, the likelihood of reform is limited by a general tendency on the part of the public to avoid the subject of death altogether.

PROBATE

The word *probate* comes from a Latin root meaning "to prove" and refers to the process of proving, or accepting as approved, the will of a dead person. The probate court registers a will, wherein it becomes the official last will and testament of the individual who signed it. The probate court also appoints guardians of minor children, names an administrator of the estate if there is no will, and can be involved in supervising the assessment of value, settlement of taxes and debts against the estate, and the distribution of remaining assets to your heirs if you made a will or to your legislated beneficiaries if you died intestate. Probate is a county court and in some locales is called surrogate, chancery, prerogative, or orphans' court.

The original purpose of the probate process was to ensure that the assets of the deceased were distributed properly and to provide an official forum in which debts or claims against an estate could be resolved and the government could collect its taxes. Today, however, probate has earned a bad reputation.

Why Avoid Probate?

Probate has been called a "lawyer's racket"[2] and a "corrupt system."[3] The problem with probate is that it is a process providing considerable room for abuse. Formal probate supervision of an estate can entail naming and bonding a personal representative who will oversee hiring others for a myriad of tasks, including accounting, appraising, liquidating, managing and selling assets, notifying creditors, submitting claims, and more. These tasks can involve a lot of people, all of whom take fees. Appraising and assessing jobs can go to cronies of the court. Archaic procedures can require elaborate paperwork and time-consuming bureaucratic obstacles. The average probate proceeding takes up to a year. An overburdened court system can cause delays simply by neglect or ineptitude. And probate makes your will a matter of public record. In other words, anyone can find out what you owned, what you owed, and who got what.

Based, as is the rest of our legal system, on English law, probate has been part of the established order for a long time. In England, however, the probate system came under attack at the turn of the century as an out-of-date system, rife with favoritism and maintained solely as a cash cow for the legal profession. It was substantially reformed in the 1920s.

In the United States the Uniform Probate Code was an effort at reform proposed in the early 1970s. It has had only a mixed success. Some states have adopted or adapted portions of the code, while others have ignored it altogether. Reformers generally feel that while the system itself has been made simpler, costs and delays have remained unacceptably arbitrary. One statistic states that it takes seventeen times as long to process an inheritance in the United States as it now does in Great Britain—and costs one hundred times as much.

Should I Worry About Probate?

You can calculate the amount of your property that will pass through probate before you choose whether it's worth taking the time, effort, and cost to avoid it. If you decide you want to avoid probate, there are a number of ways to do it, all totally legal and aboveboard. Basically, avoiding probate means transferring property outside of your will. Generally speaking, assets owned solely by you at the time of your death pass through probate. Assets held jointly, or in a trust, or insurance benefits going directly to a beneficiary do not. If you are working with a lawyer, s/he can help you figure this out. If you are doing it yourself, a good self-help guide will show you how to figure which of your assets are probatable and which are not.

There have been a number of books written decrying the abuses of the probate system and advising how to avoid it. The best-known among them is Norman F. Dacey's *How to Avoid Probate.* (See listings at the end of this chapter.)

If your estate is relatively modest, you can probably do basic probate avoidance yourself. However, if your situation is complicated, it is smart to seek the advice of an expert. The best methods for avoiding probate will vary as rates, regulations, tax laws, and financial options change. Planning properly can require the advice of a lawyer specializing in the subject or the services of an estate-planning professional.

ESTATE PLANNING

Broadly defined, there are two kinds of wills:

1. A *basic will,* or as it is often called, a "simple" will
2. An *estate plan,* the more complex package for which a will forms the foundation

Up to this point we have been discussing the simple will. In the simple will you dispense of your property, name your executor, appoint a guardian for minor children, establish simple trusts, and take other substantive actions.

However, if you have a sizable estate, you will want to consider an estate plan. With estate planning you can develop a variety of methods for the transfer of money and property.

The aim of estate planning is to minimize taxes and avoid probate (or court costs and complications). The importance of estate planning depends on the size of the estate.

How to Judge the Size of Your Estate

A good rule of thumb is as follows: If your estate consists of readily transferable property (cash, bank accounts, real estate, or personal property, such as a car, jewelry, art, etc.), the total value of which is less than $600,000 (the amount of the federal tax exemption), and you live in a state with low or negligible death taxes, then you can probably manage with a simple will and do-it-yourself probate avoidance. (Many books on will writing have appendices that include a detailed schedule of state death taxes, or check with your local county court.) If the total is over that figure, then you should consider estate planning. The larger the estate, the more expedient it is to minimize probate and taxes.

SMALL ESTATES SETTLEMENT

If your estate is small, it may not need to go through a formal probate. Your survivors may face only a simplified version of the process called "family settlement," "small estates settlement," or "voluntary administration." The cutoff point varies from state to state. You can find out how it works by checking with the probate court in the county in which you legally reside, which will provide you with information on the settlement of small estates. Many states also simplify or eliminate probate for property left by one spouse to the other.

TAXES

Death and taxes have long been linked in comic play. There's a good reason for this. You need a sense of humor when thinking about either subject or you're going to get pretty depressed. When you die, your estate can be subject to state and federal estate taxes, gift taxes, inheritance taxes, and a bunch of tricky stuff like generation-skipping tax, pickup tax, the so-called second tax, and others. Not to mention the fact that your estate must pay both federal and state *income* tax. They get you coming and going, so to speak.

But don't panic. It isn't as bad as it sounds. In fact, some estates are pretty much exempt from most of these death taxes. As of 1987, the federal estate tax exemption is $600,000. If your estate comes in under this amount, you pay no federal estate tax at all. In addition, property left to a surviving spouse is exempt.

State taxes vary, but many states exempt substantial amounts of property. (For instance, in New York, estates under $108,000 are exempt from taxation, as is all property transferred to the surviving spouse.) Speaking generally, for many people, state taxes are not going to be significant enough for them to go to the time, effort, and cost of trying to avoid them. Of course, you should check the tax rates in your state to assess your own situation. You can do this by going to the probate or surrogate court in your county (they should have an information booklet available that includes a tax schedule for your state) or by checking the tax schedules that are included in selected books on wills and estate planning. (See listings at the end of this chapter.)

If your estate is sizable, however (above the $600,000 federal exemption level), it's a real good idea to invest some money in estate planning to reduce taxes. This is because federal tax rates start at 37 percent for nonexempt property and can go as high as 55 percent.

The tax-law revisions that went into effect in 1986–87 have influenced estate planning of this type, and experts agree that as the government seeks to increase revenue in the future, there will probably be more changes. Such esoteric devices as the "grantor-retained income trust," the "self-canceling installment note," the "Q-tip trust," the "split purchase," and the "Crummey Clause" are some of the tricky financial moves that can be employed to the estate planner's advantage. As you can imagine, this kind of planning can become quite intricate and requires expert advice from professionals in the field.

In addition to taxes on the transference of property at death, an estate must pay income tax as well. There are two types of income tax due after you die: (1) tax on income you received for the year during which you died (even though you may be unreachable yourself, the government still wants its money) and (2) tax on income earned by your estate. (Some estates earn more after the death of the testator than most people see in a lifetime, such as Agatha Christie's estate or that of Elvis Presley. If this is likely in your case, see a lawyer.) Your estate remains a taxable entity until its assets have been fully distributed.

ADDITIONAL CONSIDERATIONS

Here are some other points to consider when you are writing your will.

Funeral Directions, Body Disposition, Organ Donations

It is common practice to leave instructions for disposition and commemoration requests in your will. However, sometimes a will isn't readily available as soon as it need be in matters of immediate concern, such as organ donation or prompt disposition. It is important to make this information directly accessible to those who will need to know by writing a Letter of Instruction. (See section later in this chapter.)

It is recommended that you also include such instructions in your will, because it serves to reinforce the validity of your requests should they be challenged or questioned for any reason.

Directions regarding life-sustaining treatment decisions should be delineated in a separate document especially for that purpose such as a living will or a medical durable power of attorney. (See chapter 3 for complete information on advance directives.)

Pets

We hear stories of people bequeathing a fortune to a pet, but the much more common circumstance is to overlook an animal's needs altogether. While children are not considered property by law, pets are and as such can be inherited or sold. If there is no provision for your pet in your will, or if you die intestate, the animal can be treated the same as a piece of furniture.

It is legal and appropriate to provide for pets in your will, most simply by naming a friend who has accepted the responsibility of caring for the animal and making a provision of funds available to that purpose.

Revising Your Will

It is important to update your will when something changes affecting the status of your provisions (i.e., the birth of a child, the death of a beneficiary, a change in property ownership, etc.).

You cannot revise your will by adding handwritten or typed changes. If you do so, you will likely invalidate the entire document.

Simple changes can be made by adding a *codicil* to your will. A codicil is a separate document created to make uncomplicated changes or revisions. A codicil must also be signed, dated, and witnessed; in fact, it must be executed with the same formalities as the will itself. If you need to make substantial changes, you should write a new will.

Revoking Your Will

When you write a will, you generally begin with the statement that this is your will and that it revokes all previous wills and codicils. This is the best way to revoke previous documents because it is clear and straightforward. Tearing up a will or burning it or otherwise destroying it can be a tricky matter. Legally, it's a question of intent. It could be claimed that the original will is still in effect if no revocation had been stated in a subsequent will, especially if copies of the original exist.

The point to remember is that your will is an action with legal intent and the document itself represents that action. If you've taken the action and you wish to cancel it you must take specific steps according to the laws of your state or make a new will and expressly revoke all previous wills and testaments.

You can revoke or change your will as often as you wish, there is no legal limitation.

Where to Keep Your Will

Often people keep their will in a safe deposit box. This is not the best place for it. In many states, safe deposit boxes are sealed upon the death of the signatory (whether you rent the box jointly or in your name only). It cannot be opened unless a representative of the state tax commission is present. (Sometimes exceptions can be made in order to find the will, but this requires that special arrangements be made and adds another layer of bureaucratic complication to what is already a time-consuming process.)

Try finding a safe place in your home—a fireproof metal box, perhaps. If you work with a lawyer to draw up your will, leave it on file at his or her office. Be sure that your family or someone close to you knows where it is located. Remember, your will won't do anybody any good if it can't be found. It is an important document and should be thought of as an asset in itself and cared for accordingly.

Copies

The word *copy,* when it is legally applied to a will, means a separately executed, signed, and witnessed document. (States differ regarding the recognition of duplicating originals.) Keep in mind the difference between a *photocopy* (or Xerox) and a *copy* in the legal sense. You can, of course, make photocopies of your will, but they are not legal documents.

It is important to make a *record* of your will and let someone know where it is kept. A record simply notes that your will exists and tells where to find it. (See "Preparing a Letter of Instruction" section in this chapter.) Remember, if your will is never found, it will be assumed you died intestate.

You may wish to inform your family or appropriate individuals of the contents of your will or to give them copies. In general, however, it is not advised to have a lot of copies (or even photocopies) floating around, because if any changes are made—codicils added or clauses revoked—all copies must be retrieved and amended or destroyed. Otherwise, conflicts or confusion may arise with regard to your wishes after you have died.

If your preference is privacy, your will can be completely confidential during your lifetime. There is no legal requirement that any copies or photocopies be made. If you wish, no one need know anything about what you have decided until your will is registered with the court after you die.

NEW WAYS TO DO IT

Computer Software

The most recent innovation in will writing is computer software programs for the general public. Lawyers have been using such programs since the early 1980s and have increased their reliance on them significantly over the last few years. Now anyone with their own personal computer can take advantage of this technology.

These software packages usually include a disk and a manual explaining the program and instructions for its use. A good one can be just the ticket if you regularly use a personal computer and need a simple will or basic estate planning. It can also serve as the basis of a more comprehensive estate plan. It is important to choose a software program that takes into account variations in state law and allows for regular updating.

There aren't a large number of these programs from which to choose, but the ones on the market are pretty good. Costs range from about $30 to $60, depending on whether you find a sale at a computer store or have to send away to the company. The program we tested (WillMaker; see listing at end of this chapter for further information) is available for Apple II, IBM, Macintosh, and the Commodore 64 computers.

Videotape

You may have seen articles about, or advertisements for, what are often called "video wills." Actually, the term *video wills* is a misnomer. As of this writing, state laws have not changed to allow a videotape (or an audiotape) to serve as a legal substitute for a written will. A tape can *supplement* a will, but it is not considered legally binding.

Primarily, videotape is used to make a record of the testator's state of mind at the time he or she wrote the will. Generally speaking, a lawyer recommends doing this when a will includes unexpected disinheritances or provisions that might be challenged after the testator dies. Seeing a videotape in which Uncle Charlie states clearly why he's leaving little Billy zip can readily convince Billy that he doesn't have a case for challenging his uncle's will. Actually, Uncle Charlie doesn't need to say *why;* the objective is not to show why he has made the decision but to show that he has made it while lucid and of his own free will.

Some people use videotape to express other sentiments or simply to say good-bye. If you are interested in making a videotape to supplement your will, your best bet is to contact a commercial video production company and ask if they do this type of work or if they can recommend someone who does. Often the same kinds of companies that tape weddings and other special occasions have experience in doing "last testament" tapes. Look in the yellow pages under "Video" or "Video Production Services" for companies whose advertising includes the phrase "medical/legal" production. Or ask your lawyer. If s/he uses video to establish the validity of unexpected or unusual testamentary decisions, s/he may be able to recommend a video producer. The cost is usually based on an hourly rate that can range from $90 to $300 per, so it is wise to call around and compare.

But remember, a videotape or audiotape is not a legally binding will. You must prepare a document that is legally admissible according to the laws of your state in order to ensure that your wishes will be honored by the court.

Will Kits

Another service that is advertised either in print or on radio or television and made available through the mail is the will "kit." Such kits are usually made up of a selection of forms and a booklet or brochure describing how to write your will using the enclosed forms.

It has been our experience that such kits are usually on the skimpy side and do not adequately explain the various possible contingencies; nor do they always allow for variations in state law. The companies providing these kits are not renowned for stability and often disappear after operating for a brief period of time.

While the kit might be advertised for a relatively small amount of money, you may receive information worth considerably less than what you paid. Ordering through the mail makes it impossible to know what you might be getting, whereas books are reviewed and available for consideration before making a purchase.

If you are looking for an easy and economical way to make up a simple will, it is usually more cost-effective and reliable to buy a good do-it-yourself book. Will kits generally cost more and inform less.

THE WILL OF ANOTHER

It can be very difficult to approach another person about their will. Our general reticence on the subject leaves us without the language or the shared expectations necessary to handle the whole thing with any ease. Still, it's important to give it a try. As we have already seen, dying intestate can cause problems.

The honest approach seems to be the most reliable. Simply stating that you know complications arise when we don't plan ahead, that it's important for others to be aware of personal wishes, and that you are available to help with this planning if necessary can be the best way to confront the matter.

It may seem especially difficult to approach another person about preparing a will when s/he is seriously ill or dying. But surprisingly, often a terminally ill person will not have addressed the practical consequences of dying. Because it may be the last chance to answer the questions that only s/he can answer, it becomes all the more important to ask. Sometimes you will find it is a relief to the dying person to know that someone is going to be honest with him or her and can help take care of business.

Even if an elderly relative is in the best of health, it is often quite difficult to ask if s/he has prepared a will. Elderly parents who, when younger, wrote a will to name a guardian for their minor children may not have updated that will for years. If you are responsible for, or care about, someone who is dying or elderly, it is important to make sure s/he has made a will and that the appropriate people know where it is located.

If a person needs assistance, you can help prepare the necessary information, such as making a list of assets, clarifying and making a written record of his or her instructions, or encouraging him or her to name an executor or engage a lawyer, if that is required or desired.

Some books that include advice on this subject are Robert Buckman's *"I Don't Know What to Say . . ."* and Mark A. Edinberg's *Talking with Your Aging Parents.* In the particular case of AIDS, a helpful guide is *When Someone You Know Has AIDS* by Leonard J. Martelli. In addition, the American Association of Retired Persons (AARP) publishes books and pamphlets addressing the practical needs of the elderly, including the need to prepare a will. (See listings at the end of this chapter for further information.)

PREPARING A LETTER OF INSTRUCTION

There are many practical questions that will arise upon your death. Some of them will be answered by your will. Some won't. An additional document, usually called a Letter of Instruction, can be an enormous help to your survivors during a difficult time. It can answer one of the first questions they will have: "Where is your will?" It can also answer a myriad of later ones.

After someone has died, survivors often find themselves asking: "What would s/he have wanted?" As a rule we don't tell each other what we really want. This causes a number of problems. Still, while we are alive there is the possibility of asking and answering. Once we are dead it is truly too late. Simple, practical questions can become difficult, emotional points of contention. A Letter of Instruction can eliminate confusion and disagreement as to your wishes—"what you would have wanted" is made clear.

A Letter of Instruction lists personal property, assets, and liabilities, gives locations of important papers (deeds, insurance policies, business records, your will), and spells out your preferences about disposition and commemoration. It is a personal document, not a legal one; thus, changing or updating it does not require the legal formalities necessary to update a will. In their very helpful book *Wills, Funerals & Probate,* Theodore Hughes and David Klein put it this way.

> Your will should dispose of your possessions in rather general terms and should not attempt to enumerate everything you own. Your will may, of course, bequeath certain possessions (a piece of jewelry, for example, or an antique desk) to a specific person, but it should not attempt to specify the disposition of every stock, bond, savings account, recreational vehicle, or other possession, because these change continuously over time. Yet it is extremely important that you maintain a current record of everything you own so that your survivors will not overlook items of value simply because they don't know of their existence or whereabouts.[4]

Another important distinction between the Letter and your will is this: If your will goes through probate, it becomes a public document. If you want to say something personal or leave a special message for someone, it is better to do so in a letter rather than taking the chance that it might become part of the public record. Hughes and Klein say,

> You may, for example, want to use your Letter to heal a long-standing breach in a relationship or to explain its causes or origins. You may want to express affection or respect that you are reluctant or embarrassed to express while you are alive. You may want to explain or apologize for certain of your own actions that at one time or another created problems or raised questions for your survivors.[5]

A letter to your survivors can achieve such a goal without making the matter public.

If you have a problem talking about death but want to be sure that the practical necessities are taken care of, you can simply write everything down in your Letter of Instruction, giving directions to your survivors and describing the arrangements you have made. Just be sure someone knows where it is.

Since the Letter isn't a formal legal document, it doesn't need to follow any particular format, and you can write it in whatever way is comfortable for you. It can literally be a letter to your loved ones. Or if you prefer, there are forms available for preparing a Letter of Instruction, listing inventories, accounts, policies, etc. Although you will probably want to adapt any standardized form to your own individual needs, it can be very helpful to work from such a document. They can sometimes be found at stationery stores or bookstores. Banks and other financial organizations often provide Letter of Instruction forms. Ask at the customer service department of any large banking institution.

RESOURCES AND SUPPORT

Books

Henry W. Abts III. *The Living Trust: The Fail-Proof Way to Pass Along Your Estate to Your Heirs Without Lawyers, Courts, or the Probate System.* Chicago: Contemporary Books; Markham, Ontario: Beaverbooks, Ltd., 1989.
[Explains how to avoid probate by creating a living trust.]

Jens C. Appel III and F. Bruce Gentry. *The Complete Will Kit.* New York: John Wiley & Sons, 1990.
[Includes estate inventory worksheets and story tracing a family estate to illustrate property transfers.]

Paul P. Ashley, updated by Jennifer L. Olanie. *You and Your Will: The Planning and Management of Your Estate.* Rev. and updated ed. New York: New American Library, Mentor Books, 1985.

Louis Austin. *The Living Trust Alternative.* Kansas City, Mo.: Hudspeth Publishing Co., 1988.
[How to plan a living trust to avoid probate.]

Martin S. Bender. *Everyone Needs a Will.* Holbrook, Mass.: Bob Adams, Inc., 1990.
[Sample forms, organized by marital status and with regard to children.]

Alexander Bove, Jr. *The Complete Book of Wills & Estates.* New York: Henry Holt and Co.; Markham, Ontario: Fitzhenry & Whiteside Ltd., 1989.
[Includes codicil forms and special will provisions.]

Robert Brosterman and Thomas Brosterman. *The Complete Estate Planning Guide.* Rev. ed. New York: New American Library, Mentor Books, 1987.

Denis Clifford. *Plan Your Estate: Wills, Probate Avoidance, Trusts & Taxes.* Berkeley, Calif.: Nolo Press, 1990. Available in bookstores or through Nolo Press, 950 Parker Street, Berkeley, CA 94710; (415) 549-1976 or 1-800-992-NOLO.

[This comprehensive do-it-yourself book includes charts of tax rules for every state and tear-out living trust forms.]

_____. *Simple Will Book: How to Prepare a Legally Valid Will.* Rev. ed. Berkeley, Calif.: Nolo Press, 1990. Available in bookstores or through Nolo Press.

[A clear guide and workbook that includes sample wills, tear-out forms, charts, alternative clauses, and many examples.]

D. Lawrence Crumbley and Edward E. Millam. *Keys to Estate Planning and Trusts.* Barron's Business Keys Series. New York: Barron's, 1989.

Norman F. Dacey. *How to Avoid Probate!* Rev. ed. New York: Macmillan, Collier, 1990.

[This book caused a stir in the legal community when it was first published. It is now considered to be the definitive indictment of the probate system. Includes instructions on setting up a variety of trusts and sample wills.]

Theodore E. Hughes and David Klein. *A Family Guide to Wills, Funerals & Estate Planning: How to Protect Yourself and Your Survivors.* New York: Charles Scribner's Sons, 1987.

[Includes information on "small estate" settlements, tax tables, and state requirements governing wills.]

David C. Larsen. *You Can't Take It with You: A Step-by-Step Personalized Approach to Your Will to Avoid Probate and Estate Taxes.* New York: Random House, Vintage Books, 1988.

Toni P. Lester. *How to Settle an Estate or Prepare Your Will.* New York: Putnam, Perigee Books, 1988.

[Appendix includes U.S. Estate Tax Return Form.]

Cliff Roberson. *Avoiding Probate: Tamper-Proof Estate Planning.* Blue Ridge Summit, Penn.: Tab Books, Liberty House, 1989.

[Includes discussion of living trusts. Appendices reproduce IRS publications 559 "Tax Information for Survivors, Executors and Administrators" and 448 "Federal Estate and Gift Taxes."]

Alex J. Soled. *The Essential Guide to Wills, Estates, Trusts, and Death Taxes.* Updated and expanded ed. Washington, D.C.: American Association of Retired Persons; Glenview, Ill.: Scott, Foresman and Co., AARP Books, 1988. Available in bookstores or through the American Association of Retired Persons. For complete information write AARP Books, 1900 East Lake Avenue, Glenview, IL 60025.

[The extensive appendix includes both federal and state tax schedules, state-by-state validation requirements, and laws of dissent and distribution.]

Barbara R. Stock. *It's Easy to Avoid Probate.* Updated ed. Orlando, Fla.: Linch Publishing, 1985. To order call 1-800-327-7055.

Books Containing Related Information

Don Biggs. *How to Avoid Lawyers: Step-by-Step Guide to Being Your Own Lawyer in Almost Every Situation.* New York: Garland, 1991.
[Contains chapter on wills. Includes state-by-state validation requirements.]

Consumer Law Foundation. *The Complete Legal Kit.* Philadelphia: Running Press, 1988. Available in bookstores or from Running Press Publishers, 125 Twenty-second Street, Philadelphia, PA 19103; (215) 567-5080.
[A book of forms, including a chapter on wills and estate planning.]

Jean Crichton. *The Age Care Sourcebook: A Resource Guide for the Aging and Their Families.* New York: Simon & Schuster, Fireside Books, 1987.
[Contains a section on wills and information on how to help aging parents deal with preparation of a will.]

Hayden Curry and Denis Clifford. *A Legal Guide for Lesbian and Gay Couples.* 5th ed. Berkeley, Calif.: Nolo Press, 1989.
[Contains sections referring to wills and estate planning.]

Mark A. Edinberg. *Talking with Your Aging Parents.* Boston: Shambala Publications, 1988.
[Includes a chapter on talking about legal and financial matters.]

Stephen Elias. *Legal Research: How to Find and Understand the Law.* 2nd ed. Berkeley, Calif.: Nolo Press, 1986.
[A layperson's guide to doing legal research.]

Leonard J. Martelli with Fran D. Peltz and William Messina. *When Someone You Know Has AIDS: A Practical Guide.* New York: Crown, 1987.
[Includes advice about how to discuss wills and other practical matters with someone who is dying.]

John Regan, J.S.D., with Legal Counsel for the Elderly. *Your Legal Rights in Later Life.* Washington, D.C.: American Association of Retired Persons; Glenview, Ill.: Scott, Foresman and Company, AARP Books, 1989.
[Includes chapters on making health care decisions, estate planning, and wills.]

Norma S. Upson. ***When Someone You Love Is Dying.*** New York: Simon
& Schuster, Fireside Books, 1986.
[Offers practical and sensitive advice about discussing, with a terminally ill loved one, the writing of a will. This book is currently out of
print, but worth looking for. Check your local library or used-book
store.]

Agencies/Service Organizations: Legal

Commission on Legal Problems of the Elderly, American Bar Association
1800 M Street, NW
Washington, DC 20036
(202) 331-2297
Provides information and guidance in emerging areas of law and generates
pro bono, reduced-fee, and community education programs for senior
citizens. Publishes information on wills, and other brochures and books.
Call to request a publications list.

HALT—An Organization of Americans for Legal Reform
1319 F Street, NW
Suite 300
Washington, DC 20004
(202) 347-9600
A national public interest group whose concerns include reduced probate
fees and simplified probate procedures. They respond to written questions
and inquiries; no phone consultations.

Local and Regional Bar Associations
If you use a bar association or lawyer's organization for referrals, always
remember that such referrals are not a seal of approval. The best way to find
a good lawyer is to ask a friend or associate who knows one. Local and
regional *family service associations* or *social service agencies* or *area agencies on
aging* sometimes provide information on how to find low cost legal counseling. Your public library can help you find the appropriate agency.

Other Service Agencies

On the East Coast:
Gay Men's Health Crisis
Legal Services Department
129 West 20th Street
New York, NY 10011
(212) 337-3504

Provides counseling about wills free of charge to people with AIDS or ARC (depending on size of annual income and estate). Publishes free booklet, "Legal Answers About AIDS," which includes information on wills, living wills, and powers of attorney. (GMHC also publishes a number of helpful books, covering a wide range of issues, for people dealing with AIDS.)

On the West Coast:
AIDS Legal Referral Panel (a project of Bay Area Lawyers for Individual Freedom)
San Francisco, California
(415) 291-5454
Provides free counseling on wills to anyone diagnosed with AIDS or ARC. Provides other legal services (fees on sliding scale).

Gay Legal Referral Service
San Francisco, California
(415) 621-3900
A state bar–approved lawyer referral service. Call for further information.

In the Midwest:
AIDS Legal Council of Chicago
220 South State Street
Suite 2030
Chicago, IL 60604
(312) 427-8990
Represents people with AIDS and ARC and makes referrals. Fees are based on a sliding scale.

Howard Brown Clinic
Social Services Department
945 West George Street
Chicago, IL 60657
(312) 871-5777
Clinic makes referrals to volunteer lawyers for AIDS patients registered with Social Services Department.

Computer Software
Personal Lawyer
Bloc Publishing Corp.
800 SW 37th Avenue
Suite 765
Coral Gables, FL 33134
(305) 445-0903

Includes last will and testament, powers of attorney, guardianship, and lease agreements. Buy at stores that sell software products or directly from Bloc Publishing Corp. Available for IBM and compatibles.

Will Planner

Noetic Technologies
P.O. Box 3085
Englewood, CO 80155-3085
(303) 770-2380
Half of this program offers on-line help and explanations concerning wills and estate planning. The other half produces wills and trusts. Program can estimate value and taxes of your estate. Will Planner automatically places clauses valid for your state. Buy at stores that sell software products, through mail-order catalogs, or directly from Noetic Technologies. Available for IBM and compatibles.

WillMaker

Nolo Press & Legisoft Inc.
950 Parker Street
Berkeley, CA 94710
800-992-NOLO
Program is accompanied by a book that includes information about estate planning, wills, and instructions for using the program. WillMaker automatically tailors your will to law of the state in which you reside. Buy at stores that sell software products, through mail-order catalogs, or directly from Nolo Press. Available for Apple II; IBM and compatibles; Macintosh; and Commodore 64.

WillPower

Jacoby & Meyers
1156 Avenue of the Americas
New York, NY 10036
(212) 536-7600
Includes all standard will provisions, plus an on-screen worksheet for determining the value of your estate. All instructions are on-screen. The program is available from stores that sell software products or can be purchased directly from Jacoby & Meyers. Available for IBM and compatibles.

2

Disposition and Commemoration

Two powerful human emotions—the fear of death and the love of bargains—
inexorably conflict in any serious consideration of what to do with an expired
loved one, all the more so if the loved one is oneself.

David Owen, "Rest in Pieces"

We live in a consumer society that somehow, while ignoring the
reality of death altogether, still manages to maximize its sales potential. The items and procedures necessary for disposing of a dead
human body have been made expensive, complicated, and in the
finest tradition of consumerism, a virtual requirement.

The deregulation of the cemetery business has allowed the industry to take advantage of telemarketing, direct mail, and other modern marketplace tools, resulting in an increase in the number of
people who make arrangements for disposition ahead of time. In
1987, 700,000 Americans prearranged their funerals. In 1989, the
number increased to 900,000 and it is expected to continue to rise
still further.

One industry specialist said, "I've been in this business since 1956 and God, how it's changed. We send out brochures now and people can return cards if they are interested. Telemarketing has become a major part of recruiting and so have neighborhood canvasses, print ads, and billboards."[1]

A longer perspective reveals a much greater change, from a time before the funeral industry existed at all. Until the end of the nineteenth century, the average American died at home, surrounded by family and friends. Most communities included a group of women who took on the task of preparing the body ("the laying out of the dead") while the local carpenter, or the men in the family, built a simple wood coffin. Burial took place on the family farm, in the town cemetery, or in the church graveyard. Taking care of the dead was a family or community activity, not a commercial one. Today it is a business, a trade plied to a particularly vulnerable clientele.

Why Plan Ahead?
Whether influenced by advertising or the desire to get a good buy, planning ahead for your own disposition and commemoration is a good idea. For one thing, you *can* save money if you preplan. For another, it gives you a choice. If you care about what is done with your body after you die, you need to make your preferences clear now. Most of all, planning ahead is an act of simple consideration. It is hard to overstate how helpful planning ahead will be to those who love you most.

If no plans have been made, survivors, in a state of grief, sadness, and perhaps shock, will most often take the line of least resistance and passively rely on the funeral industry to "take care of it." All too often, this results in paying prices higher than necessary for services no one involved really wants.

As pointed out by the editors of *Consumer Reports* in their book *Funerals: Consumers' Last Rights,* ". . . for many people the cost of buying a funeral and burial for a family member is one of the largest single expenses they will have to bear, exceeded only by the cost of a house, a car, a college education, and (perhaps) a catastrophic illness."[2] Today the average funeral runs from $3,000 to $5,000 and can easily exceed $10,000. Simple disposition and a personal commemoration can be accomplished for a fraction of that amount.

In addition to easing the emotional and financial burdens on your survivors, preplanning allows you to select the kind of disposition and service you desire. This becomes especially necessary should you want a personalized commemoration or memorial. If you want your ashes scattered over Le Dôme in Paris or a party held in your name on the top of a mountain in Colorado, you'll need to preplan.

If you wish to make anatomical gifts—donating organs for transplant or your body for scientific or medical research—you'll have to make arrangements ahead of time.

Preplanning becomes particularly important if you are involved in a "nontraditional" relationship (an unmarried or same-sex couple, for instance). In the absence of binding written instructions that specifically address the questions of disposition and memorial services, control will revert to your next of kin: your closest biological family relation. Unless you put it in writing, no one need acknowledge the friend or lover whom you would prefer to have making decisions. In the worst case, this can result in funeral and disposition arrangements that directly contradict your wishes.

If you are terminally ill, you may find it comforting to make decisions and plan ahead, knowing that those you love will be spared both the confusion of not knowing what you wanted and the stress of not knowing what to do.

Easy Does It
While it is important to be precise and comprehensive in preparing a will, it can be counterproductive to get too detailed about planning your disposition and funeral. Unless you are terminally ill, the place and time of your death are unpredictable. All sorts of variables can change your situation: You can move, marry, divorce, or experience the early death of those you expect to survive you. Preparing a detailed and exhaustive record of specific requirements for your funeral can create as many problems for your survivors as if you hadn't planned at all. Answering a few important questions is the idea here (unless, of course, you wish to make very detailed plans for whatever personal reasons you may have.)

Making some general decisions and sharing them with those closest to you is highly recommended. Consider your options; talk with your family or friends and let them know how you feel and what you want.

As you would expect, major funeral industry organizations such as the National Funeral Directors Association (NFDA) and the Cremation Association of North America (CANA) have advocated planning ahead. However, many groups with less vested interest, such as the American Association of Retired Persons (AARP) and the Consumers Union have also endorsed the strategy of preplanning. Some of these groups have made it easier to plan by publishing information and advice on how to go about this chore with a minimum of fuss and anxiety. These aids and guidelines are readily available, but most people don't know how to find them. This chapter will describe the basic process and tell you what to look for, what to look out for, and how to obtain more information.

THE DIFFERENCE BETWEEN PREPLANNING, PREPAYING, PREARRANGEMENT, AND PRENEED

Preplanning means just what it says, planning your disposition and funeral ahead of time. *Prepaying* means paying for these things in advance. *Preplanning* is a good idea. *Prepaying* is iffy. Most consumer advocates caution against it.

Preneed and *prearrangement* are terms coined by the funeral industry that are usually used to indicate both planning *and* paying. Watch out for this kind of hazy terminology and don't pay for anything until you read the section on prepaying later in this chapter.

Planning ahead can be as simple or as comprehensive as you wish. You can make the basic choices and let it go at that, or you can really get into it and choose flowers, music, write your own obituary, compare prices, and shop around. But you don't have to spend a cent ahead of time. If you want to provide funds to cover costs, you can do so in any number of ways that do not require going through the funeral industry.

SCOPING IT OUT

Preplanning for death can be divided into two categories: choosing a means of disposition and planning a commemorative event of some type.

1. *Disposition.* When someone dies, their body must be attended to—quickly. How do you want your body disposed of?

2. *Commemoration.*   The observation of an individual's death. How do you wish to be acknowledged and remembered?

Disposition is required; commemoration you can do or not, as you wish.

DISPOSITION

Geography, religion, secular beliefs, climate, topography, and social systems have all played a part in establishing the disposition customs of cultures throughout history. The procedure is traditionally determined by the four elements: air (exposure), water (ocean burial), earth (burial), or fire (cremation).

Certain cultures have relied almost exclusively on exposure to dispose of bodies, placing the corpse on a platform, in a tree, or on a hillside, to be weathered by elements or stripped by scavenging birds and animals. Since the sixth century B.C., for instance, Zoroastrians have regarded corpses as so unclean that they would contaminate earth, fire, or water. They therefore chose the organic method of exposure and consumption to dispose of dead bodies. Other cultures, among them Tibetans and many Native American tribes, preferred exposure because it was most efficient and natural (and in the case of Tibet, geographically prudent, as the ground is often quite frozen and firewood is hard to come by).

Some societies have developed what many would consider to be fairly exotic customs. People in Indonesia, on islands in the Caribbean, and along the Amazon River, for example, traditionally consumed the decomposed or cremated remains of the deceased, mixed with rice, various beverages, or banana mush. (If you are tempted to deem such a practice uncivilized, keep in mind that the vast majority of people in the world consider the customary American practice of embalming downright barbaric.)

Other peoples, especially seafaring cultures, have chosen water as their medium for burial. Sometimes bodies were weighted to sink underwater, left on reefs, or allowed to float and be eaten by sharks. In many cultures that relied on water burial, from the Norse in Scandinavia to the islanders of the South Pacific, bodies were set adrift in boats or canoes.

Contemporary Western culture has turned away from the ancient (and economical) means of exposure and water burial as methods of bodily disposition. Exposure to the air, regarded as a health hazard, is illegal in the United States. No one living in a major metropolitan area is going to argue with this. Sea burial, although a legal option where circumstances allow, has fallen into disfavor—unless the body has first been cremated and reduced to ash and bone fragments. With the options of air and water essentially eliminated, Western culture has focused primarily on disposition through earth or fire.

The methods practiced in North America these days are as follows:

- Burial, below ground in a grave or aboveground in a tomb or mausoleum.

- Cremation, or reduction of the body through intense heat to ash and bone fragments, which are then buried, stored, or scattered.

- Organ donation for transplantation or body donation for medical or anatomical research, followed by burial or cremation.

In addition, there are a few less orthodox propositions, including freezing and mummification, but they are not, by any stretch of the imagination, widely practiced. Other efforts to apply entrepreneurial zeal to the question of disposition have included the plan of a former astronaut to send ashes into space orbit and a scheme to convert cremated remains into gemstones to be displayed or worn. Let's start with the most common choice, burial.

BURIAL

Human beings have been burying their dead for over 60,000 years. Neanderthals and other Paleolithic peoples placed the dead in the earth (along with their food and tools), individually and in groups, covering them with rocks or dirt.

We are not alone in this practice. Elephants, as described by the noted anthropologist Richard Leakey, have also occasionally covered their dead, although what this ritual means to the elephants is not exactly clear to us. But then, the practice we've developed wouldn't make much sense to them, either. Money is key. The unremitting demand for land among the living has inhibited plans to expand cemeteries and has increased the cost of land in which to inter the dead. Americans spend about $1 billion on cemetery plots every year. Writing about changes in the funeral industry as the population bubble grows older, reporter Michael Specter predicts that amount will increase.

> Baby boomers are buying cemetery plots in record numbers. . . . They are out there hustling for the "right" cemetery spot in much the same way they have scoured the nation for the most sophisticated cabernets, the most authentic Italian espresso machines, and the best Aprica strollers. . . . Before 1960 it was rare to find any healthy young person searching for his own grave. During the '60s only ten percent of all such purchases were made far in advance. . . . That figure grew to 20 percent in the '70s and 40 percent in the '80s. And nobody sees any end soon to this bull market . . . the careful grave-watchers at the American Cemetery Association don't expect the real land crunch to hit until the year 2000, when most boomers will have hit 50. . . .[3]

Although the increase in burial costs, the decrease in available land, and the urbanization and mobility of the American public have made cremation a viable option for an increasing number of people, earth burial is still the most popular form of disposition. For some it is the only way to show the appropriate reverence; others welcome the idea of being buried next to their loved ones, and still others prefer the idea of a "final resting place" where survivors can come to mourn or commemorate in a quiet, contemplative environment.

Buying a Burial Plot: Not Your Usual Kind of Real Estate Investment

Unless you have a private family burial ground or own your own land and are considering a home burial (see later in this chapter), you will need to buy a plot of land in a cemetery if you wish to be buried. Nonprofit cemeteries are owned and operated by churches, religious groups, and cooperative groups as well as the municipal, county, and federal government in many communities. Private organizations, both fraternal and corporate, run profit-making cemeteries.

There are two basic types of cemeteries common today. The traditional cemetery allows the installation of upright stone monuments as memorials to the dead. Memorial parks and gardens, first established about sixty years ago, are architecturally landscaped with trees, flowers, and sweeping lawns. Memorial parks generally allow only flat slab memorials that lie flush in the ground and blend in with the carefully designed landscape. In any case, they can be fancy or simple, Forest Lawn or Boot Hill, and the cost varies accordingly.

Burial plots are generally about three feet by eight feet. Plots are available for couples. (Cost usually varies according to whether caskets are buried side by side or double depth, one on top of the other, an increasingly common practice due to scarcity of burial space.) Family plots are also available, although many consumer advocates point out that today, when so many people move so often, they can be a wasted investment.

Prepurchasing

Buying a burial plot is different from other types of real estate investment. It may appreciate in value, but it cannot be sold, as can the freehold ownership of a house, for instance. Some states prevent the selling of plots at a profit, and many cemeteries reserve resale rights for themselves. Check it out before you purchase.

Under a preneed or prepaid cemetery plan, a specific cemetery will reserve a grave for your eventual interment in return for prepayment, in full or in installments. Just as in preneed funeral purchases, prepayment of cemetery plots requires the consumer to take certain precautions. In *The American Way of Death,* Jessica Mitford chronicled a host of abuses, including the sale of nonexistent or already-taken plots. Although subsequent regulation of the funeral industry has curtailed such practices, you would still be wise to check before laying out your money. The licensing and ownership of a cemetery can be verified through the local Better Business Bureau or state regulatory agency.

If you are satisfied that you are dealing with a reputable, reliable cemetery, funeral provider, or memorial society, find out whether you can transfer your agreement to a cemetery in another location or sell your lot if you move.

You may also want to consider questions about care and maintenance. Do the grounds, graves, and markers seem well maintained? If so, who pays for it and how? Many cemeteries today have "perpetual care" funds that claim to cover the cost of maintenance indefinitely. Ask who administers the fund, whether it covers the upkeep of grave markers or monuments as well as the grass, and how much of the cost of your burial plot will be applied to this fund. Such care usually does not refer to the upkeep of specific grave sites but rather to the cemetery as a whole. Many advocates recommend that consumers get perpetual-care agreements in writing.

Grave Liner or Vault
Most cemeteries require that a liner or vault be placed in the excavation to prevent the ground from collapsing over time. This is not a state law but is quite customary. As described in *It's Your Choice*, a very helpful planning guide published by the American Association of Retired Persons and written by Thomas C. Nelson,

> A grave liner is a boxlike structure, most often made of concrete, with a loose-fitting slab cover to support the earth that will be filled in over it. A burial vault is a more substantial structure, often steel reinforced and metal lined or coated, with a tight-fitting molded lid that provides a seal when it is put into place. . . . There are only a few local jurisdictions where legal requirements will force you to buy a liner, but since sunken graves add to a cemetery's upkeep costs, many (though not all) cemeteries require some kind of grave liner. Check directly with local cemeteries to find out what their requirements are. Do not necessarily rely on what a funeral director tells you. If you do not wish to purchase a liner or a vault, you may be able to find a cemetery that does not require one.[4]

A liner is less expensive than a vault and will serve the purpose equally well. It can usually be purchased through either a cemetery or a funeral home (although many choose not to stock the less expensive liner and will tell you that only a vault is available) but is generally cheaper when purchased through the cemetery. If a funeral director claims that an expensive, airtight vault will preserve a body for significantly longer than the cheaper concrete vaults, it's a bad sign. This is a claim that used to be made regularly by many funeral industry people. It is not true.

Aboveground Entombment
Cemeteries commonly offer the option of aboveground burial or entombment. A mausoleum tends to serve not only as a burial place but also as a monument to the deceased individual (or family).

The practice of using stone tombs to house and protect the dead dates back to the ancient East and is at least 5,000 years old. Some of the most famous mausoleums include the Egyptian pyramids, India's Taj Mahal, and Lenin's tomb in the Soviet Union.

When a body is entombed, the casket is placed into a mausoleum crypt rather than an underground grave. This aboveground structure, usually situated on cemetery grounds, is generally built of marble, granite, or similar stone. The tomb itself is sealed with a marble or granite face, accompanied by a memorial inscription or a plaque.

Home Burial

If you want to be buried in your own backyard, you'll need to do some investigating ahead of time. Depending on where your backyard is located, you may or may not be able to have a home burial. If you own land in a rural or semirural area, most states will permit home burial, under certain circumstances and with certain restrictions (having to do with water-supply sources, underground cable, etc.), determined by the zoning ordinances in your local area.

If you are interested in exploring the possibility of taking care of disposition more personally or with the help of friends and family, you should read *Caring for Your Own Dead* by Lisa Carlson, the most practical and informative book available on the subject. Carlson describes the history of disposition in this country and how it has changed dramatically over recent years. She proposes that for some people handling death arrangements personally will not only save a considerable amount of money but might also provide a sense of control over events that can help them through the grieving process. This book takes a look at an alternative that used to be the norm and provides a great deal of pragmatic advice for those who are seeking such an alternative. (See listings at the end of this chapter.)

Coffins and Caskets

Coffins or caskets (the words have come to mean the same thing) have been used for over 5,000 years, reaching their highest development in the intricately detailed sarcophagi of ancient Egypt. Some of these elaborate coffins provided painted directions to the next world in addition to glorified representations of the deceased.

Although most people tend to think of caskets in their traditional rectangular form, there is room for variation and originality. In

Austria in the 1970s, members of a club for "Vertically Buried Loved Ones" placed bodies upright in plastic tubes that were then deposited in a deeply dug hole. And in the United States the family of a Chicago gambler once paid over $7,000 to fashion a coffin in the shape of a Cadillac Seville. An attempted mass-market innovation was the glass coffin (which weighed 1,500 pounds when empty). It never really caught on. The durable yet relatively lightweight fiberglass coffin has steadily gained in popularity.

The casket is often the single most expensive purchase in the disposition package. If you would prefer an inexpensive casket, you may need to specifically request that a funeral director or casket dealer show them to you. Many state and local laws require caskets displayed in a showroom to have a card attached to each model that lists the price, composition, and model number. Some funeral homes and casket dealers, however, may not display their economical models as prominently as their more expensive models.

In some areas you can find casket makers who operate independently of conventional funeral homes. These third-party providers make their products available in direct competition with funeral directors. If you are able to find funeral products from a third-party provider you may be charged an extra "handling" fee by the funeral home. As described in a report submitted to the Federal Trade Commission:

> Casket-handling fees are charges assessed by funeral providers for products furnished by third-party marketers. Handling fees are a relatively recent phenomena as third-party vendors have been encouraged by the Funeral Rules unbundling requirements to enter the market to sell caskets in direct competition with funeral homes.[5]

Independent casket makers are few and far between, but if there is one in your area, you may find him or her listed in the yellow pages of the telephone directory under "Funeral," or ask a local furniture or cabinet maker.

Headstones and Statuary

Grave markers range from small wooden plaques to huge, elaborate monuments. In many European cities the cemeteries are filled with marvelous funerary sculpture. Judi Culbertson and Tom Randall have produced a charming series of illustrated guides to the world's great cemeteries (entitled *Permanent Parisians, Permanent Londoners,* etc; see listing at the end of this chapter.). In it they describe the continental attitude:

> In Europe an interest in cemeteries is not regarded as morbid or unnatural. On November first and second thousands of Parisians flock to Père Lachaise to celebrate All Saints' Day and the Day of the Dead. Much French funerary sculpture is designed to be appreciated (and sometimes to give a warning or impart a private joke)."[6]

In Italy as well, the cemeteries are filled with extraordinary headstones and monuments, creating intriguing sites to explore and, in some more spectacular cases, significant tourist attractions. In Victorian England, where death was celebrated and romanticized among the middle and upper classes, graveyards were built that today present some of the more interesting examples of neogothic architecture and history.

In the United States, however, cemeteries are usually not so much fun. Many restrict the type of marker or monument one can install. Check to see what type is allowed and be sure to ascertain *all* the charges involved (inscription, installation, etc.) and whether or not a marker or gravestone can be purchased from a source other than the cemetery. Upright markers can cost as little as $350 or as much as you want to spend for an elaborate monument. Flush markers (those that lie flat in the ground), in stone or bronze, range from $250 to $600.

An increasingly common restriction in many cemeteries prohibits upright headstones altogether, limiting memorials to flush markers. Although cemetery owners claim to be motivated by aesthetics and the desire to maintain an "unbroken landscape," an even stronger impetus is the fact that headstones are a maintenance nightmare. In addition to being a target for vandals who knock them over, upright tombstones, unlike flush markers, require cemeteries to abandon their large power mowers, which often cannot fit between two tombstones, in order to cut the grass around the monuments. Cutting grass with hand-held mowers takes more time and costs cemeteries more money.

The Cost of Burial
There are numerous charges involved in burial, and they all add up.

Cemetery plot.   Costs vary considerably from sparsely settled rural areas to large metropolitan centers, but speaking generally, you can expect to pay anywhere from $100 to $3,500 for a cemetery plot. In crowded urban areas, grave sites may cost thousands of dollars, and exclusive or "select" cemeteries and memorial parks may charge exorbitant fees. Westwood Village Memorial Park in Los Angeles, where Marilyn Monroe and many other stars are buried, requires a minimum entry fee of $15,000.

Grave liner or vault.   A simple liner can cost $200 or $300 and up. A vault can cost considerably more. Heavier steel or copper vaults may range from $2,000 to $8,000.

Aboveground entombment.   Mausoleum space can cost anywhere from $1,500 to $25,000, in addition to the cost of opening and closing the crypt. Some, such as the mausoleum with a stained-glass representation of the New York skyline prepared for Harry Helmsley, can cost hundreds of thousands of dollars or more.

Casket.   The cost of a casket today ranges from a few hundred dollars to thousands of dollars, depending on the style, shape, and materials used. A plain pine or particle-board box or a cloth-covered wooden casket can cost from $200 to $700. Caskets made of harder woods like oak, walnut, and mahogany may range from $1,200 to $8,000. Metal caskets may run from $2,500 to $5,000 for a copper casket or as much as $15,000 or more for a steel or bronze casket.

In addition, there are a number of other cemetery expenses for which you can be charged, including opening and closing the grave and recording the burial in the cemetery's books. The total amount of a cemetery's earth burial charges, including the plot itself, the grave liner, and opening and closing the grave (but *not* including the price of a casket and funeral services), may range from $500 to $10,000.

If you are a veteran, you are entitled to free burial in a military cemetery (and a free headstone or grave marker from the Veterans Affairs Department, whether or not you are buried in a national cemetery). Also eligible are surviving spouses who do not remarry and unmarried minor children.

CREMATION

The major alternative to burial in the United States is cremation. Although evidence exists that bodies were burned as far back as the Neolithic period, cremation was first formally introduced into Western culture by the Greeks (around 1000 B.C.), who, upon finding that enemies desecrated the bodies of their dead soldiers, protected them by cremating them and shipping the ashes home for burial.

Viking cultures once set their dead leaders afloat in ships that were then ignited and set afire on the water. In a 1980 film entitled *Rocket Gibraltar,* an old man tells his grandchildren of this ancient custom and how he wishes it were still practiced today. He wistfully describes what it would mean to him when the flames were finished and the morning had come—"fresh and beautiful, vanished completely, like a dream."

Today cremation is a common practice in many countries. In the East it has long been the primary method of disposition. Japan makes it mandatory, and in England cremation has become by far the most popular method of disposition. In the United States, the practice has gained steadily in popularity over the last fifteen years. Cremation, which followed only 8 percent of all deaths in 1977, has risen to over 15 percent today. In Hawaii, it has already surpassed burial, while in California over one-third of all corpses are now cremated.

The reasons for the rise in popularity of cremation are numerous. It can be a bargain compared to earth burial (although, depending on the funeral or memorial service chosen to accompany the cremation, this may not always be true). Some choose it due to the increasing scarcity (and costliness) of cemetery land. Others see it as a quick, clean, and simple method to dispose of the body. In addition, the urbanization and increasing mobility of American families have diminished the sense of heritage and homeland that once demanded the return of a body for burial in a "family plot" near the family homestead. Today over 900 crematories exist in the United States. Most are associated with a cemetery or funeral home.

Ashes to Ashes

When a body is cremated, intense heat reduces it to ash and bone fragments. The cremated remains, called "cremains" in the funeral industry, can then be gathered and placed in an urn or other container for burial, storage, or scattering.

Generally, a body arrives at the crematory in a container chosen by the family of the deceased. It can range from a canvas bag or corrugated cardboard box to a pine box or even a full casket. *Note:* The Federal Trade Commission forbids members of the funeral industry to falsely claim that a casket is *required* for cremation. There is no such law. Of course, you can choose an expensive casket if you so desire, but before spending a fortune, keep in mind that the body will be cremated in the same container in which it arrives.

At the crematory, the container is placed in a *retort*—a specially designed furnace in which temperatures will reach 1,800 degrees Fahrenheit or greater. Within two to three hours, the process of combustion and evaporation in the cremation chamber reduces the body to a pile of cremains, which collects below the cremation chamber. Depending on the size of the body, cremation will yield from three to nine pounds of fragments, which can then be pulverized if further reduction is needed. (Because cremains are gravelly, they will generally need to be crushed, especially if the family intends to "scatter" them.)

Urns

Many people choose to have cremains placed in an urn, to keep or to bury or to transport before scattering. Urns, which range in cost from $25 to thousands of dollars, come in a variety of materials, styles, and sizes (and can be custom-made to order). Materials include everything from simple plastic to bronze, hardwoods, and marble. The urn can be just large enough to hold the cremains of one person or larger to accommodate more than one. It can be kept wherever you wish, displayed in a mausoleum or "urn garden," or buried in a cemetery plot.

Burying Ashes

If you decide to bury the ashes, you can do so in a standard cemetery plot, on private land, or in a special "urn garden" located within a cemetery or memorial park. Most cemeteries will allow more than one cremated body to be buried in a single plot. Burial of urns in a cemetery will carry the added fees for opening and closing the grave and will usually entail purchase of a memorial stone or grave marker as well. In addition, some cemeteries require a vaultlike container for the burial of a cremation urn.

Another option is a *columbarium,* a building with walls of recessed niches for storing urns. Usually located in a cemetery, columbaria offer the same types of choices as other memorial settings, including differing styles, materials, and sizes of niches. Costs are correspondingly wide-ranging—from $150 up to whatever the traffic will bear.

Scattering

Sometimes cremains are placed in a canister or temporary container in which the ashes can be held just long enough to be transported to a scattering site. Ashes can be scattered at sea, by air, or in a fixed location.

Each state has its own rules governing where and how you can scatter cremains. Most states do allow scattering as long as all bone fragments in the cremains have been pulverized into unrecognizability. Some states require a permit to strew ashes, over either sea or land, while others restrict the locations in which it can be done. However, as Theodore E. Hughes and David Klein point out in *A Family Guide to Wills, Funerals, & Probate,* "It is difficult to see how this prohibition can be enforced if survivors choose to do it privately and inconspicuously."[7] If you want to learn the regulations in your state, you might ask a funeral director or contact a crematorium.

If you feel that your survivors would welcome a fixed, identifiable place to visit, you may want to consider what crematories call "scattering gardens." For a fee, you can have your ashes scattered in a garden located on or near crematory property.

The Cost of Cremation

Cremation in itself, which carries no cemetery charges, generally costs less than burial aboveground or below. The basic cost of a professionally arranged cremation (including crematory charges of $50 to $200, plus a funeral director's services in transporting the body and handling paperwork) may range from $800 to $3,000.

DIRECT DISPOSITION: A LOW-COST ALTERNATIVE

Burial and cremation are most commonly performed through the auspices of a funeral home, a commercial business providing the necessary services of disposition coupled with a profusion of trappings. While most of these extras have come to be associated with the "appropriate" commemoration of the dead (and in some cases are even incorrectly assumed to be required by law or regulation), they are not necessary to the basic requirements of disposition, and they do cost a lot of money. An efficient and economical alternative method of dealing with disposition is called, appropriately enough, direct disposition. With direct disposition the body is transferred directly from the place of death to the place of burial or cremation, which eliminates embalming, viewing, storage, and other costly features of the conventional funeral process. Basically, direct disposition simply bypasses the funeral home, resulting in a considerable savings.

In response to the high costs of disposition, a company calling itself The Telophase Society (which today handles over one-sixth of all deaths in San Diego County and provides services in California, Oregon, and Washington) began offering low-cost, no-frills cremations in 1971. After Telophase won a number of suits brought against it by funeral and cemetery operators, other "direct cremation" companies joined the field. One of these, The Neptune Society, licensed in California, New York, and Florida, currently has 250,000 members signed up for its cremation services.

Although still denigrated as "burn and scatter" or "bake and shake" outfits by traditional funeral directors, these direct-disposition companies offer a valuable service by providing low-cost cremation to those who want it. Many will handle the paperwork needed to obtain and file a legal death certificate and cremation permit and/or to receive death benefits from Social Security or the Veterans Administration. (See chapter 9 for information on filing death certificates and applying for death benefits.)

Most profit-making direct-cremation companies charge an initial membership fee of about $25, which covers registration and administrative costs. Membership will allow you to preselect the type of cremation service you would like. Cost of services "at the time of need" range from about $200 to $900.

Although many of these groups call themselves societies (e.g., The Neptune Society or Memorial Cremation Society), they are not the same as memorial societies (described later in this chapter). As pointed out by the Continental Association of Funeral and Memorial Societies:

. . . memorial societies are nonprofit consumer groups democratically controlled by their members. They usually offer a choice of services and advice on preplanning. Direct cremation services are profit-making businesses. . . . [They] usually charge lower fees than funeral directors. If there is no memorial society in your area, you may find that direct cremation services offer the lowest cost method of disposing of human remains.[8]

Direct or immediate burial can be had in the same way. The body will be transported to a cemetery and promptly interred in a plain softwood or pine coffin. Charges generally run between $400 and $1,200, plus cemetery charges (cost of burial plot, opening and closing of grave site, etc.). Remember, if you wish to be buried rather than cremated, you will need to purchase a burial plot, which adds to the cost of direct disposition.

To find a direct-disposition company, look in the yellow pages of the telephone book for firms that say "Immediate" or "Direct Cremation" or "Minimal Cost Cremations or Burials." These companies sometimes advertise on the obituary pages of the newspaper.

These basic services can be provided by standard funeral homes as well as direct-disposition companies, but most funeral directors would rather sell you a much more elaborate package. The AARP planning guide *It's Your Choice* has this admonition: "If you talk with a funeral director, be wary of being talked out of a direct disposition and into a traditional funeral. Know what you want, and make sure you get it."[9]

MAKING ANATOMICAL GIFTS

You can do two rather extraordinary things with a dead body: You can use it for research and teaching, or take parts from it to repair living bodies. Making a gift of your body can be done in a number of ways. You can bequeath particular organs for transplantation, donate all organs and tissues, or give your entire body to a medical school.

Organ Donation
In 1954, surgeons in Boston successfully transplanted a kidney for the first time. Since then, the practice of transplantation from do-

nors to recipients has expanded to encompass a wide variety of organs, including livers and hearts as well as kidneys. Bones and tissue (including cartilage, marrow, skin, eardrums, and corneas) have also been transplanted with success. In addition to skin and corneas, transplantable human tissues include other eye parts, blood vessels, ligaments, tendons and other connective tissue, pituitary glands, the dura mater and other brain tissues, eardrums, middle ears, and ear bones, heart valves, and other organ subparts.

The practice of transplantation became more common in the 1980s with the introduction of cyclosporine, a powerful immunosuppressive drug that significantly reduced the chances that a host's body would reject transplanted donor organs.

Some Interesting Issues Surrounding Organ Donation and Transplantation

The ethical questions involved in the practice of organ transplantation are too numerous to go into here but are nonetheless interesting. For the most part, they center around the problems raised by the shortage of organs compared to the number of people who want transplants. How to decide who receives what? Should age be a factor? Should money be a factor? Should recipients be given a second transplant if the first one isn't working out? Continued medical developments now allow for multiple organ transplants, but this practice will add to the shortage.

The United Network for Organ Sharing (UNOS) is the primary organ-distribution network system in the United States. Established in 1984 by the National Task Force on Organ Transplantation, UNOS coordinates regional organ-procurement agencies and transplant centers. This system operates under the principle that organs, once removed from the donor, are a "national resource" and as such are to be disseminated to the most appropriate recipient based on a point system reflecting strict medical criteria for blood and tissue matching. However, the selection of waiting recipients is often influenced by a number of factors not easily controlled or regulated. Investigative reporter Mark Dowie has written a fascinating and revealing account of organ transplantation entitled *"We Have a Donor."* In it he says, "The organ-as-national-resource theory remains just that—a theory. An organ is still, de facto, the property of the center that harvests it. . . . The final choice of a recipient remains the privilege of surgeons and committees in the transplant units."[10] And is sometimes influenced by other factors as well. When you see parents on national television pleading for a liver for their dying child, they may well be bypassing this system.

In attempting to address the shortage, some recommendations suggest expanding "presumed consent" laws (laws that allow removal of organs *unless* the deceased has indicated otherwise) and making payments to donors. Currently it is illegal to sell or purchase body parts. However, as pointed out by Joel Swerdlow in the Annenberg Washington Program Recommendation for a National Transplantation Policy, "[current law] . . . does not regulate or even anticipate potentially excessive earnings by organizations that procure, process and distribute tissues and organs. Since a fully utilized body generates so much medical business, the possibility of abuse, or even scandal, is real."[11]

Indeed, there is a big potential profit in organ and tissue marketing. At this time, the business of donation, procurement, and transplantation of body parts is confined to the public sector, but it is hard to believe that a society as dedicated to profit making as ours will be able to resist moving this "product" into the marketplace.

A Big Demand

All of these issues are intensified by the fact that there is a great demand for healthy organs. In 1990, over 21,000 people were on waiting lists, over 15,000 for kidneys alone, and these lists are continually growing. A new name goes on the organ waiting list every half hour.

A lot less publicized than organ transplants is the transplantation of bone, tendon, ligament, or connective-tissue implants to more than 200,000 people in the United States each year. Another 30,000 receive corneal transplants. Organs and tissues are also used for research and medical study.

While tissues and corneas can be taken from almost anybody, major organs are another story. In a definitive essay on anatomical donation, author David Owen puts it this way:

Only about one percent of all the people who die are potential kidney donors, for instance, and kidneys are actually removed from only one in five of these. The reason is that a suitable organ donor is that rarest of individuals, a person in marvelous health who is also, somehow, dead. Major organs for transplantation have to be removed while the donors' hearts are still beating, which means that all donors are brain-dead hospital patients on artificial respiration. The ideal donor is a young man who has played a game of basketball, run a few miles, and then had a safe dropped on his head.[12]

Being a Donor Isn't Dangerous

It is not uncommon to fear that declaring yourself a donor might make organ-hungry surgeons eager to proclaim you brain-dead. Actually the opposite is closer to the truth. Two physicians with no vested interest, who will not be involved in the transplantation, must find the a patient "utterly and irretrievably deceased." After being declared brain-dead, an organ donor must be maintained on a respirator as a "beating heart" cadaver until the organ-procurement process begins.

Whole-Body Donation

The dissection of human bodies provides an invaluable part of medical education. Since private donations constitute the principal source of donor bodies, both teaching and research hospitals depend on bequests in order to complete the education of medical school students. Cadavers are dissected in anatomy classes or used for biomedical education and research. If you wish, you can indicate whether you would prefer to have your body used in anatomy classes or for research.

Some medical schools will pick up the body at the time of death; others require that it be delivered. None will pay extra costs if you die in a distant place. Donating your body to science is even cheaper than direct disposition. After the school term has ended, medical institutions cremate or bury cadavers at no charge to the family. If the family so desires, many schools will return the body for disposition. In the first case, there is no charge, but if you want the body back, you must cover subsequent costs.

Most medical schools prefer only whole-body donations (although many accept bodies from which eyes have been removed). According to David Owen, "Medical schools do reserve the right not to honor pledges. All schools turn down bodies that have been severely burned, for obvious reasons. Other requirements vary. Pennsylvania rejects bodies that are 'recently operated on, autopsied, decomposed, obese, emaciated, amputated, infectious, mutilated or otherwise unfit.' " With the exception of corneas, you cannot donate your organs for transplant *and* your body for research. It has to be one or the other.

How to Make an Anatomical Bequest

ORGANS AND TISSUES   If you have decided that you wish to be an organ donor, the easiest way to indicate your preference is to obtain an *organ donor card,* also known as a *uniform donor card.* This card, currently held by 19 percent of American adults, will identify you as a willing potential organ donor. It grants permission and instructs doctors and other medical personnel to regard you as a donor of organs for transplantation in the event of your death.

If you would like an organ donor card or form, you can obtain one from organ donor agencies in your community—the local hospital, the county or state office of the National Kidney Foundation, or a community eye bank. Or contact The Living Bank, Medic Alert, Organ Donors Canada, or the Continental Association of Funeral and Memorial Societies. (See listings at the end of this chapter.)

You can also procure an organ donor card from your local Department of Motor Vehicles. Depending on the practice in your state, you may check a box on your license, have your license stamped, or have a separate card attached to your license that testifies to your wishes. Indicating your preference about becoming an organ donor is not compulsory except in Colorado, where drivers must check off a box stating whether they would or would not like to become organ donors. (Sixty percent say yes.)

However, in making a decision to be an organ donor, the single most important thing you should do is to *inform your family and ensure their cooperation in fulfilling your wishes.* As emphasized by David Owen,

> You could die with an organ-donor card in every pocket, and another one pasted on your forehead, and still no one would touch you if your current or separated but not divorced spouse, son or daughter twenty-one years of age or older, parent, brother or sister twenty-one years of age or older, or guardian, in that order, said no. . . . If you want to be an organ donor, carrying a card is much less important than making sure your relatives know your wishes.[13]

This is because doctors don't want the complication of a legal hassle with surviving next of kin and medical profession policy generally restricts acting without their consent. Physicians will not remove organs without permission from the living relatives.

WHOLE BODY   If you wish to donate your body for medical research or the training of medical school students, you should contact the school or hospital to which you would like your body to go. The more prestigious institutions, such as Harvard Medical, sometimes have more contributions of this sort than they need, but most such establishments have developed some reciprocity on this matter, and if accepted, a body will be put to good use in one place or another.

The medical institution you choose will inform you of its procedures regarding anatomical gifts. In most cases, they will provide you with an *instrument of anatomical gift,* or *certificate for bequeathing body,* which you will need to sign and have witnessed.

Again, be certain to discuss your intentions with both your family and your doctor. Family members need to be informed in order to avoid opposition that could delay or even prevent bequeathal following your death.

You should make alternative disposition plans in case, for whatever reason, your anatomical bequest is not accepted.

REVOCATION   If at any time after you have declared your intention to make an anatomical gift you entertain second thoughts, you can easily change your bequest. Simply destroy your universal donor card or your instrument of anatomical gift and let your relatives and your physician know that you have changed your mind about the donation.

A Final Point
Donating organs, bones, or tissues doesn't rule out a funeral or even open-casket viewing, if that is your wish. Funeral homes can usually make a body suitable for viewing in a conventional manner.

Whole-body donation involves a special type of embalming that preserves the body for many years. If you wish to have a funeral with the body present, you must find a funeral director who will contact the medical institution for special embalming instructions. Most people who make whole-body donations opt for a memorial service.

EMBALMING

The practice of embalming was begun around 4000 B.C. by the ancient Egyptians, who treated internal organs with pine oils, packed the body with herbs and salts, and immersed it in a salt solution.

In the United States, embalming, once considered paganistic, did not become widely acceptable until the Civil War, when the practice was used to transport the bodies of soldiers back to their homes (a practice that continued in all subsequent wars in which the United States was involved). After the Civil War, embalming was promoted as a means of allowing public viewing of the body (and incidentally as a method of preventing premature burial) and quickly became the centerpiece of the new funeral industry.

The success of the National Funeral Directors Association in promoting the process is demonstrated by the fact that today embalming has become an expected and virtually unquestioned practice following most deaths in the United States—the only country in the world where this is true. The people of many other cultures regard embalming as somewhat barbaric. Indeed, even in the United States, certain religions, especially Orthodox Judaism and Islam, forbid the practice altogether on the grounds that it desecrates the body.

The cosmetic embalming process practiced by the funeral industry does not preserve the body for very long. Rapid decomposition, although temporarily halted by embalming, will resume within several weeks. Indeed, one of the provisions of the Federal Trade Commission's 1984 Funeral Rule prohibited funeral providers from misrepresenting the preservative value of embalming and that of caskets, vaults, and grave liners as well. No funeral product or service can prevent deterioration indefinitely. (A different type of embalming, done to preserve a body for medical research, can last up to twenty years.)

Although it has become common practice, embalming is neither always necessary nor legally required except in certain circumstances. Some states mandate embalming if a lengthy delay exists between the time of death and the date of disposition. Other states or counties require it in case of death due to a communicable or contagious disease. Finally, if the body must be transported by common carrier (i.e., plane or train), some state laws (or the policies of some common carriers) may require prior embalming. (In *Caring for Your Own Dead,* Lisa Carlson includes a state-by-state listing of these requirements. Her book also gives a history of embalming, a discussion of the issues involved, and descriptions of the various procedures.)

AND NOW FOR SOMETHING COMPLETELY DIFFERENT

Although almost everyone in the United States chooses the traditional disposition methods of burial or cremation, recent years have seen the introduction of some alternatives promoted by a few enterprising entrepreneurs.

Cryonics

In 1967, James Bedford became the first person to undergo cryonic suspension. When the company that froze him, Cryonics Interment Inc., later went bankrupt, the corpse was shipped to Riverside, California, home of Alcor, the largest of the three main cryonics organizations that still exist today. The other two cryonics groups are Trans Time, located in Oakland, California, and the Cryonics Institute, headquartered in Oak Park, Michigan.

About five hundred people have already signed up to be frozen after they die, or as those in the cryonics industry optimistically call it, "undergo deanimation." The premise underlying this euphemism assumes the possibility of "reanimation," or the reversal of the dying process. Fifteen or more people and three animals have already been frozen, awaiting the day when medical breakthroughs may be able to reverse the process of dying and cure the ailment that killed them.

By law, those who choose to be frozen have opted for an entirely legal means of disposition. They have donated their bodies for scientific research to ostensibly nonprofit organizations that conduct cryonics research on anyone who makes themselves available for cryonic suspension services (and pays a hefty fee). However, few laws govern the cryonics industry. It requires neither licensing nor accreditation (although the procedures that ready a subject for freezing generally demand the services of a licensed mortician or coroner).

The lack of regulation in the cryonics industry has already led to some difficulties. Several cryonics organizations have gone out of business, leaving frozen corpses to thaw out and decompose when power was shut off. It was also discovered that other bankrupt companies had never frozen clients in the first place.

The Cryonics Process
The cryonics process cannot commence until you have died (or "deanimated"). After a doctor has declared you legally dead, the body is packed in ice and hooked up to a heart-lung machine. Doing so lowers the body's temperature while simultaneously keeping oxygen pumping through the blood, heart, and lungs in order to minimize the damage done to cells and tissues. Then blood is drained from the circulatory system and replaced with glycerol (antifreeze) and other "cryoprotectants," chemicals intended to prevent blood from freezing and damaging cells and to protect tissues from ice formation. After being wrapped in plastic, the body is next submerged in a bath of dry ice and silicon or rubbing alcohol until the body temperature has gradually (over a period ranging from one to twelve days) plummeted to −110 degrees Fahrenheit. It is then placed in an insulated sleeping bag and lowered headfirst into a stainless-steel thermos, called a dewar, which is filled with liquid nitrogen. In the dewar, the body will cool (over three weeks) to −320 degrees, and supposedly be maintained until the day when it is to be revived and cured.

One company also offers what they call "neuropreservation." If you have chosen neuropreservation, the cryonics team will "surgically isolate" (i.e., remove) your head just before the dry-ice bath. When cooled, it will be bagged and canned for cold storage in a communal tank with eight to ten other canned heads. In theory, when thawed, these heads will be surgically reattached to another body or used as a source of cells with which to clone a new body.

Costs
Prices quoted by cryonics groups run anywhere from $30,000 to $100,000, plus membership fees and additional charges. Neuropreservation begins at a minimum of $25,000 a head. The companies recommend that you buy a life insurance policy, naming the cryonics company as beneficiary, in order to cover the costs of the services.

The Trouble with Cryonics

Potential cryonics customers have more to worry about than the cost, however. The biggest problem is the most obvious one: Not a single frozen subject has ever been revived. Although sperm, eggs, bone marrow, skin, blood cells, and even embryos have been frozen, thawed, and brought to life, the reanimating of human beings seems no more likely in the foreseeable future than cloning.

Cryobiology is the legitimate study of the effects of very low temperatures on living organisms and biological systems. Cryobiologists, who regularly freeze and thaw tissue for transplants and therefore come closest to the aim of cryonicists, are among the harshest critics of cryonics. Unable to use frozen hearts, kidneys, or other organs for transplants, these scientists have little patience with those who claim that they will soon be able to freeze and thaw an entire human being. Arthur Rowe, M.D., editor in chief of *Cryobiology*, summed up the opinions of most of his colleagues when he told a journalist, "To believe in cryonics, you would have to believe you could make a cow from hamburger."

The problem, as cryobiologists see it, is that cryonicists will need to overcome the damage done simply by freezing tissue. When body temperature dips below the freezing point, the spaces between cells crystallize, cells rupture, organs tear, and flesh cracks.

An even more difficult problem facing cryonicists, however, is the fact that you have to be declared dead before you can be legally frozen. (This prohibition has already landed Alcor in legal trouble in one case in which it beheaded a woman and froze the head prior to establishing brain death and obtaining a death certificate.) Since its subjects are already dead, cryonic suspension is *not* truly suspended animation. Those who become frozen are thus depending on science to find both a cure for what killed them and a way to bring the dead back to life.

Finally, apart from financial, scientific, and medical drawbacks, the possibility of reanimation also raises ethical questions. If reanimation were possible, the resulting overpopulation would create enormous strains on housing, unemployment, health care resources, medical insurance, and Social Security benefits. Consider the questions this would raise regarding ownership and inheritance of property, life insurance benefits, and remarriage of widows and widowers. In this kind of environment, Dennis J. Doherty, a professor of Christian ethics at Marquette, wonders how long the reanimated will want to remain alive. "How long would one want to live before realizing that death is not an enemy?"

Mummification
Recently, attempts have also been made to revive the ancient art of mummification. Summum Bonum, a Salt Lake City winery, caught the attention of both Phil Donahue and the *Wall Street Journal* in 1988, when it claimed to be founding the world's only commercial mummification facility. Although the company says it has signed up over one hundred people for its services, it has so far mummified only a cat and a dog.

For a base price of around $8,000 the company plans to soak corpses in scented oil, wine, herbs, and chemical preservatives for several weeks before wrapping them in cotton or linen and placing them in a plaster and fiberglass cocoon. The mummified body would then be sealed inside an airtight mummiform, a handcrafted, possibly bejeweled container of gilded bronze or gold shaped to present a likeness of the deceased. This mummiform, which can cost anywhere from $100,000 to $1 million, can then be placed in a family mausoleum for display. Like the cryonics industry, the fledgling mummifiers suggest life insurance as a way of financing the exorbitant costs involved in this method of disposition.

COMMEMORATION

Evidence discovered in Iraq suggests that funerals, complete with the laying of flowers at the burial site, date back at least sixty thousand years. The clinical psychologist Therese Rando, who specializes in grief and bereavement, points out that "virtually all societies and cultures have been found to have some form of funerary rituals." She quotes D. G. Mandelbaum in his work *The Social Uses of Funeral Rites,* who says:

> Certain things must be done after a death, whether it occurs in a very simple or in a highly complex society. The corpse must be disposed of; those who are bereaved—who are personally shocked and socially disoriented—must be helped to reorient themselves; the whole group must have a known way of readjustment after the loss of one of its members.[14]

In most cultures since the Stone Age, people have believed that the correct performance of funerary rites permitted the dead to depart to their proper place and condition after death. In other words, the funeral was for the benefit of the dead. Today we more often consider death rituals to be for the benefit of the living.

Speaking generally, in the past, when our beliefs were centered in an agrarian-based ideology that tended to characterize death as part of a cyclical passage, death rituals were designed to help effect that passage or crossing. Ancient works, such as *The Egyptian Book of the Dead* and *The Tibetan Book of the Dead,* are essentially guidebooks to assist the dead in their journey. Today our beliefs are centered in an urban-based psychology that tends to characterize death as a stopping point or an end. Death ritual is designed to aid the living, who fear that stopping point and the irrevocable loss it implies.

In this more recent tradition, sociologists and psychologists see ritual as important in bringing survivors together to accept the reality of the death, remember the deceased, share grief, and support each other in mourning.

Therese Rando describes the factors that have resulted in these changes, including a secularization and reorganization of society that makes us more mobile, less inculcated in community, and thus less inclined to turn to communal ritual for support and succor.

> Advances in medical science, changes in mortality rates, and the segregation of the ill and elderly, together with the previously mentioned social transitions, have made death seem remote in America. It is no longer a part of everyday existence. In earlier times, children and adults were repeatedly exposed to experiences that familiarized them with death. The deaths of everyone in the extended family, from infants to elders, were as witnessed as the births. Nature also was observed in its continual cycle of life and death. For people in preindustrialized America there was a sense of unity, of an integrated process that took one from birth to death and related both events. That sense is now lacking in contemporary society, and it partially accounts for a widespread American tendency to deny death and the need for funerary rituals.[15]

In his classic work *Dealing Creatively with Death: A Manual of Death Education and Simple Burial,* Ernest Morgan lists a number of social and emotional needs that death rituals can meet for survivors. They include:

- Reestablishing relationships with others in the community, so that life can resume for the living in a more normal way;

- Identifying with and echoing the values of the deceased;

- Affirming their own values in the face of another's death;

- Relief of guilt (chiefly through the acceptance and support of others) for any shortcomings or failings in their relationships with the deceased;

- Rehabilitation of the memory of the deceased, especially after a long and disfiguring illness;

- The opportunity to deepen religious or spiritual life; and

- Sharing in one another's emotional support, encouragement, and strength.[16]

SERVICES AND CEREMONIES

The death ceremonies practiced most commonly in the West today are *funerals* and *memorial services.* By definition, a funeral is a ceremony held with the body present, and a memorial service is a ceremony held after the body has been disposed of. Sometimes both events will be scheduled, with the funeral itself reserved for family and close friends and a memorial service held later for a larger group.

Another type of ceremony is called a *commitment* or *committal service.* Held at graveside or in a chapel located at the crematory, this brief ceremony accompanies final disposition of the body. Generally attended only by family members or close friends, it often supplements, rather than replaces, a traditional funeral.

The Traditional Funeral
The traditional American funeral is still by far the most popular commemoration ceremony in the United States. Usually arranged through a commercial funeral home, this ceremony generally takes place in the funeral-home chapel or in a church. The body is present in either an open or a closed coffin, a ceremony is held that is hopefully in keeping with the beliefs of the deceased (religious or otherwise), and the coffin is then transported to the grave site for burial or a crematory for cremation. In some cases, a visitation or

wake, in which mourners view the body, may precede, follow, or occur during the funeral service.

This ceremony can be very simple, or it can be as elaborate as you wish. Like weddings, funerals run the gamut and are influenced by the life-styles, finances, and personal taste of the individuals involved. However, unlike most weddings, funerals are not joyous occasions allowing time to plan ahead for all the details, think about choices, and comparison shop. We tend to turn all this over to a funeral director, and since s/he is almost always dealing with people who are sad, tired, or shocked, not to mention uninformed and in a real big hurry, the funeral director pretty much has the upper hand, from a consumer's perspective.

The Cost of a Funeral

The standard adult funeral includes a lot of items and services, the cost of which can really add up. A 1988 study for a popular financial monthly reveals both specific amounts and the manner in which services are priced.

- Professional services (can include recording and filing paperwork, coordinating between survivors and clergy, pallbearers, organist, clergy, etc.)—$350 to $1,700
- Moving the body from the place of death to the funeral home—$50 to $300
- Embalming—$95 to $380
- Refrigeration (as an alternative to embalming)—$45 to $125
- Cosmetic preparation of the body—$65 to $235
- Burial clothing—$35 to $100
- Visitation-room rental fee—$45 to $260
- Chapel rental—$95 to $200
- Honoraria for clergy—$25 to $250
- Hearse—$95 to $125
- Utility or lead car in funeral procession—$50 to $100
- Limousine rental (per car)—$95 to $125[17]

In addition, there are what are called "cash advance" items. The funeral director will advance the cash to pay these costs, which will be added to the bill, often with a service or handling charge attached. These are such items as flowers provided by the funeral home, an organist or other music, and memorial cards or register books. These amounts are in addition to the cost of a casket and cemetery or crematory charges (see previous section).

Although the funeral industry once sold all of these services as a package, the FTC's Funeral Rule (passed in 1984) forbids funeral providers from mandating prearranged packages. One provision of the rule states that funeral directors must "allow consumers to select and purchase only those goods and services they desire (instead of . . . predetermined packages)."[18] Although many funeral homes still offer package deals, which may cost as much as 15 percent less than it would to buy each product and service separately, theoretically you can now arrange your own funeral package, purchasing only the items that you want.

But the biggest influence on cost involves the number of services and products that you choose to purchase. If the "unit" service, which generally includes everything but the casket and cash-advance items, matches your preferences, you can often save some money by purchasing such a funeral package.

The Memorial Service

A memorial service is a commemoration ceremony in which the body is not present. It usually takes place after disposition and can be held practically anywhere—in a funeral home, place of worship, communal hall, someone's house, or out-of-doors. The location of a memorial service can be a very personalized choice. The singer Janis Joplin left money in her will for all her friends and fellow musicians to gather at the Noname Bar in Sausalito, California, for a party in her memory. It was said to have been a very successful commemorative event.

A memorial service generally affords more latitude for originality of planning and spontaneity of expression than does a traditional funeral. It can be tailored to individual predilections. Since this service does not require the transportation or display of the body, there is more flexibility in scheduling time and place. Although, like funerals, they are generally held within three or four days of death, memorial services can be scheduled considerably later and at the convenience of mourners—in the evening or on a weekend, for instance.

You can arrange a memorial service independently, through a nonprofit memorial society, or through a funeral director. The latter, however, usually advocate full funerals based on the principle that viewing the body aids the grieving process. A funeral director isn't really the most disinterested adviser in this matter. (It's like the old joke about asking a barber if you need a haircut.) As described by Hughes and Klein (in their aforementioned *A Family Guide to Wills, Funerals & Probate*),

> Some psychologists (and virtually all funeral directors) firmly believe that it is only after viewing the body that survivors accept the reality and finality of the death and that such viewing actually facilitates the grieving process. . . . Other psychologists (and many clergymen), however, argue the opposite point of view with equal conviction. They do not feel that viewing a highly cosmeticized corpse helps the survivors accept the death, and they feel that in some circumstances viewing the corpse may be a traumatic experience.[19]

The costs of a memorial service are generally much less than a full funeral because you are bypassing many of the expenses incurred in preparing a body for viewing.

Help with Planning in Detail
If you wish to plan your funeral or memorial service in detail, the following books may be of help to you. *Dealing Creatively with Death* by Ernest Morgan; *Caring for Your Own Dead* by Lisa Carlson; *The Wheel of Life and Death* by Philip Kapleau; and *Funerals: Consumer's Last Rights* by the editors of *Consumer Reports*. Both *Giving Sorrow Words* by Candy Lightner and Nancy Hathaway and *Grieving: How to Go on Living When Someone You Love Dies* by Therese A. Rando are primarily about grief, but they include information of interest on funerals and commemoration. (See listings at the end of this chapter.)

It's Your Funeral
And of course you need have no formal funeral or memorial service at all. Those who believe that lavish funerals waste the resources of the living while producing little benefit for either the dead or the

living may find it most appealing to dispose of the body immediately and economically with no accompanying public ceremony.

THE FUNERAL INDUSTRY

In the United States, the funeral industry is so entrenched that it may come as a surprise to learn it has been so for little more than one hundred years. Funeral directors or morticians (who were then called undertakers) began promoting their trade after the Civil War, with special emphasis on the skill required for embalming. The profession received an important boost near the turn of the century, when an increasingly urban population no longer commonly held wakes in private homes. The funeral parlor was born.

Today the funeral industry is big business. Americans spend over $6 billion a year on funeral costs. More than twenty thousand funeral homes exist in the United States.

The majority of funeral homes, however, average only one funeral per week, with no conceivable way to increase demand for their services. For years, this fixed market has forced them to add the cost of overhead on to the bills of its customers.

When funeral homes held a virtual monopoly on the industry, they could charge whatever they liked. In 1963, Jessica Mitford exposed the practices of the funeral industry in her landmark work *The American Way of Death*. She charged the funeral industry with exploiting the dead, taking advantage of the bereaved, making enormous profits, and packaging expensive funerals with no thought given to what customers wanted. Such practices led to the growth of memorial societies (see discussion later in this chapter) and direct-disposition agencies that offered simplified, economical funerals.

Despite their denunciation of the industry, even critics agree that funeral directors can perform a much-needed service. A good funeral professional can provide you or your survivors with helpful information and assistance in planning your funeral. If you wish, s/he will take care of all arrangements to move the body from the place of death to the funeral home, dispose of the body according to your wishes, and coordinate the logistics involved in a ceremony. S/he may also handle paperwork or help fill out the various forms required—from death certificates and disposition permits to applications for Social Security and/or Veterans Administration death benefits. Finally, if well-trained and understanding, a funeral professional can help ease the stress and pain felt by survivors.

The growing strength of memorial societies and direct-disposition firms has had a more powerful impact on increasing funeral-industry services than it has on decreasing the cost of traditional funerals. Today most funeral directors (over one-third of whom are now women) have received training not merely in anatomy, chemistry, embalming, and accounting but also in public health, sociology, and grief and bereavement counseling.

New Developments

In the increasingly competitive funeral market, morticians have found it necessary to court customers through advertising, mass mailings, and even telemarketing—as well as through the more traditional calendars and church bulletins. Over three hundred small, independent funeral homes have joined together in a national network called Trust 100, cutting costs by purchasing advertising and products in volume.

The main impetus behind the creation of this cooperative network of independent funeral homes has been the growth of Service Corporation International (SCI), the funeral industry's giant conglomerate, which commands over $800 million in annual funeral revenues. SCI, a publicly traded corporation that already owns more than 500 mortuaries and 100 cemeteries and is continuing to acquire more every year, provides its funeral homes with bulk purchasing discounts and accounting and advertising assistance. SCI also operates crematories, casket makers, flower shops, and other manufacturers of funeral products and supplies—as well as selling insurance policies for prepaying burial expenses.

Another recent development is what has been called the "gentrifying" of the funeral business. The styles of funeral services, items, and artifacts now available include some novel innovations, such as cremation urns sculpted out of boulders, caskets with personalized interiors (pinstriping or a romantic Laura Ashley pattern are two popular styles), and fantasy funerals (designed by film and theater producers). Computer software programs used by funeral directors produce personalized memorial programs, obits, and sympathy letters.

These developments may be seen as fashionable, faddish, or just plain commercial—the funeral industry trying to catch up with a modern, high-tech world. Reporting on this trend, *Esquire* magazine describes the entry of video on the funeral scene:

> Today's well-equipped funeral chapel needs a television and a VCR so mourners can watch *The Tribute Program,* a six-minute replay of highlights of the deceased's life. Introduced last year by National Music Service Corporation, a supplier of background music to funeral homes, *The Tribute Program,* features snapshots of the guest of honor that dissolve to color scenes of mountains, the seashore, forests, or any of hundreds of stock video images in the company's library. The family selects the backgrounds and chooses a piece of music for the song track and a quotation that appears at the end of the program. . . . In addition to serving as a visual memory and keepsake that can be replayed at home, *The Tribute Program* also fills out a skimpy service. "It's no substitute for a good old-fashioned eulogy, but it fills a need," says a spokesman. "It can give people something to gather around."[20]

THE FTC FUNERAL RULE

In 1984 the Federal Trade Commission adopted what has become known as the Funeral Rule, which regulates methods of pricing and disclosure in the industry. (Although currently up for review, all regulations specified in the 1984 Funeral Rule remain in effect as of this writing.)

The Funeral Rule requires that funeral providers furnish the consumer with price information over the telephone if requested and with a complete list of prices, including caskets, if you visit in person. After you make your purchase, the funeral director must give you an itemized list of the services and goods you have selected and the price of each item as well as the total price. The rule also requires funeral providers to offer the option of unfinished wooden boxes or corrugated containers as an alternative to caskets in the case of direct cremation.

Funeral providers are forbidden to make false statements that oblige the consumer to purchase certain items or services, and they must furnish a written confirmation of any legal, cemetery, or crematory policies that require the selection of particular products or services.

MEMORIAL SOCIETIES: AN ALTERNATIVE TO THE FUNERAL INDUSTRY

A memorial society is a private, consumer-oriented, nonprofit organization helping to provide economical and dignified disposition and commemoration. Membership is open to anyone who wants to join. Although some societies have been organized by churches, they are nondenominational in membership and services offered. A memorial society functions basically as a funeral cooperative and is generally staffed and operated primarily by volunteers drawn from its membership. (They are also sometimes called funeral societies.)

The first such group was formed in 1939 in an attempt to redress the high cost of dying. Even before Jessica Mitford's exposé, memorial-society members had soured on the funeral industry in the United States. A 1962 survey by Robert Fulton showed that memorial-society members, in contrast with nonmembers, viewed funeral directors as primarily business people, rather than as professional service people fulfilling the needs of the public. Seeing funeral costs as exorbitant, these members strongly advocated cremation, body donation, and the simplification of funeral rites. Almost thirty years later, most of the 1 million members still adhere to these positions. In 1963, the Continental Association of Funeral and Memorial Societies (CAFMS) was organized; eight years later, a similar organization, the Memorial Society Association of Canada (MSAC), formed.

Some memorial societies also serve as consumer watchdogs and funeral-information bureaus. Members often testify at federal regulatory and legislative hearings regarding funeral-industry practices and disseminate information, advice, and counsel to the general public on funeral planning, consumer choices, death, and the funeral industry.

Most will provide members and nonmembers alike with a worksheet that promotes advance planning of disposition as well as funeral or memorial services. If no memorial society exists in your area, the CAFMS or the MSAC will provide you with educational materials on arranging a low-cost funeral.

www. vbiweb. champlain. edu/famsa/directory.ht

How Do Memorial Societies Work?

Memorial societies work in the same way that a food cooperative does. Members pay a nominal onetime fee generally ranging between $10 and $25, which covers organizational costs and the initial paperwork recording your funeral choices.

The society works directly with local funeral directors, cemeteries, and crematories, establishing contracts for simple funerals or memorial services and disposition at reduced rates. The size of their membership generally gives them considerable bargaining power, allowing for significant discounts on products and services for its members.

Many members choose simple funerals costing $1,000 or less. Memorial societies can arrange either burials or cremations, usually at a lower cost than funeral homes. In comparing the services provided by funeral homes and memorial societies, one study found that the cost of an immediate burial arranged through a memorial society ranged from $400 to $875, compared to $425 to $1,230 for an immediate burial contracted through a funeral home. For direct cremations, the price ranged from $340 to $935 when arranged by a funeral home but only $160 to $530 through a memorial society.[21]

How to Find a Memorial Society

Today about two hundred of these groups are located throughout the United States and Canada. To learn if there is a memorial society near you, look in the yellow pages of the phone book or contact the Continental Association of Funeral and Memorial Societies. (See listings at the end of this chapter.) *Note:* As mentioned previously, a number of direct-disposition firms call themselves "societies" (such as the Neptune Society, the Telophase Society, and other profit-making outfits). These are not nonprofit memorial services. Although some offer valuable and much-needed services, they are in actuality profit-making businesses, rather than cooperatives.

PREPAY/PRENEED

With interest in preplanning funerals on the rise, the hottest growth area in the funeral industry today centers on what morticians call "preneed" sales: prearranged, prepaid funeral arrangements. Prearrangement in the funeral business has quadrupled since 1984, and about two-thirds of the funeral homes in the United States currently help customers plan—and often pay for—their own funerals. Almost one-quarter of all funerals today are financed through some sort of "pay now, die later" system. Virtually all of the funeral industry's advertising dollars and marketing strategies now go into attempts to attract the preneed market.

Buyer Beware

Outside of the funeral industry, most financial analysts and consumer advocates who have studied prepaid plans advise against them under most circumstances. Two of the strongest advocates of preplanning, CAFMS and AARP, discourage prepayment in most cases.

CAFMS generally opposes prepayment plans for three reasons: If your survivors don't know that you have already paid for your funeral and disposition arrangements, your money will have been wasted. If you move, you may not be able to transfer your arrangement to another funeral home. And if you die and have not yet paid your final installment, your agreement may not be in force.

The AARP urges extreme caution, including consultation with an attorney, before signing any prepaid document. They warn against prepayment agreements that tie consumers exclusively to one funeral provider and plans that do not guarantee a set price for the funeral arrangements. They also advise members to make sure that all money for prepayment will be placed in a state-regulated trust fund. This guarantees that unscrupulous funeral directors, otherwise free to spend the money at any time, will not squander your funeral funds. Unregulated trusts tend to invite potential fraud or abuse. "If the funds will not be placed in trust, prepayment should not be made under any circumstances."[22]

The AARP publishes a booklet entitled *Product Report: Prepaying Your Funeral?* It is an informative guide and can be had by contacting AARP. (See listings at the end of this chapter.)

Consumer Reports magazine advises its readers to put aside their own money rather than entrust it to a funeral director or a trustee to invest for them. Certificates of deposit or money market funds, for example, that are earmarked for funeral expenses will generally earn a higher rate of return than prepayment trust funds.

You can take out a standard-term life insurance policy that will cover your funeral costs. Despite the claims of some insurance companies, these policies, if not attached to a specific program of funeral services and merchandise, are not truly "preneed" or "burial insurance." However, if the beneficiary knows your wishes and will carry them out, a standard insurance policy can function as a de facto prepayment plan.

As another alternative, you can establish a Totten Trust. A Totten Trust is essentially a self-administered savings account in your name designed for a specific purpose and designated "in trust for" a named beneficiary. It can be opened at a credit union, bank, or other savings institution and is wholly controlled by the consumer.

Rather than designate a funeral provider as the beneficiary (as is the practice in industry prepayment plans), name a trusted friend or family member who will use the funds in the trust according to your wishes. Your Totten Trust beneficiary can arrange for your disposition and commemoration in accordance with any specifications you have provided. This strategy, too, will yield a plan for prearrangement that closely resembles the funeral industry's prepayment programs.

LETTER OF INSTRUCTION

Once you have made your plans, it is most important to communicate them to those who will survive you. You should talk with your family, close friends, or others who may need to know (lawyer, clergy, etc.), but the most beneficial thing you can do is to write a Letter of Instruction. As described in chapter 1, a Letter of Instruction is a document listing personal property, assets, and liabilities, giving the location of important papers, deeds, policies, and such items as safe-deposit-box keys, etc. It is also the best place to record your preferences and plans for disposition and commemoration.

You should describe in detail any preplans you have arranged and specify any purchases or financial agreements you have made. (Name the funeral home, memorial society, direct-disposition firm, etc., and include a copy of any contract, policy, or agreement you have signed, with the names and phone numbers of those who should be contacted.) Keep your Letter where it can be readily found by your survivors.

A Letter of Instruction can be written informally. It is not a legal document and needn't be officially prepared according to any particular format—it can be a simple letter, from you to those you love.

Indeed, the act of planning ahead is a kind of proof of your love—a practical gift of genuine consideration.

RESOURCES AND SUPPORT

Books

Lisa Carlson. *Caring for Your Own Dead.* Hinesburg, Vt.: Upper Access Publishers, 1987. Available in bookstores or from Upper Access Publishers, One Upper Access Road, Hinesburg, VT 05461; (802) 482-2988.
[This unique book furnishes detailed information for those who desire to make their own funeral arrangements and provide for body disposition without a funeral director. Information is provided on burial and cremation costs; body and anatomical donation; death certificates; and other requirements surrounding caring for the dead. Includes a state-by-state listing of relevant statutes and regulations. A valuable directory of hard-to-find information.]

Consumer Reports. *Funerals: Consumers' Last Rights: The Consumers Union Report on Conventional Funerals and Burial . . . and Some Alternatives, Including Cremation, Direct Cremation, Direct Burial, and Body Donation.* New York: W. W. Norton, 1978.
[Contains detailed information on the practices and economics of the funeral industry. Although some of this information is dated, much remains very useful today. The book is currently out of print, but worth looking for. Check with your local library or used-book store.]

Jessica Mitford. *The American Way of Death.* New York: Simon & Schuster, Touchstone Books, 1978.
[The renowned exposé of the modern American funeral industry, currently out of print, but worth looking for. Check with your local library or used-book store.]

Ernest Morgan. *Dealing Creatively with Death: A Manual of Death Education and Simple Burial.* 11th ed., revised and expanded. Edited by Jennifer Morgan. Burnsville, N.C.: Celo Press, 1988. Available in bookstores or from Celo Press, 1901 Hannah Branch Road, Burnsville, NC 28714; (704) 675-4925.
[This book is the classic in the field. It includes discussions of simple burial and cremation, memorial societies, and commemoration. It also contains helpful appendices and a detailed listing of eye banks, medical schools, and other organizations that take anatomical gifts in Canada and the United States.]

Thomas C. Nelson. ***It's Your Choice: The Practical Guide to Planning a Funeral.*** Washington, D.C.: American Association of Retired Persons; Glenview, Ill.: Scott, Foresman and Co., AARP Books, 1987. Available in bookstores or through the American Association of Retired Persons. For complete information write AARP Books, 2720 Des Plaines Avenue, Suite 113, Des Plaines, IL 60018.
[Discusses options and offers advice on disposition and funerals. Appendices include price comparison forms and personal planning forms.]

Elmo A. Petterle. ***Legacy of Love: How to Make Life Easier for the Ones You Leave Behind.*** Bolinas, Calif.: Shelter Publications, 1987. Available in bookstores or through Shelter Publications, Inc., P.O. Box 279, Bolinas, CA 94924; (415) 868-0280.
[A workbook for planning disposition, funerals, memorials, and other arrangements when death occurs.]

Books Containing Related Information

Judi Culbertson and Tom Randall. ***Permanent Parisians: An Illustrated Guide to the Cemeteries of Paris.*** Chelsea, Vt.: Chelsea Green Publishing, 1986. Available in bookstores or through Chelsea Green Publishing, P.O. Box 130, Post Mills, VT 05058; (802) 333-9073.
[The first in a charming series of guides to the most interesting historic grave sites of the famous, the powerful, and the eccentric. Illustrated. Series includes *Permanent New Yorkers, Permanent Californians,* and the upcoming *Permanent Londoners.*]

Hayden Curry and Denis Clifford. ***A Legal Guide for Lesbian and Gay Couples.*** 5th ed. Berkeley, Calif.: Nolo Press, 1989.
[Includes a brief section on preplanning for same-sex couples as a means of avoiding later conflicts; appendix includes tear-out forms.]

Earl A. Grollman, ed. ***Concerning Death: A Practical Guide for the Living.*** Boston: Beacon Press, 1974.
[Includes essays on coroners, funeral directors and funerals, selecting cemeteries, choosing a memorial, and cremation.]

Dale V. Hardt. ***Death: The Final Frontier.*** Englewood Cliffs, N.J.: Prentice-Hall, 1979.
[Includes a survey of philosophical, cultural, and religious views on burial customs and cremation.]

Theodore E. Hughes and David Klein. ***A Family Guide to Wills, Funerals & Probate: How to Protect Yourself and Your Survivors.*** New York: Charles Scribner's Sons, 1987.
[Chapter on preplanning your funeral includes discussion of various

choices for disposal, including cremation and organ and body donation; commemoration alternatives are also discussed.]

Philip Kapleau. *The Wheel of Life and Death,* New York: Doubleday, 1989. [Includes comments and suggestions on funerals, commemoration, and various types of services.]

Candy Lightner and Nancy Hathaway. *Giving Sorrow Words: How to Cope with Grief and Get On with Your Life.* New York: Warner Books, 1990.
[This book on grief includes a chapter covering funeral and memorial services and their importance to the grieving process as well as some interesting examples of personalized ceremonies.]

Charles Panati. *Panati's Extraordinary Endings of Practically Everything and Everybody.* New York: Harper & Row, Perennial Library, 1989. [Includes a history of the development of cemeteries and interesting facts and anecdotes about death and dying.]

Therese A. Rando. *Grieving: How to Go On Living When Someone You Love Dies.* Lexington, Mass.: Lexington Books, 1988.
[Includes a chapter on personal bereavement rituals and funerals. Discusses therapeutic values of funerals and offers suggestions for designing your own rituals to give more meaning to the process.]

Harry Van Bommel. *Choices: For People Who Have a Terminal Illness, Their Families and Caregivers.* Toronto: NC Press Limited, 1990; distributed in U.S. by Seven Hills Book Distributors. Available through Seven Hills Books, 49 Central Ave., Cincinnati, OH 45202; 1-800-545-2005.
[Includes options to consider when planning your own funeral arrangements. The book lists detailed instructions to be left to your survivors about your plans and wishes for funeral and cemetery services and covers Canada, the United Kingdom, and the United States.]

Agencies/Service Organizations

AARP (American Association of Retired Persons)
1909 K Street, NW
Washington, DC 20049
(202) 872-4700
A large nonprofit membership organization providing a wide range of educational and community service programs. The AARP offers a number of helpful publications at no charge for both members and nonmembers, including: "Prepaying Your Funeral: Some Questions to Ask"; "Cemetery Goods and Services"; and "Funeral Goods and Services." AARP free publi-

cations are available by sending a postcard to: AARP Fulfillment at the above address. Or call to request a catalog of all AARP publications.

American Cemetery Association
Three Skyline Place
Suite 1111
5201 Leesburg Pike
Falls Church, VA 22041
(703) 379-5838
The major cemetery and memorial-park trade association. They can answer questions regarding cemetery rules and practices in addition to making referrals. The ACA will help arbitrate complaints concerning their own members or refer you to an appropriate agency or organization.

Cemetery Consumer Service Council
P.O. Box 3574
Washington, D.C. 20007
(703) 379-6426
Sponsored by four of the major industry groups to resolve consumer complaints. Has free pamphlet explaining services.

Continental Association of Funeral and Memorial Societies
7910 Woodmont Avenue
Suite 1208
Bethesda, MD 20814
(301) 913-0030
Consumer-membership organizations advocating memorial societies as a means of ensuring dignity, simplicity, and economy in funeral arrangements. Each local society is independent, and the level of service provided may vary. The national office of CAFMS can refer you to a local society in the United States, or help you establish one if none exists where you live. CAFMS also has available anatomical donor cards and information concerning anatomical gifts. A pamphlet listing the societies throughout the United States is provided at no charge.

In Canada, memorial associations are a confederation, the Memorial Association of Canada, but have no national office. Check your local telephone directory for a memorial association in your area.

Cremation Association of North America
111 East Wacker Drive
Suite 600
Chicago, IL 60601
(312) 644-6610

www. vbiweb. champlain. edu/famsa/directory. htm

A national trade association with free pamphlets discussing cremation. They can also make referrals.

FSCAP (Funeral Service Consumer Assistance Program)
National Research and Information Center
1614 Central Street
Evanston, IL 60201
1-800-662-7666
An independent organization that arbitrates consumer complaints concerning funeral-related purchases. They will handle prelitigation or postlitigation complaints. Write an initial letter describing the problem to FSCAP; their staff will respond with follow-up.

Jewish Funeral Directors of America
250 West 57th Street
New York, NY 10107
(212) 757-0578
A national trade association of funeral directors serving the Jewish community. Has free pamphlets available and can make referrals over the telephone.

National Funeral Director's Association
11121 West Oklahoma Avenue
Milwaukee, WI 53227
(414) 541-2500
The largest educational and professional association of funeral directors. Provides a number of free pamphlets available to consumers, including: "A Way to Remember: Choosing a Funeral Ceremony"; "Death Away from Home"; "Embalming"; "Funeral Etiquette"; "The Traditional Funeral"; "What Are My Options? A Guide to Final Disposition"; and "Yes, Funerals Are for the Living." The NFDA represents the funeral industry, and they definitely have something to sell. This material can be a helpful source of information, but remember, it is written from their point of view.

National Funeral Directors and Morticians Association
P.O. Box 377993
Chicago, IL 60637
(312) 752-7419
A national association primarily of African-American funeral providers. Will make referrals by telephone.

St. Francis Center
5417 Sherier Place, NW
Washington, D.C. 20016
(202) 363-8500
This nonprofit, nonsectarian organization sells a pamphlet detailing "How to Make Your Own Coffin" (plans available for $1.00, plus self-addressed, stamped envelope with $.58 postage). They also provide professional counseling, training sessions for caregivers and health professionals, and practical support for the dying and the bereaved.

U.S. Federal Trade Commission
Public Reference Section
6th and Pennsylvania, NW
Washington, D.C. 20580
(202) 326-2222
Oversees the enforcement of the Funeral Industry Rule. Will answer consumer questions over the telephone; however, complaints must be made in writing and sent to the FTC's Correspondence Branch, Washington, D.C. 20580. Copies of public documents, such as the pamphlet "Consumer Guide to the FTC Funeral Rule," are available at no charge.

Anatomical Gifts
The following organizations can provide information about anatomical gifts and organ donor cards:

The Living Bank
P.O. Box 6725
Houston, TX 77265
1-800-528-2971

Medic Alert Foundation
P.O. Box 1009
Turlock, CA 95381-1009
(209) 668-3333

Organ Donors of Canada
5326 Ada Boulevard
Edmonton, Alberta, Canada T5W 4N7

United Network for Organ Sharing
1100 Boulders Parkway
Suite 500
Richmond, VA 23225-8770
800-24-DONOR

3

Life-and-Death Decisions

Biomedical developments of the past several decades have made death more a matter of deliberate decision. For almost any life-threatening condition, some intervention can now delay the moment of death. . . .

President's Commission for the Study of Ethical Problems in Medicine and Biomedical and Behavioral Research

When you have planned for the disposition of your body and your property, there is an additional concern for which you will want to provide—the possibility that you may become incapacitated and unable to indicate your wishes regarding your own life and death.

Your Right to Self-Determination
Today it is quite conceivable that while your brain and your body can have ceased to function, machines will keep you "alive" artificially. Once this occurs, dying is no longer an inevitability, it has become a decision. The question is, whose decision?

Of course, anyone would choose to maintain life while recovery or healing takes place. The problem arises when death is postponed

78

without any chance of healing or rehabilitation. You may be placed on life-support technology or treatment when there is no known way to bring you back to capacity or even to consciousness. The case of Karen Ann Quinlan brought this dilemma into public view. The case of Nancy Cruzan brought it to the Supreme Court. Subsequent and similar cases proliferate, fraught with legal, ethical, and financial concerns. It can happen to you.

Another contingency created by today's medical practices is the invasive or debilitating treatment of terminally ill patients in the last stages of the dying process. While some people wish to exhaust every possible treatment up to the last moment of life, others find many medical procedures too painful, incapacitating, or futile to continue through the end stages of a terminal condition. They prefer to cease fighting and spend their time peacefully with family or friends. In such a case, a patient has the right of "informed refusal." You can say no.

Often, however, a terminal patient can't articulate his or her desires, and in the hectic hospital environment, informed refusal of extreme measures can be ignored or dismissed by busy medical professionals.

As you are dying, you may wish to have every possible treatment measure employed to the end, or you may want only comfort measures taken. The choice is yours. But you may lose the chance to choose if you don't use it now.

When You Can't Determine Anything
It is generally accepted that people have the legal right to decide for themselves whether or not they wish to accept medical treatment of any kind. The confusion develops when you are unable to make your wishes known. If you are incapacitated or incompetent, others are faced with the question of what you "would have wanted"—and you're not even dead yet!

Although most legal and health care professionals agree such decisions should be made by the patient, if the patient didn't make them and is now incapable of doing so, who does? And on what basis?

Traditionally, when someone becomes incapacitated, a court proceeding appoints a guardian or conservator who then has the authority to make decisions on behalf of the incapacitated person. This is a time-consuming process and can be emotionally and financially draining. In the past, it was a fairly infrequent occurrence, and the need to prepare ahead for incompetency was rarely considered. But now we are part of a population that lives longer, develops degenerative diseases, and is maintained with life-prolonging technology. In short, it is now much more common for people to live past their capacity to maintain themselves or their affairs.

Another unpleasant possibility is that of a severe accident—one that would have left you unquestionably dead just twenty years ago. Today, however, emergency and trauma care can resuscitate the heart and respiratory functions even when brain function is lost. We may be left without any decision-making capacity at all.

Personally, I'd Rather Not Think About This. . . .

It is very dispiriting to think about the many dreadful things that can happen to us, and usually it's better not to. It gets in the way of a good time. However, there *is* an appropriate place for raging paranoid fantasies, and planning ahead for incapacity is it. Now is the time to take a minute and consider the possibilities in order to protect yourself and those you love. Here's why.

Today if you are seriously ill or injured, you will almost certainly be taken to a hospital. Thirty years ago, fewer than half of us ended our life in a hospital; now over 80 percent will wind up there as we are dying. In the hospital all treatment is aimed at keeping the mechanisms of the body functioning while a dangerous situation is reversed or a precipitous decline is halted. If you are going to recover, these measures can save your life. If you are not going to recover, the same measures can leave you a physical shell, maintaining basic functions long after the reason for doing so has evaporated.

At what point do extraordinary efforts bring more misery than surcease? Most of us never give it any thought. We rely on the medical profession. The medical profession is inclined to keep you "alive" at all costs, and it may well be at *all* costs—emotional, psychological, and financial as well as physical.

The Monetary Costs of Life-Prolonging Treatment

In a modern urban hospital the cost of intensive care services runs between $2,000 and $3,000 per day. One study showed that the cost of treatment with a respirator for more than forty-eight hours averaged $40,000.[1] Longer periods of life-support technology and services can cost hundreds of thousands of dollars. And the bill comes due whether you live or die (or are indefinitely comatose). If technological progress has brought us legal, medical, and moral confusion, it has also brought financial terrorism.

Longer-term maintenance on minimal life-support systems may run as low as several hundred dollars per day, but when you consider that such maintenance can be required for months or even years, you can understand why many families wind up filing for bankruptcy to qualify for Medicaid in order to pay for long-term care.

Private insurance policies usually cover only 80 percent of the charges billed for end-of-life or critical care. Since these charges are so high, the remaining 20 percent can be a debilitating expense for survivors. Given the current structure and state of our health care system, these expenses are more likely to escalate than to decrease.

The cost of maintaining a human life beyond the point of its "natural" death has serious consequences. Those who love you the most will pay the most. Setting limits now will save them more than pain. It could save their own future.

PLANNING AHEAD FOR INCAPACITY

A new kind of legal document has evolved to deal with what has been called "the impact of technology and social change on the experience of dying."[2] A directive prepared in advance of need, this document may be called a "living will," a "proxy," or a "medical durable power of attorney." It may be an official document provided by the state in which you reside, a form you fill out, or a power of attorney form provided by your lawyer. Its primary purpose is to state the conditions under which you would refuse the continuation of life-prolonging procedures and/or to designate a proxy—someone you name to make decisions on your behalf, should you become incapacitated.

Basically, there are two ways to protect yourself. You can state your own wishes in writing, and you can name someone else to speak on your behalf.

- *The living will* (also called a declaration or directive to physicians). A living will is your own personal statement about what medical treatment you want and don't want should you become incapacitated.

- *Durable power of attorney for health care* (also called a proxy or a medical power of attorney). A DPA, or proxy, is a way to appoint another person to state your wishes or to make decisions on your behalf should you become incapacitated.

The Living Will or Physicians' Directive

Developed in 1967 by attorney Louis Kutner, the first living will provided a way for people to set out in advance their personal wishes regarding end-of-life medical treatment. Gradually, the term has come to be commonly used to describe such documents.

A living will is not like a conventional will. It has nothing to do with the transference of property. It is about what happens as you die rather than after you die—a statement of your preferences regarding the limitation or removal of life-prolonging procedures when death is imminent.

A living will does not advocate "mercy killing" or any kind of premeditated act to cause death (which is illegal in the United States). Nor does it limit "comfort measures" (generally considered to be defined as "medication, nursing care, and other treatment administered for the purpose of keeping you as comfortable and free from pain as possible").[3] A living will protects your right to refuse "heroic" measures that prolong the dying process, should that be your wish.

Medical Durable Power of Attorney or Proxy

A medical durable power of attorney (DPA) authorizes another person (a proxy or agent) to make medical decisions for you when you become incapable of making them for yourself. It may also be called "limited durable power of attorney for health care" or simply "medical proxy."

When you name someone to be your proxy, you are giving that person significant power and responsibility. Depending on your state's law, your proxy may:

- Give, withhold, or withdraw consent to specific medical or surgical measures with reference to the principal's condition, prognosis, and known wishes; authorize appropriate end-of-life care, including pain-relieving procedures.

- Grant releases to medical personnel.

- Employ and discharge medical personnel.

- Have access to and disclose medical records.

- Resort to court, if unavoidable, to obtain authorization regarding treatment decisions.

- Expend (or withhold) funds needed to carry out medical treatment.[4]

As you can see, these are extensive powers. Thus, it is vital that you talk with your proposed proxy and discuss in detail the various possibilities and your preferences. This person should be someone who understands your values and is aware of your personal beliefs and principles. You will be trusting him or her to act according to your wishes, even if it becomes painful or runs counter to what s/he might personally prefer.

Choosing a Proxy
In their helpful book, *Making Medical Decisions: How to Make Medical and Ethical Choices For Yourself and Your Family,* Thomas and Celia Scully describe in detail the factors to consider when choosing an advocate. They point out that although a family member will be the first called, s/he may not necessarily be the best person to act as your advocate in an emergency or when the prognosis is terminal. They also recommend that your advocate be an assertive person who will act in a determined manner to ensure that your rights are protected. This practical book summarizes contemporary medical ethics and provides the kind of detailed information you need to know in order to protect yourself in a wide variety of circumstances.[5]

STATES, STATUTES, AND THE STATUS OF THE LAW

Most states have passed some form of legislation relating to advance directives. The substance of these laws varies significantly from state to state, as do their titles ("Medical Treatment Decision Act," "Living Will Statute," "Natural Death Act," "Rights of the Terminally Ill Act"). While none of the laws are identical, they do share common characteristics.

- Recognition of an adult individual's advance directive regarding medical care in the event of a terminal condition

- Immunity from legal liability for medical caregivers who honor directives as required by the statute

- A suggested form for the declaration, which in most states may be varied with personal directions

- Definitions of the terms of the statute, such as "life-sustaining procedure" and "terminal condition"

- Procedures for execution of declarations, such as witnessing requirements and easily met revocation procedures

- A requirement that the declaration of a qualified patient be made part of the medical record

- A requirement that physicians who are unwilling or unable to honor a declaration must make a reasonable effort to transfer, or must permit the transfer of, the patient[6]

These statutes are, however, quite varied in their particular definitions and limitations. For instance, some allow for the cessation of certain types of treatment but not others (such as artificial feeding). And most state laws apply only to patients who have been diagnosed as having a "terminal condition" and do not include those who are permanently unconscious or in a vegetative state as a result of an accident or, for instance, a stroke.

The legal status of advance directives and health care proxies is still evolving. While the concept is recognized in some form or another in all states, a DPA or a living will may or may not be specifically *authorized by statute* in any one state.

A recent U.S. Supreme Court decision[7] reinforced a state's right to enact legislation on life-support cessation and indicated that an individual's rights are best protected by a written advance directive. It is now generally accepted that a living will or proxy DPA is the way to address the question of an individual's "right to die."

WHICH DIRECTIVE
IS RIGHT FOR ME?

Preparing an advance directive may seem confusing because there is no uniform legislation and no uniform document. You can use a generic living will form, or the durable power of attorney format that is available in some self-help books and through your lawyer, or one of the number of medical directives that have recently been developed, or the form adopted by your state *if* your state has enacted a law. The question is, of these choices, which will best protect you?

While both a living will and a DPA can answer some of the same needs, there are differences between them. Which one is best for you will be determined by your personal situation and the state in which you reside.

If there is someone with whom you feel comfortable giving over the legal right to act on your behalf, naming a proxy provides protection for what may be unforeseen circumstances. However, if there is no one to serve as your proxy or you live in a state that does not clearly authorize agents to make life-support decisions, a living will may be more appropriate.

If you live in an unconventional situation (i.e., a same-sex couple or nonbiologically related family) and your choice of proxy may be challenged by your next of kin, it is wise to prepare your directive with the help of an experienced and sympathetic lawyer. There are cases on record in which the wishes of a gay partner in a medical emergency have been ignored completely. Should there be any conflict or disagreement, the law will move irrevocably in favor of the biological relative (father/mother, sibling, or adult child). The best way to protect yourself is to complete the DPA form appropriate for your state *and* to consult with a good attorney. A useful book, including detailed instructions and advice, is *A Legal Guide for Lesbian and Gay Couples* by Hayden Curry and Denis Clifford. (See listings at the end of this chapter.) This book is useful not only for gays and lesbians but for anyone who lives in an unconventional situation and wants to ensure that his or her rights are protected.

If the wording and stipulations of your state law are in accord with your own personal preferences, you're in luck. Simply get a copy of the form as mandated by the statute and fill it out. If the limitations in your state law do not accord with your preferences, you may also wish to prepare a generic living will to cover those points of concern to you.

To learn about the law and obtain the correct form for your state, contact the Concern for Dying/Society for the Right to Die. Living will forms may also be available from state and local agencies on aging or your state Department of Health. (See listings at the end of this chapter.) In some states the attorney general's office can inform you about local legislation and advise as to how you can obtain the correct form for your state.

CONCERN FOR DYING/SOCIETY FOR THE RIGHT TO DIE

The two foremost organizations concerned with the issues of life-support cessation are the Society for the Right to Die and Concern for Dying. (The two groups plan to merge by mid-1991, forming the National Council on Death and Dying.)

Providing legal advice and information on the individual's right to self-determination, they are dedicated to protecting the rights and improving the care of dying patients and have been active in promoting legislation and filing "friend-of-the-court" briefs in leading "right to die" cases.

One of the most important services they provide for the general public is the distribution of living will forms that are easy to understand and complete as well as literature explaining your rights, answering questions, and demystifying the law. If you contact them, they will send you information on the law as it pertains to your state of residence and the correct form (or forms) to give the best protection in your case. They are a nonprofit organization supported by contributions and memberships, and they provide this service free of charge.

Using the forms provided by this group, most people can prepare a fully valid living will or proxy, or both, without hiring a lawyer. However, depending on your situation and because the law on this issue is unsettled, you may want to consult an experienced attorney if you have any special concerns. (If you are preparing a medical DPA and you live in a state that has not enacted a statute specifically pertaining to medical care, the Society for the Right to Die recommends that you seek the advice of an attorney to be sure your DPA will work with your state's laws and precedent.)

REVOCATION

Any of these documents can be revoked at any time. If you wish to terminate your living will, you may do so by verbally notifying your family, your doctor (or the appropriate health care professional), and/or by destroying the document.

A DPA should be revoked in writing (a simple signed and dated declaration of your wish to revoke). The reason for this is that a DPA actually gives another person the power to act legally on your behalf. You will want to be sure to record the legal revocation of that power should you change your mind.

WHERE TO KEEP YOUR ADVANCE DIRECTIVE

Put the original of your advance directive in a safe place in your home or office (not a safe-deposit box). Give your doctor a copy. (This could be a good opportunity to discuss the matter with him or her.) Additional copies should be placed with any medical institution that maintains your records (e.g., an insurance company, veterans group, or health care organization). Obviously, if you have chosen an attorney in fact, s/he should know where your advance directive is located and have access to the original.

One of the services offered by the Concern for Dying/Society for the Right to Die is a Living Will Registry, enabling you to register your advance directive with a centralized file. For a very minimal fee they will keep a copy of your directive, available upon request, and provide you with a wallet-sized card indicating that you have a living will and naming the person to call in an emergency. This can be very helpful, especially for those without close family.

WHAT ARE MY CHOICES?

What are the medical-treatment decisions your family may face at the end of your life? What exactly are "life-prolonging procedures" or "life-support systems," anyhow?

Technically, life support can be anything that artificially extends a life, either by maintaining the function of a vital organ or a process of the body. Initially defined by the use of equipment, such as a ventilator or dialysis machine, terminating life support meant turning off the machine and thus came to be characterized as "pulling the plug." Now, however, the phrase *life support* or *life extension* generally includes artificial feeding (nutrition and hydration through a tube) and can refer to antibiotic or steroid treatment as well as resuscitation.

If you have a terminal illness at the time you prepare an advance directive, you will have some idea of the probable consequences and prognosis. If you can, it is a good idea to discuss with your doctor the procedures and treatments usually prescribed in cases such as yours so that you will be able to make specific requests about what you want and don't want as the illness progresses.

If you are healthy, you won't be able to predict what kind of critical situation might develop or what particular treatments may eventually be at issue. But you *can* set limits as to what you would be willing to do, and not do, if given the choice.

Spelling It Out

The basic decision you need to make is about life-support systems in general. Would you want them used no matter what? (You can write an advance directive to ensure that you *will* be given every possible treatment or therapy available if you worry that your physician may give up too soon.) Or would you prefer to avoid the use of life-support systems totally? Most of us fall between these two extremes and are simply trying to avoid the futile or painful protraction of the dying process or of being maintained in a vegetative state.

Some of the life-support procedures most commonly at issue in end-of-life decisions include:

- *Resuscitation.* Cardiopulmonary resuscitation, or CPR, includes "such emergency procedures as mouth-to-mouth resusci-

tation, external chest compression, electric shock, insertion of a tube to open the airway, injection of medication into the heart or open chest heart massage."[8] In many hospitals and nursing homes you can request a *"Do Not Resuscitate"* order (DNR or "No Code"). Thus, if you are at the end stages of a terminal illness or if CPR is futile as a measure to improve your condition, you may forgo this often violent procedure. (For instance, patients with advanced Alzheimer's disease may not wish to be resuscitated when their heart stops beating.)

- *Mechanical breathing.* A machine called a ventilator (or respirator) forces air into the lungs and maintains respiration. A life-saver in the short term, this technology can cause long-term difficulties, such as oxygen toxicity, lung damage, and the extreme discomfort that comes from intubation, the procedure in which a tube is passed down the throat or through the nose, causing gagging and leaving the patient unable to eat or to speak.

- *Artificial nutrition and hydration.* There are several different methods of artificial or tube feeding, the most basic of which is the simple and commonplace IV (intravenous line). The more invasive types include feeding through a nasogastric tube (inserted through a nostril and into the stomach), through a tube inserted into the stomach (gastrostomy), or into the upper end of the small intestine (jejunostomy). The nasogastric tube method causes gagging and discomfort in a conscious patient, many of whom try to remove the tube, creating additional medical and treatment complications. In an unconscious patient the issue often centers around discontinuing this treatment once it has been started. For some people, this implies starving the patient to death, although medical evidence has indicated that these patients do not experience hunger, thirst, or pain during this process. As a result of this controversy, living will statutes in a number of states prohibit the removal of tube feeding once it is in place.

These are the kinds of choices you can readily make in an advance directive: how and under what circumstances do you want such treatments used in your own case?

Some Examples and Advice

Although you can't predict the future or allow for every possible circumstance, it is important to be as clear as you can be in stating your preferences. A number of the books listed at the end of this chapter detail the types of medical interventions you will want to consider. Concern for Dying/Society for the Right to Die also publishes a book and other helpful material describing treatments and explaining your choices.

In his book *The Essential Guide to a Living Will,* journalist B. D. Colen describes the pros and cons of the various types of life-extension treatments and methods. He provides an informative primer on hospital procedures that can be invaluable if you are facing hospitalization or have been diagnosed terminal and shows how important it is to communicate the "outside limits you want to put on the medical care you may be given." He includes a copy of his own living will that provides a good example of the kinds of choices that can be made. (See listings at the end of this chapter.)

Another example is Mary Kay Blakely, author of *Wake Me When It's Over,* who, after her personal experience in a comatose state, wrote: "My living will—prepared two years after it was needed—gives my family the option of 'heroic measures' for three months, then states my desire for the termination of all treatment."[9] And the anthropologist and physician Melvin Konner, in an article about Alzheimer's disease, describes how, when asked, "How long do *you* want to live?" he replied: "My answer, without hesitation, is that I do not want to outlive my brain."[10]

TALKING ABOUT IT

Most people don't find life-support-treatment cessation the stuff of great dinner conversation. Even more than our reluctance to consider the subject of death, we are especially disinclined to discuss the pros and cons of the persistent vegetative state.

However, talking about cessation of treatment is extremely important not only because it will help clarify your wishes to those who may be responsible for ensuring your rights but also because it will actually legally strengthen your position should your case wind up in dispute either in the hospital or in the courts. The law looks to find evidence of any indication that you did or did not want to set limits on extraordinary treatment, and verbal evidence has proved to be critical in some cases.

As we have said, discussion with your proxy should be very comprehensive and clear. But you should also talk with your friends and family in general. Discuss your wishes and the reasons for the decisions you've made. If your spouse, mate, or live-in partner is not your proxy, be sure to talk with him or her, explaining your decisions so that s/he is not surprised by your actions or by your choices. It is important that there be a consensus between those involved; otherwise, difficult legal problems can arise. If you have a lawyer, s/he should be apprised of your wishes as well as consulted on ensuring your rights.

Talk to your doctor and/or any health care professionals you see regularly. It is most important not to surprise your family physician. The determination of incapacity is a medical decision, not a legal one. Your doctor will almost certainly be involved in this matter, and if s/he doesn't know how you feel about life-prolonging measures, s/he cannot be expected to act in accordance with your wishes. If your doctor does not agree with you, it is best to know now, while choices can be made, rather than to find out after the fact and wind up in litigation, or worse.

If you don't have a doctor, it is all the more important that your family or friends be aware of your preferences. It will fall on them to make your wishes clear to medical professionals.

Letting your loved ones know when you would want them to let you die is certainly as important as discussing your personal preferences in life.

You're the Only One
Who Knows What You Want

Often people really want someone else to tell them what to do, especially when decision making is difficult. Oncological surgeon Barry Shapiro describes his experience with this problem:

> Patients are often bewildered, frustrated, even angered, at being "forced" to decide their future . . . to face a dilemma, by being made part of a very difficult decision-making loop. . . . Medicine is now an interactive process between doctor and patient. The physician has the responsibility to provide the patient with a cogent explanation of his treatment and reasonable options whenever invasive care is necessary.

The patient has the responsibility to integrate the treatment options and make a final, informed decision.[11]

In sum, don't confuse what a doctor tries to do with what a doctor cannot do, which is to make *your* decision for you. You're the only one who knows what you would want.

RESOURCES AND SUPPORT

Books

George J. Alexander. *Writing a Living Will: Using a Durable Power-of-Attorney.* New York: Praeger, 1987.

Denis Clifford. *The Power of Attorney Book.* 3rd ed. Berkeley, Calif.: Nolo Press, 1990. Available in bookstores or through Nolo Press, 950 Parker Street, Berkeley, CA 94710; (415) 549-1976 or 1-800-992-NOLO.
[Discusses all forms of power of attorney; appendix includes tear-out forms.]

B. D. Colen. *The Essential Guide to a Living Will.* New York: Simon & Schuster, 1991.
[Journalist B. D. Colen writes regularly on the latest developments in bioethics. In this book he provides an overview of hospital procedures, including a description of invasive procedures and life-extension technology. The author offers as an example his own living will.]

Bradley E. Smith, with Jess Brallier. *Write Your Own Living Will.* New York: Crown Publishing Co., 1991.

A number of new books on living wills and other advance directives are now being published. Keep your eyes open for the most recent and up-to-date.

Books Containing Related Information

George J. Annas. *The Rights of Patients: The Basic ACLU Guide to Patients' Rights.* 2nd ed. Completely revised and up-to-date. American Civil Liberties Union Handbooks. Carbondale, Ill.: Southern University Press, 1989.
[Chapter on care of the dying includes discussion of living wills, right to refuse treatment, durable power of attorney, and other rights of the dying. Appendices include Patient Bill of Rights Act and Right to Refuse Treatment Act.]

Robert N. Brown with Legal Counsel for the Elderly. *The Rights of Older Persons.* 2nd ed. Completely revised and up-to-date. American Civil Liberties Union Handbooks. Carbondale, Ill.: Southern University Press, 1989.
[Chapters on guardianship, civil commitment, and the right to refuse medical treatment.]

Hayden Curry and Denis Clifford. *A Legal Guide for Lesbian and Gay Couples.* 5th ed. Berkeley, Calif.: Nolo Press, 1989. Available in bookstores or through Nolo Press, 950 Parker Street, Berkeley, CA 94710; (415) 549-1976 or 1-800-992-NOLO.
[How to protect your personal autonomy. Chapter on medical emergencies includes discussion of durable power of attorney and living wills; appendix includes tear-out forms.]

Legal Counsel for the Elderly. *Decision-Making, Incapacity and the Elderly: A Protective Services Manual.* Washington, D.C.: Legal Counsel for the Elderly, 1987; supplement, 1989. Available from Legal Counsel for the Elderly, 1909 K Street, NW, Washington, DC 20036; (202) 833-6720. Write or call for a publications catalog.
[A manual for attorneys, patients'-rights advocates, paralegals, and other advocates who represent older persons. Includes information on powers of attorney, guardianship, and living wills.]

Thomas A. Raffin, M.D., Joel N. Shurkin, and Wharton Sinkler III, M.D. *Intensive Care: Facing the Critical Choices.* New York: W. H. Freeman, 1989.
[An informative, easy-to-read book for laypeople describing procedures, benefits, and risks of intensive care; when such care is and is not appropriate; costs and efficacy.]

John Regan, J.S.D., with Legal Counsel for the Elderly. *Your Legal Rights in Later Life.* Washington, D.C.: American Association of Retired Persons; Glenview, Ill.: Scott, Foresman and Co., AARP Books, 1989.
[Chapter on planning for possible incapacity includes discussion of living wills and durable power of attorney.]

John A. Robertson. *The Rights of the Critically Ill.* Rev. ed. American Civil Liberties Union Handbooks. New York: Bantam, 1983. Available in bookstores or from the American Civil Liberties Union, 132 West 43rd Street, New York, NY 10036; (212) 944-9800.
[Includes information on the right to refuse treatment and the right not to be resuscitated.]

Eugene D. Robin, M.D. *Matters of Life & Death: Risk vs. Benefits of Medical Care.* New York: W. H. Freeman, 1984.
[Utilizing a risk-benefit analysis, this book is aimed at the medical consumer. Includes discussion of intensive care units, critical-care units, and care for the terminally ill.]

Thomas Scully, M.D., and Celia Scully. *Making Medical Decisions: How to Make Difficult Medical and Ethical Choices for Yourself and Your Family* (originally published as *Playing God: The New World of Medical Choices*). New York: Simon & Schuster, Fireside Books, 1989.
[A practical guide to medical ethics for the layperson. This helpful book includes discussion of living wills and durable power of attorney; numerous references and appendices, such as the Patient's Bill of Rights and the AMA Statement on Withholding or Withdrawing of Life-Prolonging Medical Treatment.]

Irving J. Sloane. *The Right to Die: Legal and Ethical Problems.* Legal Almanac Series no. 90. New York: Oceana Publications, 1988.
[Mainly a discussion of legal aspects; includes living wills, consent to treatment, and Uniform Rights of the Terminally Ill Act.]

Agencies/Service Organizations

AARP (American Association of Retired Persons)
1909 K Street, NW
Washington, DC 20049
(202) 872-4700
A large nonprofit membership organization providing a wide range of educational and community-service programs. AARP offers a number of publications with information about planning ahead, autonomy, and choice at no charge to members and nonmembers. Included among these are "Tomorrow's Choices: Preparing Now for Future Legal, Financial, and Health Care Decisions," and "A Matter of Choice: Planning Ahead for Health Care Decisions." The AARP's free publications are available by sending a postcard with your request to AARP Fulfillment at the above address. Or call to request a catalog of all AARP publications.

Center for Medical Consumers
237 Thompson Street
New York, NY 10012
(212) 674-7105
A resource for medical information, providing an alternative for consumers, including information on death-care issues; they maintain a library open to laypeople and publish a monthly consumer newsletter.

Dying with Dignity
175 St. Clair Avenue, West
Toronto, Ontario, Canada M4V 1P7
(416) 921-2329
Distributes living wills and durable power of attorney forms to Canadians. It also seeks to educate the public and health care professionals on self-determination and personal autonomy in matters of death and dying. They also can provide counseling to individuals struggling with these issues.

Emanuel Directive
General Internal Medicine Unit
Bulfinch 1
Massachusetts General Hospital
Boston, MA 02114
A highly detailed directive to help sort through the medical interventions you may wish to consider in preparing an advance directive. To obtain the directive, send $2.00 to the above address, in care of Dr. Linda Emanuel.

Gay Men's Health Crisis
Legal Services Department
129 West 20th Street
New York, NY 10011
(212) 337-3504
Provides legal counseling to people with AIDS or ARC; has developed a useful medical directive and power of attorney. (GMHC also publishes a number of helpful books, covering a wide range of issues, for people dealing with AIDS.)

Concern for Dying/Society for the Right to Die
250 West 57th Street
New York, NY 10107
(212) 246-6973
These two groups work to protect the rights and improve the care of dying patients. The society is a legal advisory and legislative action group providing information on the individual's right to self-determination and is active in promoting legislation and filing briefs in leading "right to die" cases. They offer counseling and can make legal referrals. Concern works with the lay public and professionals involved with the terminally ill to increase understanding of patients' legal rights, promote collaborative decision making, and strengthen the patient-caregiver relationship. Both organizations publish handbooks, newsletters, and other printed material. If you contact them, they will send you the advance directive(s) that will give you the best

protection under your state's laws. The two organizations plan to merge sometime in 1991 to form the National Council on Death and Dying.

Also: *Local and regional agencies on aging,* the *state Department of Health,* and your *state attorney general's office* may have information on advance directives or living will forms for your state.

Other Service Agencies
On the East Coast:
Legal Counsel for the Elderly
1909 K Street, NW
Washington, DC 20036
(202) 833-6720
Operates a national legal hotline for older adults and many programs for District of Columbia residents. Also sponsors legal hotlines for residents of Florida, Michigan, Ohio, and Pennsylvania. Call the Washington, D.C., number for the hotline in those states.

Whitman Walker Clinic
Legal Services Project
1407 S Street, NW
Washington, DC 20009
(202) 797-3527
Free legal consultations with volunteer attorneys (for people with AIDS or ARC) on wills, estate planning, and living wills. Publishes a free booklet entitled "Legal Answers on AIDS" that includes information on medical directives and personal autonomy.

In the Midwest:
AIDS Legal Council of Chicago
220 South State Street
Suite 2030
Chicago, IL 60604
(312) 427-8990
Provides information on medical directives and powers of attorney for people with AIDS. Fees are based on a sliding scale.

Columbus AIDS Task Force
1500 West Third Avenue
Suite 329
Columbus, OH 43212
(614) 488-2437
Makes referrals to attorneys for people with AIDS in the Columbus area.

On the West Coast:
Gay Legal Referral Service
San Francisco, California
(415) 621-3900
A state bar–approved lawyer referral service. Call for further information.

Video

In Your Hands: The Tools for Preserving Personal Autonomy
Modern Talking Picture Service
5000 Park Street, N.
St. Petersburg, FL 33709
(813) 541-7571
Narrated by Helen Hayes, this 16½-minute video contains information on living wills, medical directives, and powers of attorney. The video is available for a 3-day rental and is accompanied by a 31-page Program Guide and copies of a 12-page viewer's pamphlet. Produced by the American Bar Association's Commission on Legal Problems of the Elderly.

Death Care

II

4

Making Decisions
for Another

Sometimes the machines are a blessing and sometimes they are a curse. But
we haven't invented laws or rules yet to tell the difference.

Anonymous Physician

In Chicago, a man pulls a gun in a hospital room and demands to
be left alone with his unconscious son. He unplugs the ventilator
that has kept the child breathing for nine months and, weeping,
cradles the comatose body in his arms until the boy dies. The father
is arrested for murder.

Six years after suffering irreversible brain damage in a car crash, a
thirty-one-year-old woman lies immobile in a Missouri rehabilitation
center, her body so severely contracted that her fingernails cut into
her wrists. Cared for by nurses, her stiff torso is washed, wiped clean,
and turned every few hours to prevent bedsores. Surgically implanted tubes provide nutrition and hydration. Her parents ask that
the tubes be removed, saying their daughter would never have
wanted to continue living in such a state. The rehabilitation center
refuses. A trial judge orders the parents' decision upheld. The Mis-

souri Supreme Court overrules, denying permission. The U.S. Supreme Court upholds the state's right to intercede. The case goes back to the trial judge, the state withdraws its objections, new evidence is heard, and the judge reiterates his original decision. The feeding tube is removed. Seven years, eleven months, and fifteen days after losing consciousness, the young woman dies.

In upstate New York an eighty-six-year-old stroke victim lies motionless, in a comatose state for five months. Because she had expressed the desire not to linger in such a condition, relatives obtain legal permission to have her artificial feeding tube removed, thus "allowing her to die." Just as they are about to implement the court order, she regains consciousness unexpectedly. When told what has occurred, she says, "These are difficult questions," and lapses back into unconsciousness.

These dramas are extraordinary examples of situations that are becoming more and more ordinary. We hear about them when they develop into court cases or when an individual resorts to extreme measures. But whether we see them on the nightly news or never hear of them at all, there are many people struggling with this nightmare—someone they love is not really living and not really dead.

Seventy percent of all Americans will find themselves facing a similar circumstance. In chapter 3 we learned about advance directives and the importance of preparing ahead for incapacity. Here we will take a look at what happens when there is no advance directive and you must make a decision that affects the way in which another person will live or die.

Whose Decision Is It?

If you are the spouse, parent, adult child, or sibling of an unconscious, comatose, or otherwise incapacitated patient, you may well be asked to participate in making treatment decisions. Health care professionals traditionally turn to close family members to answer the questions the patient can't answer. As Ruth Macklin, a leading philosopher and medical ethicist, states: "Although there is still considerable legal uncertainty in situations in which patients have expressed no wishes about medical care before becoming unable to participate in decisions, the practice almost everywhere is for physicians to consult family members and be guided by their wishes."[1]

If the patient planned ahead and prepared a living will, a medical durable power of attorney, or other advance directive, this document will provide a guide to the patient's wishes. If s/he has appointed a proxy or a durable power of attorney for health care, now is the time for the proxy to assume responsibility. If you have agreed to serve as attorney in fact or been named as a proxy in a living will, you'll have talked with your friend or relative about what to do. If the patient has a legal guardian or a court-appointed conservator, that individual may or may not have authority over *medical* decisions.

Settings and Circumstances

When we are actually in a hospital where someone we love, or for whom we are responsible, is in critical condition, it is very difficult to be cool, calm, and collected. Emergency rooms are often cluttered and messy; intensive care units are crowded, noisy, and filled with intimidating machinery. The appearance of the patient may be anything but peaceful. Someone in a brain-damaged state may lie with their eyes or mouth open, blinking, apparently awake, or jerking reflexively. S/he may respond to some stimuli; physicians may disagree as to whether s/he can feel pain or may not be able to tell you for certain. The real picture might well be one that horrifies and frightens you.

Your initial reaction to seeing a loved one in such a condition will likely be shock and fear. It is quite possible you will feel numb or disoriented. It is important to take the time and to get the assistance you need in order to make reasoned and compassionate choices and not to act out of your own pain or need in the confusion of the moment.

If the threat is immediate and all the action takes place in an emergency situation, your choices are considerably restricted. A hospital emergency room is an exception to the doctrine of informed consent. Under such conditions, medical professionals will take immediate action to curtail a life-threatening condition and will not take the time to discuss treatment decisions with the patient or the immediate family. Maintaining and stabilizing vital functions becomes the sole focus of activity. Questions about consequences are put on hold.

More often, however, a condition is progressive through stages that allow for discussion and consideration. It is possible that you will have time to make some decisions. The trick is to use that time well.

Rather than one single decision leading to a clear-cut result, you will frequently be faced with a series of decisions as circumstances progress and new conditions present themselves. "If a fever develops, should antibiotics be used?" "For how long?" "If respiration fails, should resuscitation be attempted?" "Under what conditions?" "Should a feeding tube be removed?" "Now or later?" "Under what circumstances?"

A prominent physician and ethicist has pointed out that ". . . if a person needs life support to survive, the question of his or her chances to regain a good quality of life can be asked over several days, and indicated action can be taken: either fighting for the patient's survival or assisting the patient to die with dignity and peace."[2]

BASIC GUIDELINES

While cases vary considerably, there are some general guidelines that can be helpful if followed. You will need two different types of information.

1. What exactly is the patient's medical condition?
2. What would s/he have wanted in this situation?

One of the best books available on this subject is called *Making Medical Decisions: How to Make Difficult Medical and Ethical Choices for Yourself and Your Family* by Thomas and Celia Scully. (See listings at the end of this chapter.) In it the authors present a list of questions to ask the physicians and health care professionals involved. The answers to these questions will give you a real sense of the patient's condition.

1. What happened? How serious is this condition?
2. Why is he unconscious? (e.g., lack of oxygen to the brain, bleeding, stroke, shock, drug overdose, or increased pressure on or in the brain.)
3. Is he in any pain?
4. Is he in coma? Is the coma irreversible?
5. Is he brain-dead or likely to be soon? When will you know?
6. Is he likely to regain consciousness? How long will that take—weeks, months? Will he wake up completely?
7. Will he be permanently unconscious? Will he enter the persistent vegetative state? When will you know?

8. How long does he need to be on the respirator? Can he live without it?
9. If the heart stops, should he be resuscitated?
10. If he gets an infection, should he be treated with antibiotics?
11. If he doesn't begin to eat or drink, should he be continued on IV or tube feedings?
12. If he lives, will he be in pain? Able to do anything for himself? Or will he need special care of some kind?
13. If he lives, will he be aware of his surroundings? Able to communicate with us in some way?
14. If he lives, will he be able to make decisions for himself, or will he need a guardian?
15. What do you suggest at this point? Should we get other opinions and talk to additional specialists?[3]

What Would the Patient Have Wanted in This Situation?

If there is no advance directive, it is very important for you to try to remember whether there has ever been any verbal directive, conversation, or remarks in which s/he indicated an opinion or a personal feeling about life-support treatment or cessation. Are there others who might know? Scully and Scully suggest asking family members, friends, co-workers, the patient's attorney, clergy, or doctors who have cared for the patient in the past.

Questions you might ask yourself include:

• Did the patient ever speak to you about such a possibility?

• Did you ever discuss it in general terms or talk about specific cases in the news?

• Did the patient know anyone who was on life support? If so, how did s/he react to the situation?

• Is there a debilitating condition the patient would have found intolerable?

• Does the patient have a strongly held philosophical or religious belief that might help guide you in making a judgment about their wishes?[4]

It can be most difficult to actually put yourself in the place of the one you love or for whom you are responsible. Usually we make decisions based on what *we* want, which is normal and appropriate. Now we need to decide based on what is best for another and to think as much as we can from the other's point of view, not what is best for us but what is (or was) important to the person who now cannot choose.

The possible actions you may be asked to consider taking, or may wish to ask about taking, can be divided into three general categories, (1) declining futile treatment, (2) discontinuing debilitating treatment, and (3) ending life-support measures. These actions will involve:

- Limitations on resuscitation efforts
- Limitations on initiating life-support measures
- Withdrawal of "ordinary" life-support measures
- Withdrawal of "extraordinary" life-support measures

Let's look at each one of these treatment options:

Do-Not-Resuscitate Orders

First-aid cardiopulmonary resuscitation (CPR) is a basic tool in emergency medical treatment. We've all heard of those cases in which CPR, practiced on the scene, saved someone's life. This first-aid technique involves clearing the throat passage, placing your mouth over the victim's mouth, and blowing air into the throat passage while applying rhythmic pressure to the chest to encourage the heart and lungs to resume function. When the victim is otherwise capable of recovery, CPR can be a miraculous lifesaving measure. But resuscitation as practiced routinely in hospitals on elderly or terminal patients is a different matter.

If you are in a hospital and your heart or lung function fails, you will be "coded"—emergency CPR will be performed. This can involve providing oxygen (through a mask or tube in the windpipe); chest compression to massage the heart or electroshock to shock the heart into beating again; and the injection of drugs, sometimes directly into the heart itself, to maintain heartbeat.

Ethics specialist Ruth Macklin describes CPR:

If any procedure in modern medicine deserves to be called "aggressive," it is CPR. As commonly practiced, a resuscitation team rushes to the bedside, where one member of the team jumps onto the patient and pounds on his chest while others insert lines and tubes, give injections, and do whatever is necessary to get the patient's heart beating again. It is usually a messy affair, with blood and other body fluids spattering everyone within reach.[5]

When first developed, CPR was a "heroic" or extraordinary measure. As it became more and more routine, it became clear that sometimes the practice hurt more than it helped. The authors of *Intensive Care: Facing the Critical Choices,* a well-written and informative book about medical treatment and choices, say, "CPR is simply not effective in very sick people. One study reports that CPR revives only 37 percent of patients in the ICU and only 17 percent live to be discharged from the hospital."[6]

CPR is an invasive therapy with chancy results. Resuscitation can leave the patient brain damaged or comatose. The National Conference on CPR and ECC (electrocardiac conversion), which was sponsored by the National Academy of Sciences, stated: "The purpose of CPR is the prevention of sudden, unexpected death. CPR is not indicated in certain situations such as in cases of terminal irreversible illness where death is not unexpected."[7] If you are at the end stages of a painful terminal illness, respiratory failure can be a blessing.

Today most hospitals allow for what is called a *Do Not Resuscitate* order or a "No Code," an order written into the patient's chart directing that if cardiopulmonary failure occurs, the patient should be made as comfortable as possible but no resuscitation should be attempted.

If you are trying to decide whether or not to request a DNR order for your relative or loved one, Scully and Scully recommend you ask these questions:

Is the patient likely to survive the resuscitation?
Is the patient likely to be left in coma?
Is the patient likely ever to be well enough to go home?
Will s/he feel pain during the resuscitation?
Is the patient likely to wake up connected to a respirator, and if
    so, for how long?[8]

Limiting the Initiation of Basic Life Support

Once machines are in place and medications are prescribed, removing them raises the issue of life cessation and causality. Are there *basic* actions that must always be taken no matter what the potential outcome, just because they are there to be taken?

This type of question presents a classic ethics dilemma. Are there cases in which it would be better not to begin even basic treatment in the first place? It arises most often in situations involving the terminally ill elderly. When an eighty-nine-year-old is in the end stages of cancer or Alzheimer's disease and his or her heart stops, the most humane action may be to avoid doing anything. This is what DNR orders are for.

However, the same situation also arises with other types of treatment measures, including mechanical ventilation, artificial nutrition and hydration, and antibiotic drugs. Artificial feeding can create the most emotionally charged issue. Certainly food and water are basic to human needs, but when someone is critically ill, our usual notion of nutrition may not apply. Is the process of forcing liquid through a surgically implanted tube into someone's stomach dinner, or is it a medical treatment?

Standard Procedures

As these problems have become clearer, more restraint is being practiced within the hospital environment. In some cases, what once were routine procedures are being questioned before the fact. The hopelessly ill are less often moved into ICUs, marking a shift from the once prevalent tendency to apply every available therapy at all costs. Dr. William A. Knaus, an ICU specialist at George Washington University Hospital, says:

> In general we will not take patients who have widely disseminated cancer and respiratory failure because we know those patients will probably die here no matter what we do. . . . We discourage them, make sure the family knows that the prognosis is essentially zero and that ICU's can be miserable places.[9]

Drs. Raffin and Sinkler believe that physicians should reconsider some of their most automatic assumptions.

> Sometimes medications are begun as part of basic support procedure, and this ought to be rethought in certain cases. Is it an act of kindness

to pull a comatose, hopelessly ill person from the edge of a painless death and grant days or weeks of discomfort or agony in its place? The automatic administration of antibiotics and some steroids can have that effect.

They point out:

Physicians are trained to provide these basics of care almost as a reflex, often without even considering whether they are performing a truly caring act. They should think first. The patient (when possible) or the family must be allowed to make the decision whether to begin these basic support measures. Once these measures are instituted, the act of removing them requires a direct action that would not have been necessary if the measures were not instituted in the first place. The placement of intravenous lines makes it very difficult for a physician *not* to use them for treatment. Sometimes it might be better not to insert IV lines at all.[10]

Such issues are beginning to demand more public attention if for no other reason than the fact that health care resources, not to mention human hearts, are being strained to the breaking point. There is no question but that the technology is beginning to dominate what should be human, and humane, considerations. One area of continued confusion has to do with the difference between *basic* life-support measures and *heroic* life-support measures.

Ordinary and Extraordinary Life-Support Measures

If the terms *ordinary* and *extraordinary life-support measures* are used, you should ask the medical team to define exactly how they are using them and what is meant in any particular case. This is because even within the medical and legal communities the distinction between ordinary treatment and extraordinary or heroic treatment is not clear-cut. Usually these measures are defined not by the particular drugs or procedures used but by how they will affect the patient's prognosis; determined by, in Scully's words, "whether or not the benefits of the proposed treatment are in proportion to the burdens imposed on the patient."[11] Thus, while in the case of a young accident victim with a good prognosis a ventilator and intubation might be considered ordinary life-sustaining treatment (because it does indeed "sustain" life while healing can occur), in the case of an elderly patient in the end stages of a terminal condition the same treatment might well result in the painful prolongation of the dying process and constitute extraordinary treatment.

The distinction is conditional on the legal side as well. One judge, in a case regarding the cessation of life support, stated that "the terms 'ordinary' and 'extraordinary' have assumed too many conflicting meanings to remain useful."[12]

This lack of clarity can add considerable confusion to an already complex situation. Some practicing medical ethicists recommend simply thinking in terms of *humane* treatment when and if the difference between ordinary and heroic becomes clouded.

Terminology

Other phrases or concepts that may arise in discussions between the family and the health care team include the following: (These are also the principles argued when such cases wind up in the courts.)

TRACK RECORD   Track record refers to evidence as to the patient's own preferences. Does a record exist that can clearly indicate what s/he would have wanted in this situation? This record can be written or spoken, but written is better. If a living will has been signed, it constitutes the best kind of track record, but previously expressed verbal wishes have been taken into account and can constitute evidence of preference.

Unfortunately, most people don't talk together about their wishes in these matters. If they have not done so, someone has to make a "substituted judgment" on their behalf.

SUBSTITUTED JUDGMENT   That is, judgment substituted for the judgment of the incapacitated patient. This principle holds when you are making decisions based on what you feel the patient would decide were s/he able to do so; decisions based on what you know about his or her values, beliefs, and feelings—your experience of that person.

A substituted judgment can be made only if the patient was once capable of making such a decision himself or herself. However, if the patient is a child or someone who is severely mentally retarded or never capable of making an informed, autonomous decision in the first place, the idea of the patient's "best interests" may become the primary consideration.

BEST INTERESTS   This phrase refers to the notion of what is "best" based on generally accepted and widely shared criteria. In other words, most of us share common assumptions about what is okay and what is horrible—societal values. What would the values of society dictate be done for this person? If there is no other way of knowing, we look to the "norm." This principle presumes a humane approach.

You can get help in understanding these principles as they apply to your situation and in learning the legal ramifications of any action you may take by calling the Society for the Right to Die or Concern for Dying. Another resource is the hospital ethics committee.

THE ETHICS COMMITTEE

When considering the cessation of life-support measures, a family may consult with a health care team or an ethics committee. A relatively new construction, the hospital ethics committee is a group of legal, philosophical, and medical experts who specialize in dealing with ethics issues in the hospital setting. (About 60 percent of the hospitals in this country have some kind of ethics committee. In smaller institutions the job of ethics adviser may be filled by a single staff member or "ethics consultant.")

Ethics committees give advice. They do not make decisions. The committee or consultant can act in a formal manner, making a recommendation that is entered into the patient's medical record or, more informally, discussing the situation with the family or interested parties and providing information and clarifying options.

Ethics committees can help reaffirm patients' rights, guide physicians through the ethics labyrinth, inform families and friends as to the types of care that can be applied or withheld and the types of comfort measures that can be given, and reassure caregivers and families alike that in some cases withdrawing treatment is ethically defensible.

And ultimately, when it is clear that the final choice is required, it need not rest solely on one person's shoulders; it can become what Derek Humphry, in his book *The Right to Die,* calls a "negotiated death." He says:

. . . many doctors are aware that, failing resolution, keeping a hopelessly ill patient alive against his will is draining for everyone and incurs tremendous social, financial, and emotional costs. . . . Typically, over days or weeks, the patient, his physician, his family, the hospital ethics committee, hospital administrators, and sometimes lawyers form an ad hoc committee, concurring that death is inevitable and that prolonging life only adds to the patient's suffering. At a time agreed on, equipment is unplugged or other forms of treatment are discontinued. That such a phenomenon exists is perhaps inevitable in a world where technology has enabled doctors to extend the life of a dying person but has provided no explicit set of ethical or legal guidelines that will be universally applied and consistently upheld by courts.[13]

THE LAW

Although the law is established regarding a competent individual's right to refuse treatment, sometimes even such clear-cut cases wind up in the courts. When they do, it is usually because medical personnel refuse to accede to the patient's request. This can be the result of moral, ethical, or religious differences between a doctor and a patient or because of a fear of criminal liability or for political reasons (i.e., the case is seen as a chance to confirm or challenge the law toward a political end).

When the patient is competent, the autonomy precedent is consistently reaffirmed. With incapacitated patients the case law is somewhat muddled. Opposing decisions have been handed down in the same jurisdiction. A "right to die" case in one state will establish a precedent directly contradictory to that in another state or even in the same locale. The best advice, given the current unsettled status of the law, is to stay out of court if at all possible.

Ultimately, everyone has a different idea about when they would prefer to die and under what circumstances. When you are required to weigh these circumstances on behalf of another human being, it is best to be doing it with the help of supportive family, friends, and professionals. If the negotiation process isn't put into effect or breaks down for some reason (say, for instance, that family members disagree), legal problems may arise.

For advice about legal questions, contact the Society for the Right to Die, Concern for Dying, or the American Civil Liberties Union. Or find a good attorney with experience in medical ethics issues.

These resources can help whether you are in a hospital or are dealing with treatment and support decisions on behalf of a patient in a nursing home, a long-term-care facility, or your own home.

The Liability and Responsibility of Medical Professionals

Sometimes we will hear that a doctor won't remove a ventilator or otherwise end treatment because of the fear of incurring criminal liability. What about this question: If a doctor or other medical professional suspends life-support systems, is s/he liable to criminal charges or malpractice claims?

No doctor in the United States has ever been jailed or had his or her license permanently revoked for terminating life support at the request of a patient or family. As pointed out by counsel at Concern for Dying, courts have stated ". . . that the medical profession will be protected if they act in good faith, if the action is not unreasonable by medical standards, and if the procedures previously enunciated by court decisions or natural death acts are followed." They go on to say that "concern for criminal liability is generally unfounded and pointless."[14]

Surveys have shown that physicians themselves affirm the right of terminal patients to decline treatment and die peacefully, with as little suffering as possible.[15] Then why should there be any problem?

Surprisingly, most medical professionals are as uncomfortable with the idea of death as everybody else is. They, too, withdraw from the enormity of these issues and sometimes from the decision-making process as well. Doctors are trained to preserve life at all costs; they are not trained to practice death care.

And physicians are not legal experts. Many don't really know much about the law regarding self-determination and autonomy. (While surveys show physicians supporting living wills and patient autonomy, on-site clinical studies have shown that in practice they rarely talk with patients about advance directives or end-of-life decisions.)[16] Nor are they in the business of mediating disputes between family members. If the patient's family is not united in their decision, a physician will rarely act to discontinue life-support treatment of any kind.

Add to this the ever-present threat of malpractice suits in our litigious culture and it is not surprising that physicians often feel they are culpable even though the law has consistently determined they are not.

The role of the nurse is sometimes critical when it comes to life-support cessation decisions. Physicians tend to move in and out of the situation, making rounds or visiting briefly, while the nursing staff maintains an ongoing contact with the patient and the patient's family. Being generally more visible and sometimes more approachable, nurses are often the ones to whom the family goes for information and advice. They can be very helpful in answering the many questions that arise, and influential in negotiating the difficult issues involved.

WHEN THE PATIENT IS A CHILD

When the patient is a child, the legal basis for consideration is not autonomy or self-determination but what, in law, are called "objective, best-interest standards." The body of law affecting such cases is the same as that prevailing when, for instance, religious beliefs conflict with state law regarding schooling, health care, or other medical matters. The law is clear: The state can override parents' wishes in the "best interest" of the child.

Scully and Scully's *Making Medical Decisions* covers this subject. It includes a complete description of medical, legal, and ethical issues regarding life support for children. The authors encourage parents to ask questions.

> You may be wondering if it's now time to stop treatment and let your child die in peace. You may hesitate to bring up the topic for fear you'll be judged a bad or unfeeling parent. But today, more and more people are questioning just how long treatment should be continued when it seems to be getting nowhere. In short, if you're worried and wondering, don't sit around waiting for the doctor to bring up the issue. Ask.[17]

They list specific questions to ask when your child is unconscious, including:

- Is my child in permanent coma, or will he or she wake up?

- Would new methods of treating children in coma work in my child's case?

- If not, will my child be in a persistent vegetative state like Karen Quinlan? How long could he or she last that way?

- Should we stop everything and just let my child die peacefully?

- If I want to be with my child until the very end, can I stay by his or her side when life supports or other treatments are removed?

- What might I expect at that point?[18]

In practice everything depends on the particular circumstances. Generally the following points of consideration are applied: Are the measures inhumane? Is the treatment futile? Is the child in irreversible coma?

Two examples involving children illustrate the range of uses of life-extension technology. In Missouri a nine-year-old boy dying of advanced leukemia was resuscitated ten times in three days, his body convulsed and broken from the painful resuscitation procedure. His parents had to go to court to get permission to allow their son to die peacefully.

In California, a two-year-old was found floating facedown in a swimming pool. Although the child had drowned, an emergency medical team established a heartbeat, and the boy was placed on artificial systems until his father, a professional athlete on tour, could reach the hospital to participate in his "death." Then the support equipment was removed. "They did it so I would experience it, not just hear about how it was," said the father.

Neonatal Intensive Care
Another increasingly complicated ethical concern is neonatal care, and once again it is the unexamined use of the technology that creates moral dilemmas. Where once severely deformed or premature infants would die "naturally," today modern medicine can maintain life, even where it cannot cure or correct serious abnormalities.

In the early 1980s, several so-called Baby Doe cases brought ethical neonatal questions into the political arena. In these cases, decisions by parents and their doctors not to perform surgery on severely handicapped newborns were challenged by some medical administrators and special-interest groups. The subsequent series of legal battles resulted in a U.S. Supreme Court decision supporting the parents' right to make decisions but emphasizing the state's responsibility to protect the best interest of the child.[19] In medical, legal, and ethical circles the debate continues. Meanwhile, making treatment decisions remains a painful personal nightmare for parents of infants who may be sustained but cannot be healed.

Hospital ethics committees can give advice, but unfortunately there isn't a network of support groups for parents trying to make neonatal treatment decisions. (Such groups as the Spina Bifida Association or National Down's Syndrome Society tend to be organized around particular illnesses or deformities. See listings at the end of this chapter for further information.)

MONEY

Life-extension technology is expensive, and intensive care costs a lot. As described in chapter 3, keeping someone alive against all odds can bankrupt a family. But how can you check on costs and make decisions based on price tags? Many people are distraught when faced with life-and-death decisions and find it impossible to weigh the financial factors.

Even if they have the equanimity to consider the costs, most people feel guilty for thinking about money "at a time like this." Trying to be fiscally practical in such situations is very difficult and may seem inappropriate. And the medical-care system isn't designed to help you. It is very difficult to get information or an estimate of charges going in.

Insurance and Assistance
Skyrocketing costs and the crisis in the insurance industry have contributed to serious problems in this country's overburdened and inequitable system of medical care. Many experts predict worsening conditions, especially regarding the elderly dying. As the population ages (nearly 80 percent of Americans alive today will live past age sixty-five), demand for medical services continues to climb, and what the insurance industry calls "last-year-of-life" costs are becoming a controversial portion of overall medical expenses.

Today the best-protected segment of the population is the affluent elderly who have both private insurance and Medicare, which covers most hospital charges and up to 80 percent of "medical" costs (defined as physicians' services, medical services and supplies, outpatient hospital services, and therapy).

Medicare is available to most people over sixty-five and to those under sixty-five with disabilities (who have been entitled to Social Security disability payments for at least two years) and to people with permanent kidney failure. Certain low-income families, the blind, and the impoverished can receive coverage through Medicaid, a government assistance program.

Private insurance coverage varies widely but is rarely sufficient to protect fully from so-called catastrophic illness. There are many cases in which family members survive the loss of a loved one only to receive devastating bills in the mail a month later. In addition, insurance coverage can impact upon life-support decisions. Sometimes you may feel it's better to terminate certain life support, or the physician may recommend the cessation of a particular category of treatment, but find that discontinuing that category of treatment will result in losing insurance coverage.

And for those with no insurance coverage at all (37 million Americans in 1989), life-support technology is of course prohibitive.

When the question arises of continuing or terminating treatment, money is one of the factors involved whether it is discussed or not. Don't be ashamed of your concern about money and don't be afraid to ask questions. Try to talk with the hospital admitting office or ask to speak to the social worker. Sometimes the clerical staff can tell you how to go about getting information or assistance.

Some hospitals participate in the Hill-Burton Program, a federally legislated program requiring hospitals, nursing homes, and health care centers that have received federal loans for construction and renovation to provide uncompensated services to the impoverished. (Some of these services may be restricted or limited.) Patients can apply for assistance under the Hill-Burton Act even after they have been discharged, and the application can be made on behalf of a patient by family or clergy. If you think you might qualify, ask about Hill-Burton at the hospital admitting or credit office or ask a hospital social worker.

DEALING WITH YOUR OWN
UNCERTAINTY

Making treatment decisions is a very hard thing to do. It is not surprising that most people try to avoid it. But for all the reasons we have discussed, this painful experience is becoming unavoidable more often for more people.

Challenging our most intense personal beliefs as well as the social customs we regularly, and unquestioningly, practice, such decisions raise issues of responsibility, need, attachment, and often unexamined assumptions. Many difficult feelings can arise, frequently compounded by shock, fear, and grief. It is a time when private counseling can be invaluable if it is available to you. Others turn to clergy or friends for support and advice. A growing number of books are available on the subject of medical ethics, some of them written specifically to help the individual or family facing such decisions. (See listings at the end of this chapter.) If you have a spiritual belief or follow a religious practice, it can ameliorate much of the uncertainty that pervades such events and help you make choices you can live with.

In the midst of all this complexity it can be steadying to remember that this is really a question of when, not whether, a person will die, that death is not necessarily a terrible thing, and that the process of dying is as natural as the process of being born.

These are very personal decisions. Your own instincts are your best guide. No one can tell you how to do it. There is rarely, if ever, a single correct decision; it is more often a process of unfolding uncertainties. We tend to look for black-and-white answers. Here we won't even find black-and-white questions.

One of the subtler and more confusing matters raised by these choices is, when does "allowing to die" change to "assisting to die" and "assisting" change to "causing to die"? When does the cessation of life support become euthanasia? These are matters of definition. In chapter 5 we'll look at these demarcations and the changing definition of death itself.

RESOURCES AND SUPPORT

Books

Daniel Callahan. *Setting Limits: Medical Goals in an Aging Society.* New York: Simon & Schuster, Touchstone Books, 1988.
[Addresses the issue of the termination of treatment for the elderly dying. Includes suggested criteria for ethical decision making.]

Derek Humphry and Ann Wickett. *The Right to Die: Understanding Euthanasia.* Eugene, Ore.: Hemlock Society, 1990.
[Also discusses bioethics issues, including the right to refuse treatment.]

Ruth Macklin. *Mortal Choices: Ethical Dilemmas in Modern Medicine.* Boston: Houghton Mifflin, 1988.
[An examination, using actual cases, of how hospital ethics committees attempt to resolve bioethical dilemmas.]

Thomas A. Raffin, M.D., Joel N. Shurkin, and Wharton Sinkler III, M.D. *Intensive Care: Facing the Critical Choices.* New York: W. H. Freeman, 1989.
[An informative, easy-to-read book for laypeople describing procedures, benefits, and risks of intensive care and when such care is and is not appropriate; includes sections on costs and efficacy.]

Eugene D. Robin, M.D. *Matters of Life & Death: Risk vs. Benefits of Medical Care.* New York: W. H. Freeman, 1984.
[Utilizing a risk-benefit analysis, this book is aimed at the medical consumer. Includes discussion of intensive care units, critical-care units, and care for the terminally ill.]

Thomas Scully, M.D., and Celia Scully. *Making Medical Decisions: How to Make Difficult Medical and Ethical Choices for Yourself and Your Family* (originally published as *Playing God: The New World of Medical Choices*). New York: Simon & Schuster, Fireside Books, 1989.
[A practical guide to medical ethics for the layperson. Includes discussion of neonatal questions; with numerous references and appendixes, such as the Patient's Bill of Rights, the AMA Statement on Withholding or Withdrawing of Life-Prolonging Medical Treatment, and a list of national and regional centers for medical ethics.]

Irving J. Sloane. *The Right to Die: Legal and Ethical Problems.* Legal Almanac Series no. 90. New York: Oceana Publications, 1988.
[Primarily a discussion of legal aspects; includes consent to treatment and Uniform Rights of the Terminally Ill Act.]

Robert M. Veatch. *Death, Dying and the Biological Revolution: Our Last Quest for Responsibility.* Rev. ed. New Haven: Yale University Press, 1989.
[Presents current thinking in bioethics as it affects decisions about death and dying.]

William J. Winslade and Judith Wilson Ross. *Choosing Life or Death: A Guide for Patients, Families, and Professionals.* New York: Macmillan, Free Press, 1986.
[An accessible book on medical practices and the legal realities of bioethics; with helpful general information on technological medicine and patients' rights.]

Books Containing Further Information on Neonatal Bioethics

Willard Gaylin and Ruth Macklin, eds. *Who Speaks for the Child: The Problems of Proxy Consent.* New York: Plenum, 1982.

Jeff Lyon. *Playing God in the Nursery.* New York: W. W. Norton, 1986.
[Written by a journalist, often in graphic detail, this book discusses medical, legal, ethical, and other issues surrounding the withholding of medical treatment from children with severe birth defects.]

Earl E. Shelp. *Born to Die? Deciding the Fate of Critically Ill Newborns.* New York: Macmillan, Free Press, 1986.
[An examination of neonatal medicine and ethics.]

Books Containing Related Information

Robert N. Brown, with Legal Counsel for the Elderly. *The Rights of Older Persons.* 2nd ed. Completely revised and up-to-date. American Liberties Handbooks. Carbondale, Ill.: Southern University Press, 1989.

Jean Crichton. *The Age Care Sourcebook: A Resource Guide for the Aging and Their Families.* New York: Simon & Schuster, Fireside Books, 1987.
[Contains a clear explanation of Medicare and Medicaid programs and reimbursements.]

Legal Counsel for the Elderly. *Decision-Making, Incapacity and the Elderly: A Protective Services Manual.* Washington, D.C.: Legal Counsel for the Elderly, 1987; supplement, 1989. Available from Legal Counsel for the Elderly, 1909 K Street, NW, Washington, DC 20036; (202) 833-6720.
[A manual for attorneys, patients'-rights advocates, paralegals, and other advocates who represent older persons. Chapters on guardian-

ship, civil commitment, the right to refuse medical treatment, and financial planning for Medicaid eligibility.]

Agencies/Service Organizations

American Civil Liberties Union (ACLU)
132 West 43rd Street
New York, NY 10036
(212) 944-9800
A national organization with state affiliates and local chapters actively involved in the protection of constitutional rights. Write for a publications list.

Center for Medical Consumers
237 Thompson Street
New York, NY 10012
(212) 674-7105
A resource for medical information, providing an alternative for consumers, including information on death-care issues; they maintain a library open to laypeople and publish a monthly consumer newsletter.

Dying with Dignity
175 St. Clair Avenue West
Toronto, Ontario, Canada M4V 1P7
(416) 921-2329
Distributes living wills and durable power of attorney forms to Canadians; seeks to educate the public and health care professionals on self-determination and personal autonomy in matters of death and dying; also provides counseling to individuals struggling with these issues.

Concern for Dying/Society for the Right to Die
250 West 57th Street
New York, NY 10107
(212) 246-6973
These two groups work to protect the rights and improve the care of dying patients. Concern works with the lay public and professionals involved with the terminally ill to increase understanding of patients' legal rights, promote collaborative decision making, and strengthen the patient-caregiver relationship. The society is a legal advisory and legislative action group providing information on the individual's right to self-determination and is active in promoting legislation and filing briefs in leading "right to die" cases. They offer counseling and can make legal referrals. Both organizations publish handbooks, newsletters, and other printed material. If you

contact them, they will send you the advance directive(s) that will give you the best protection under your state's laws. The two organizations plan to merge sometime in 1991 to form the National Council on Death and Dying.

Additional Resources

Local and regional *family service associations* or *social service agencies* or *area agencies on aging* sometimes provide information on how to qualify for financial assistance for end-of-life medical expenses.

Currently there is no substantial network of support groups for individuals and families facing life-and-death decisions. Information and assistance tend to be organized around specific diseases and disabilities, such as the Cystic Fibrosis Foundation, American Kidney Fund, or Alzheimer's Disease and Related Disorders Association. For a listing of such support groups and their hotlines, see Jean Carper, *Health Care U.S.A.* (New York: Prentice Hall, 1987), or other references readily available at your local public library.

The National Health Information Center of the Office of Disease Prevention and Promotion, U.S. Department of Human Services, P.O. Box 1133, Washington, DC 20013-1133; 800-336-4797; (301) 565-4167 (in Maryland) offers services that include referrals to government agencies, voluntary associations, self-help groups, and support groups.

5

Redefining Death and Dying

How are we to determine whether or not it is right to either hasten or delay these natural processes? How do we decide whether the predominant force in a patient is a healing process or a dying one?

Thomas A. Raffin, Joel N. Shurkin, and Wharton Sinkler III, *Intensive Care, Facing the Critical Choices*

In the past, if you became seriously ill or injured, it was quite likely that you would die within a relatively brief period and that your death would come as a result of the natural course of your disease or injury. As we have seen, today that natural course can be interrupted. Medical technology can sustain vital functions, and the dying human body can be suspended in its progress toward death.

This is a recent phenomenon, and we've been slow in recognizing its implications because so many other aspects of death and dying have also changed. For one thing, we used to die more quickly. In his book *Age Wave*, Ken Dychtwald, an expert in the field of social gerontology, puts it succinctly: "Throughout all of human history, the average length of life was short." A child born in the colonies in 1776 could expect to live only to thirty-five, and the median age of the population of the new United States was a mere sixteen years. Death was more common in the course of one short lifetime. Most recently, the rate of increase in life expectancy has mushroomed from an average of forty-seven years at the beginning of this century to seventy-five years at its end. Today death has become less omnipresent in any single generation. We are less acquainted with the process of dying and less occupied with its consequences. This is especially true for the period following the Second World War.

Over the last fifty years, a number of major technological breakthroughs have spurred progressively effective medical procedures, treatments, and drugs. These developments eradicated many communicable diseases, which had been a leading cause of death.

At the same time, cultural changes created significant shifts in the traditional family structure, shifts that affected where we die and, subsequently, the way we learn about death. The extended family home, in which grandparents and children cohabit, all but disappeared. As we moved more often from place to place, the house itself was no longer the physical setting for primary life events. As people stopped being born at home, they also stopped dying there, making it even less likely that a child will experience firsthand the actual death process in the course of growing up. We have become unfamiliar with death.

These technological and demographic developments have raced ahead of ethical and philosophical considerations. Suddenly we are capable of maintaining the physical body in mechanical suspension while death is put on hold. But death hasn't gone away; it's still on the line, and sooner or later we're going to have to take the call.

BIOETHICS

The repercussions of medical and cultural changes, combined with developments in genetics research and other scientific disciplines, have resulted in the evolution of a new field—the field of bioethics.

Bioethics is defined as "a field of study concerned with the ethics and philosophical implications of certain biological and medical procedures, technologies, and treatments, such as organ transplants, genetic engineering, and care of the terminally ill."[1] Arthur Caplan, the director of the University of Minnesota's Biomedical Ethics

Center, calls bioethics "the attempt to decide what values will govern the practice of health care, what values *ought* to govern what people do."[2]

In think tanks, universities, and teaching hospitals all across the country, the role of the ethicist is gaining respect as more and more questions require new answers. Over the last twenty years a number of organizations have developed that are devoted to the study and analysis of these issues. One of the most notable is the Hastings Center in upstate New York, which defines as its purpose: "To confront and attempt to resolve the moral problems brought on by advances in the biomedical sciences and the professions."[3] Other such institutions include the Center for Biomedical Ethics at Case Western Reserve University. These groups do research, conduct workshops, and disseminate publications. They advise and consult on ethical issues to various industries and government and in some cases can provide information and resources for individuals as well. (See listings at the end of this chapter.)

In 1982, the President's Commission for the Study of Ethical Problems in Medicine and Biomedical and Behavioral Research was established to address some of these issues. They published numerous reports (including one called *Deciding to Forgo Life-Sustaining Treatment*) that have helped to clarify the questions, if not provide all the answers.

Practicing M.D.s are also trying to grapple with contemporary medical complexities. In 1986 the American Medical Association issued a statement on "Withholding or Withdrawing of Life-Prolonging Medical Treatment," providing guidelines for physicians who must make the determination of death.

THE DETERMINATION OF DEATH

In the movies the hero places his ear on the victim's chest, looks up at the assembled suspects and solemnly intones, "I'm afraid this man is dead." In real life this just won't do. We need a lot more evidence than a quiet rib cage to fulfill contemporary criteria for the definition of death.

Traditionally, the medical criteria for determining death focused on respiration and heartbeat. If your heart and lungs stopped, you were considered dead. But if your heart and lungs can be maintained

mechanically, what makes you "dead"? Today the center of contention in such cases is the brain. You are dead when your brain has
"died."

Brain Death

But what exactly *is* brain death? Unfortunately, the phrase is impre-
cise and is sometimes used to describe several differing conditions or
is confused with coma, which is not brain death.

Speaking generally, the medical definition of brain death can be
divided into two basic categories: cerebral death and the death of the
brain stem. The cerebral cortex (responsible for so-called higher
functions such as thinking, judgment, perception, etc.) can be irreversibly destroyed and the brain stem may still function (controlling
reflexive functions such as breathing and heartbeat).

This has led to some controversy over the use of brain function
as a criterion for defining death. Should a person be declared dead
when higher brain activity has irreversibly ceased, even though their
brain stem continues to function reflexively? Karen Ann Quinlan
existed in this state for ten years *after* her parents won the legal right
to remove mechanical life support. This condition is called "persistent vegetative state" and is defined as "permanent loss of consciousness; the brain stem is intact and functioning, but there has been
irreversible cessation of higher cortical or cerebral functions, such as
awareness of the surroundings and ability to think, reason, and
experience pleasure and pain."[4]

The persistent vegetative state is not the same as the coma state.
Although the comatose patient is not responsive and cannot be
aroused, a coma is not necessarily irreversible. Someone may be in
deep coma for a long period of time with little chance of recovery,
or they may wake up completely and recover significantly.

In 1980, the President's Commission for the Study of Ethical
Problems in Medicine and Biomedical and Behavioral Research proposed the Uniform Determination of Death Act, which is generally
considered to be the basis for current legal and medical definitions.
It includes respiratory, circulatory, and brain stem functions, thus
allowing a person to be declared dead even if their heart and lungs
are being maintained artificially. The act reads as follows:

> An individual who has sustained either (1) irreversible cessation of
> circulatory and respiratory functions, or (2) irreversible cessation of

all functions of the entire brain, including the brain stem, is dead. A determination of death must be made in accordance with accepted medical standards.[5]

Tales from the Crypt

The technology that allows physicians to measure subtler gradations of physical function (such as the electroencephalograph, which registers the famous "flat EEG" when the electrical activity of the brain ceases) has made the determination of death more complicated but somewhat more definitive than in the past. One hundred years ago a patient could appear to be dead, with no discernible pulse or heartbeat, when in fact s/he was not. Cases of premature burial were widely reported, and an enterprising little industry existed in the invention of devices to signal from the grave. In countries where the practice of embalming became commonplace, such concerns ebbed, but in fact determining the moment of death has never been an exact science.

This is because death doesn't happen "all of a sudden" but rather as part of a process, including *clinical death* (the cessation of heartbeat and respiration), *brain death* (as previously described), and *cellular death* (when the different types of cells die off at differing rates and stages). Even after all the systems of our physiology have ceased to function, our bodies remain extant—for a short time. As described so beautifully by Lewis Thomas in his classic work *The Lives of a Cell*, "Death is not a sudden-all-at-once affair; cells go down in sequence, one by one. It takes hours, even days, before the irreversible word finally gets around to all the provinces."[6]

The natural event of death has always been a gradual physiological process. Today we have the capability to stretch that process a little further, to extend the time during which the systems cease to function. If this capability can be used to heal and restore, then indeed a miracle has taken place. However, for an individual who cannot be healed and for whom the dying process is unbearably painful, this capability may not be welcome.

EUTHANASIA

Euthanasia is a word with an old-fashioned sound to it and a somewhat ominous connotation. For some it evokes euphemisms, such as putting a sick animal "to sleep." For others it is reminiscent of the horror of genocide.

In fact, the word *euthanasia* means "good death." You've heard the expression "Have a good life." In its early usage the hope for a good death was comparable. Histories of preindustrial societies often reveal various rituals in which the elderly or ill are either allowed, or expected, to hasten the end of life by accepting some kind of poison potion. In classical Greek and Roman cultures there were many circumstances under which it was considered a noble act to end your own life (to avoid humiliation at the hands of an enemy, as an alternative to execution, to escape debilitating illness), and of course the Japanese practice of hara-kiri is well known, if little understood, by contemporary Westerners. Many of these customs are based on the principle of honor before all else, but some have their antecedents in the idea of mercy, to provide relief from suffering and pain.

In this country in the early part of the century, the commonplace use of the term euthanasia implied a humane act to end suffering. But after World War II the term became redolent of concentration camps and genocide, gaining a stigma that still lingers.

Contemporary Arguments For and Against
Today there is a growing reconsideration of euthanasia, both the term itself and the issues it raises. There exists considerable debate on the subject within the medical, academic, and legal fields and an exploration of proposed legislation that would make active euthanasia legal in this country. Such proposals focus on removing the criminal penalties for actively assisting the terminally ill to die if they so wish.

The Quality of Mercy
Why is this issue being reconsidered today? Our enhanced capability to extend human life in the throes of the dying process also extends whatever pain is incurred in that process. More people are experiencing the realities of extended degenerative illness. A fatally ill person in the end stages of disease may suffer chronic and debilitating pain, vomiting, incontinence, or hemorrhaging. They may lose their sight, their capacity, or all semblance of physical control, being unable to move themselves from one position to another or even to raise an arm. Their very breathing may be painful to them. How

individuals deal with affliction varies greatly, but for some the response is to welcome death as an end to agony. Proponents of euthanasia argue that we refuse to give suffering human beings the same surcease from pain we would hasten to proffer a dying pet.

Referring to what has been called "the new euthanasia movement," Daniel Callahan, director of the Hastings Center, believes that the current move toward legalizing euthanasia stems from a growing fear of being caught in the medical system as a dying patient. He says:

> The power of medicine to extend life under poor circumstances is now widely and increasingly feared. The combined power of a quasi-religious tradition of respect for individual life and a secular tradition of relentless medical progress, creates a bias toward aggressive, often unremitting treatment that appears unstoppable.[7]

Those who speak against euthanasia often invoke what is called the "slippery slope" concept, arguing that once laws are in place legalizing active euthanasia under certain circumstances, it becomes easier to justify acting in other circumstances and that the potential for abuse is too great. They point out that history has shown how such legislation can become a gateway to a "final solution" in the guise of mercy. This argument raises the specter of "getting rid" of poor people, the infirm, and the elderly. There is the fear that legalized euthanasia for those in pain could be a step toward the legalized murder of groups deemed by government to be in some way undesirable or unfit, as in Nazi Germany.

To most advocates of legalized euthanasia, the issue is one of personal freedom and the constitutionally implied guarantee of autonomy.

How do we ensure the right of individuals to make decisions about their own bodies for themselves and at the same time protect against such possible abuses as have occurred in the past? This is the crux of the current debate, which has become invested with political, social, religious, and economic concerns as well.

MERCY KILLING AND MURDER,
SUICIDE AND SELF-DELIVERANCE

Clearly, euthanasia is a kind of killing. Active euthanasia is sometimes called "mercy killing." Part of the argument surrounding the legalization of euthanasia centers on the question of when mercy becomes murder—the distinction between allowing to die and causing to die. Causing the death of another goes against the basic tenets of most religions and, many say, of society itself.

One argument avoids the issue altogether by proposing what might be called "adequate death care," that is, care making the death process itself more bearable. This approach holds that if the dying were afforded more suitable attention, adequate pain control, and comfort measures, combined with "companionship and other therapeutic means to alleviate emotional suffering," the last stages of illness would be more tolerable, decreasing the number of terminal patients seeking to die preemptively. (See discussion later in this chapter.)

In considering the question of suicide or "self-deliverance," the authors of *The Last Dance: Encountering Death and Dying* define what they call "surcease suicide" as that which is "attempted with the desire to be released from pain, emotional or physical." They go on to say:

> To some, suicide represents a rational way out of an unfortunate predicament. This type of suicide is sometimes called "rational suicide" because the reasoning used—death will provide surcease from pain—conforms to normal logic. Others refer to this type of suicide as "auto-euthanasia," self-administered mercy killing.

Explaining the differences between autoeuthanasia and suicide the authors write,

> In this sense, euthanasia relates primarily to surcease from physical pain. Suicide, on the other hand, is generally thought of as escape from emotional or mental pain. . . . Suicide is generally considered an act of violence, whereas euthanasia is more likely to be considered a benevolent act that ensues from a decision made by the patient and perhaps is enacted with the consent of loved ones.[8]

Many others writing on this issue make the same distinction.

What's the Difference Between Informed
Refusal of Medical Treatment and Suicide?

For the most part, legal authorities agree that the informed refusal of medical treatment on the part of a competent adult is an exercise of the right of self-determination and the right of privacy and is not an act of suicide. In one such decision the judge cited the existence of ample legal precedent to allow the patient to decide to have his own life-support system removed and added that such an act was not a suicide but a removal of artificial medical systems that allowed the body's own mechanisms to come into play.[9]

In his book *Death, Dying and the Biological Revolution,* the prominent ethicist Robert M. Veatch states:

> . . . the legal right of refusal for competents is basically settled. And although physicians continue to fear that they will face legal difficulties if they honor patients' wishes to refuse treatment, there is simply no legal basis for that fear. On the contrary, there is increasing evidence that physicians who treat against the consent of the patient are potentially guilty of assault. Cases have already been brought against such physicians.[10]

The difference between removing life support to let "nature take its course" and acting so as to purposefully end a life has become more readily acknowledged in the current case law.

Suicide and the Law

The proscription against suicide is strong in Western cultures. In Europe in the seventeenth century suicide was considered a crime against God, man, and monarch, and punishment was dealt out both to the deceased (an ignominious burial and excommunication from the church) and to his or her family. Although legal strictures against the surviving family were never enacted in law in the United States, attempted suicide was a punishable crime. If you tried to kill yourself and failed, you could be prosecuted.

While suicide itself is no longer prosecuted as an illegal act, authorities treat a suicide as a homicide case until satisfied that, indeed, the deceased caused his or her own death and was not killed by another.

Assisted Suicide and the Law

Although the current debate over euthanasia and bioethics issues has influenced strict application, most states have laws on the books that make assisting suicide a felony murder.

In spite of the fact that a lot of discussion and reconsideration is going on, it is very important to remember that in the matter of actively assisting another individual to kill himself or herself, you are putting yourself at substantial risk of criminal prosecution. The need for these legal safeguards is obvious, for without them murder could be defended by a claim that the victim desired to be killed. The courts are at pains to interpret the statutes accordingly.

If a terminally ill person asks you to help him or her die and you are unsure about what to do, try to get advice from a sympathetic lawyer, a psychologist or counselor who has had experience with the dying, or a member of the clergy.

If you wish to help someone who has decided to die, you might consider contacting the Hemlock Society, a group advocating euthanasia and providing practical and legal information specific to aiding self-deliverance. (See listings at the end of this chapter.)

If you wish to convince someone to reconsider a decision to commit suicide, there are numerous suicide prevention resources nationwide. For a complete discussion of suicide prevention and a list of related agencies (as well as a list of prevention centers in the United States), see *Suicide: Prevention, Intervention, Postvention,* by Earl A. Grollman. For information on grief and bereavement following a suicide see chapter 10.

ANOTHER CULTURE, ANOTHER APPROACH

In Holland, active voluntary euthanasia by licensed physicians, while not legally sanctioned by statute or legislation, is accepted and practiced widely. Doctors follow a strict set of guidelines, which includes these points:

- The patient must be fully informed of all possible treatment options and must have given careful consideration to the decision.

- There must be no other reasonable alternative.
- A second, independent doctor must be consulted and concur.
- A full report must be filed with authorities.[11]

In addition, there are specific criteria for performing euthanasia to safeguard the rights of survivors.

Rather than creating a legislated standard, the acceptance of euthanasia in Holland has been more a matter of adding exceptions to the legal proscriptions against assisting suicide.

Over the last twenty years the Dutch have evolved a unique approach to the problem of mercy killing. Professor Pieter Admiraal, a leading Dutch advocate of what he calls "justifiable active euthanasia," has written about the process and the findings of those who study this phenomenon. He says: "We don't like to perform euthanasia and never suggest it to a patient." He goes on to point out that by the time someone reaches a decision to die, the level of suffering is almost always such that it would be inhumane to refuse.

> Very rarely does a patient in the early stages of disease decide to refuse treatment or want to die. Normally, patients want to live, want to fight their disease, want to accept all and any kind of treatment available . . . the will to live, to survive, is one of the most basic human desires.[12]

The Netherlands is sometimes held up as a positive working model by euthanasia advocates, but opponents believe it must be studied over time to see if abuses develop.

CARE, COST, AND CONSCIENCE

It would be disingenuous to present even a cursory survey of death ethics without talking about money. The moral and financial questions are intertwined—a difficult situation, to put it mildly. The economics of death and dying in the United States today are spectacularly problematic.

If you spend the last days, weeks, or months of your life in a hospital, the costs will be greater than if you spend that same time in that same hospital and recover. Health-economics experts do not agree as to why this is so but cite a variety of influences, among them the obvious fact that people who die are sicker than people who recover and thus require more expensive care; that the majority of people who die in hospitals are elderly and develop more complications, thus requiring more complex treatment than younger patients; and that efforts to extend the life of the terminally ill often include intensive care unit services, which are the most expensive services available.

While specific statistics on the costs of dying are not readily available and tend to be contradictory, the consensus is: If you get sick and die, it will cost more than if you get sick and live.[13]

Huge amounts of money go to pay for medical costs at the end of life. Because there is not enough overall to support medical care, the money that goes to maintain life for the aged competes with money for health care for the young.

Currently in bioethics there is an increasingly vocal debate about what, if any, should be the limits on the types of life-extension technology and money expended on those who are dying. This is an area of great controversy. On the one hand, there is the need to allocate limited resources; on the other, there is the specter of developing policies that could allow a precipitous "termination" of the elderly, the infirm, and the physically unfit. No one knows how this dilemma will be resolved.

Victor Fuchs, a Stanford University economist, says:

> At present the United States spends about one percent of the gross national product on health care for elderly persons who are in their last year of life. . . . One of the biggest challenges facing policy makers for the rest of this century will be how to strike an appropriate balance between care for the elderly dying and health services for the rest of the population.[14]

In an article in the *New York Times* entitled "Pain, as a Matter of Policy," Selma Abramowitz wrote of her personal experience with this dilemma when her eighty-year-old father suffered a massive stroke. For eight weeks he was treated in a major urban hospital before he died. She says:

> As the organs of his body failed, doctors were called in to examine and treat that part of the body. Not one doctor looked at the whole patient. Not one had the courage or the honesty to say, this course of treatment is of no long-term benefit. They just collected their fees.
>
> The bill for this exercise in futility will be more than $100,000 in

Medicare dollars. The cost of the emotional strain on my mother, my brother, my sisters and myself cannot be calculated. Were this just one family's sad story it would be of little consequence, but the implications are far-reaching. We can no longer view medicine as compassionate or the medical profession as having only an ethical interest in preserving life. Reimbursement policies have changed that: Treatment is now dictated by Government insurance policies and regulations.

Walk through any nursing home and see the beds of living corpses, products of medical technology, health insurance and professional irresponsibility. Ask yourself about the motive of a health care facility that goes to court to oppose the removal of a feeding tube. Are they motivated by a concern for life or for their accounts receivable?"[15]

Ms. Abramowitz goes on to propose that the ethics of death care will not change until economic and reimbursement policies change. This strong indictment of our medical care system is echoed in government studies, academic analyses, corporate reports, and the popular press. We have clearly reached a point where "medical care" must begin to include "death care."*

CONTEMPORARY DEATH CARE

Whether in an effort to reallocate scarce resources or simply to provide more humane and comfortable conditions for those who are dying (and thus decrease our fear of the dying process), a number of medical, sociology, and psychology professionals are beginning to call for a more enlightened approach to "death care."

The renowned psychiatrist Elisabeth Kübler-Ross is one of the most visible pioneers in this effort, as is Dr. Cicely Saunders, who created models and procedures for enlightened terminal care in England. Others have followed their lead in attempting to remedy the fact that dying today is very hard to do.

As with any attempt at reform, there are differing opinions as to how and what to change. But it is generally agreed that the setting, or place where we die, is important. In neglecting the whole idea of death care (as opposed to health care), we have also neglected to provide reasonable settings in which to die. The dying patient winds

---

*I use this term to mean caring for our death, as health care means caring for our health. It is intended to connote a concern for death and the way in which people are cared for when they are dying.

up in an institution that is designed to give short-term acute care or long-term chronic care, not death care. Dying in these places becomes, by default, no care.

Some critics feel the institutions themselves can be made more responsive and that the key to positive change lies in humanizing the bureaucratic aspects of health care agencies. Others believe the problems are more deeply rooted and that a fundamental reworking of our entire medical-care delivery system is necessary in order to address the problem of alienation that has become inherent in the practice of scientific medicine.

Most new approaches strongly favor a shift from the goal of curing to caring; a focus on easing death rather than a single-minded effort to avoid it.

Some argue for a return to home care as the answer. But dying at home requires a tremendous dedication on the part of family or loved ones, who may or may not be able to provide the level of attention necessary to ensure good care.

The most successful approach to date is called hospice, a *program* of care that can be applied to a variety of *places;* at home or in a hospital or nursing home–type facility, providing assistance to family caregivers. Perhaps this model is the key to positive change. (See chapter 7.)

Depending on your situation and personal preferences, a hospital, a nursing, or a family home may or may not serve as the place best equipped to give you what you want as you are dying. In chapter 6 we'll take a look at where you're likely to wind up.

RESOURCES AND SUPPORT

Books

Philippe Ariès. *The Hour of Our Death.* Translated by Helen Weaver. New York: Random House, Vintage Books, 1982.
  [A scholarly examination of attitudes toward death in Western Christian cultures. This classic work spans the Middle Ages to modern times.]

_____. *Western Attitudes Toward Death: From the Middle Ages to the Present.* Translated by Patricia M. Ranum. Baltimore: Johns Hopkins University Press, 1975.
  [Four brief essays by the pioneer social historian of death.]

Robert M. Baird and Stuart E. Rosenbaum, eds. *Euthanasia: The Moral Issues.* Contemporary Issues in Philosophy series. Buffalo: Prometheus Books, 1989.
[These essays examine both sides of the issue from the perspective of moral theorists and physicians.]

Daniel Callahan. *Setting Limits: Medical Goals in an Aging Society.* New York: Simon & Schuster, Touchstone Books, 1988.
[Addresses the issue of the termination of treatment for the elderly dying. Includes suggested criteria for ethical decision making.]

_____. *What Kind of Life: The Limits of Medical Progress.* New York: Simon & Schuster, 1990.
[Explores values and priorities of society and its health care system in the age of high-technology medicine.]

Karen G. Gervais. *Redefining Death.* New Haven: Yale University Press, 1987.
[An exploration of the philosophical, legal, and medical concepts of death and their public policy implications.]

Dale V. Hardt. *Death: The Final Frontier.* Englewood Cliffs, N.J.: Prentice-Hall, 1979.
[Includes a survey of philosophical, cultural, religious, and medical issues surrounding death.]

David Hendin. *Death as a Fact of Life.* New York: W. W. Norton & Co., 1984.
[A medical journalist discusses issues including the definition of death, euthanasia, and the responsibilities of the physician.]

Derek Humphry and Ann Wickett. *The Right to Die: Understanding Euthanasia.* Eugene, Oreg.: Hemlock Society, 1990.
[Includes historical, cultural, and legal examinations of euthanasia and the right to die.]

Jack B. Kamerman. *Death in the Midst of Life: Social and Cultural Influences on Death, Grief and Mourning.* Englewood Cliffs, N.J.: Prentice-Hall, 1988.
[A sociological look at death and dying in America.]

David Lamb. *Death, Brain Death and Ethics.* London: Croom Helm, 1988.
[An examination of the concept of death in light of modern medical technology. Includes an analysis of medical and philosophical definitions of death.]

Ruth Macklin. *Mortal Choices: Ethical Dilemmas in Modern Medicine.*
Boston: Houghton Mifflin, 1988.
[An examination, using actual cases, of how hospital ethics commit-
tees attempt to resolve bioethical dilemmas.]

Robert M. Veatch. *Death, Dying and the Biological Revolution: Our Last
Quest for Responsibility.* Rev. ed. New Haven: Yale University Press,
1989.
[Presents current thinking in bioethics as it affects decisions about
death and dying.]

Robert F. Weir, ed. *Ethical Issues in Death and Dying.* 2nd ed. New York:
Columbia University Press, 1986.
[A collection of essays on defining death, selective nontreatment of
newborns, suicide, and euthanasia.]

Books: Suicide/Self-Deliverance

Earl A. Grollman. *Suicide: Prevention, Intervention, Postintervention.* 2nd
ed., rev. and expanded. Boston: Beacon, 1988.
[Includes survey of historical and religious attitudes toward suicide;
also discusses the views of social scientists. Comprehensive appendix
includes listing of suicide prevention centers nationwide.]

Derek Humphry. *Let Me Die Before I Wake: Hemlock's Book of Self-
Deliverance for the Dying.* Eugene, Oreg.: Hemlock Society; dis-
tributed by Grove Press, 1987.
[A collection of case histories and advice on self-deliverance.]

————, with Ann Wickett. *Jean's Way: A Love Story.* New York: Harper
& Row, Perennial Library, 1986.
[A personal account of an assisted suicide.]

Betty Rollin. *Last Wish.* New York: Warner Books, 1986.
[The author helps her dying mother to carry out her suicide.]

Judith M. Stillion, Eugene E. McDowell, and Jacque H. May. *Suicide
Across the Life Span: Premature Exits.* Series in Death Education.
New York: Hemisphere, 1989.
[Includes overview of the history of suicide in Western culture. Also
analyzes suicide at various life stages.]

Books Containing Related Information

The Diagram Group. *The Brain: A User's Manual.* Expanded ed. New
York: Putnam Publishing Group, Perigree, 1987.
[Includes definition of brain death.]

Ken Dychtwald and Joe Flower. *Age Wave: The Challenges and Opportunities of an Aging America.* Los Angeles: Jeremy Tarcher, 1989. [A discussion of the coming "age wave"; includes issues affecting medical care and dying.]

Agencies/Service Organizations
Dying With Dignity
175 St. Clair Avenue West
Toronto, Ontario, Canada M4V 1P7
(416) 921-2329
Advocates recognition of voluntary euthanasia and distributes the Euthanasia Declaration. Seeks to educate the public and health care professionals on self-determination and personal autonomy in matters of death and dying. They also provide counseling to individuals struggling with these issues.

Hemlock Society
P.O. Box 11830
Eugene, OR 97440
(503) 342-5748
An educational membership organization supporting the option of active voluntary euthanasia (self-deliverance) for the advanced terminally ill adult or seriously incurably ill person. Has local chapters around the country. Offers various publications and a quarterly newsletter.

Academic and Research Centers
Some academic centers and think tanks are devoted to the study and analysis of bioethics. Listed below are several of the most prominent. These centers do not provide assistance to the general public but do sometimes publish relevant material and present lectures or symposia that may be of interest to you.

On the East Coast:
The Hastings Center
255 Elm Road
Briarcliff, NY 10510
(914) 762-8500
Issues reports and guidelines aimed at resolving the moral problems brought on by advances in the biomedical sciences and the professions. The "Hastings Center Report" is issued bimonthly.

In the Midwest:
Center for Biomedical Ethics
Case Western Reserve University School of Medicine
2119 Abington Road
Cleveland, OH 44106
(216) 368-6196

Center for Biomedical Ethics
University of Minnesota
3-110 Owre Hall, UMHC 33
Minneapolis, MN 55455
(612) 625-4917

On the West Coast:
Program in Medical Ethics
University of California—San Francisco
Box 0903, C126
San Francisco, CA 94143-0903
(415) 476-6241

6

Where Death Happens

Death has got something to be said for it;
There's no need to get out of bed for it;
Wherever you may be,
They bring it to you, free.

Kingsley Amis

The technological and medical advances of the past forty years did more than change the way we die. They changed *where* we die as well. A new kind of medicine evolved, more effective and more actively curative than before. This miracle medicine was often technological in nature and came to be practiced in, and dispensed through, institutions: hospitals, clinics, and research and teaching facilities. If you were sick, you went to the doctor; the doctor no longer came to you.

William Winslade and Judith Ross have written an instructive book on medical ethics, *Choosing Life or Death: A Guide for Patients, Families, and Professionals.* In it they describe the difference between the doctor as caregiver in the patient's home and the doctor as scientist in the institution:

141

When patients died at home (up until World War II home deaths were very common), decisions about whether to provide some kind of care that might extend life, if only for a short time, were made by physicians who knew the family, knew their circumstances and personalities and what they would prefer, even if they had not specifically expressed their preferences. . . . When there was little that physicians could do to postpone the patient's death, they cultivated the *art* of medicine; of comforting and caring for both the dying patient and the patient's family.

When effective intervention became possible, they prolonged life and did not always worry about the kind of life the patient had. . . . The ability to keep patients alive tended to prove medicine's success as a science, and *to be scientific* has been the highest accolade offered in our time. In addition, the institutionalization of medicine, whereby health care is provided not in the doctor's office nor in the patient's home but in hospitals, has made aggressive treatment more likely because the setting is more public.[1]

INSTITUTIONAL DYING

With the development of scientific medicine, hospitals evolved into institutional centers of healing, teaching, and research. With this change, the hospital became a place where disease was corrected. If a patient died there, it meant something had gone wrong. This approach creates a situation in which dying people come to be seen as a drain on the general "success rate" of the institution—an unfortunate reminder of fallibility. Jeanne Quint Benoliel, an experienced health care administrator, has written about institutional dying. She explains how this attitude developed.

In the twentieth century . . . the practice of medicine came to be structured and organized around the primacy of the cure ethic. Life-saving procedures and machines became increasingly important in the daily activities of physicians, and the solo practice of general practitioners rapidly gave way to group practice provided by specialists. As the day-to-day activities of physicians, nurses, and other hospital workers came to center on the primacy of life-saving tasks, services to meet the human needs of patients and families came to be tangential and secondary processes. These changes appeared not because the various professional groups lacked concern but, rather, because the work to be done was organized for the purpose of saving lives, and the dying patient represented failure.[2]

Scientific medicine has developed a language of "death control," but science hasn't controlled death. We still die. And when we do, we are simply dying; we are not failing.

Today 80 percent of us die in institutional settings. There is no question that institutional procedures, policies, and systems do not encourage an enlightened death experience. What does this mean to you and yours, and what, if anything, can you do about it?

Let's take a look at each of the settings in which we most commonly die—in hospitals, other health care facilities (nursing homes, long-term-care facilities, etc.), and at home.

HOSPITALS

The modern hospital is an amazing phenomenon, the central preserve of the "culture of medicine" that dominates our health care choices. Influenced in its development by social, ethnic, religious, and geographic distinctions, the hospital is a monolithic institution that is, paradoxically, diverse. The differences between a small rural hospital and a large urban medical center can be substantial, but they are both *the hospital*—the place where we go when we are most ill, the place where we go when we are dying.

By the end of the 1920s the modern hospital was the primary dispensary of medical care in this country. As described by Charles E. Rosenberg in his book *The Care of Strangers:*

It had become central to medical education and was well integrated into the career patterns of regular physicians; in urban areas it had already replaced the family as the site for treating serious illness and managing death. Perhaps most important, it had already been clothed with a legitimating aura of science and almost boundless social expectation.[3]

For the individual in an acute stage of a terminal illness whose primary desire is to seek curative treatment and to attempt every possible measure to maintain or prolong existence, it is definitely the place to be.

In the hospital setting, preserving life, maintaining or restoring health, and curing illness are the priorities. Aggressive treatment decisions are the rule rather than the exception. A 1984–85 study concluded that the treatment orientation in hospitals overwhelmingly aims toward cure rather than comfort, even among terminally or critically ill patients who had been designated DNR or "No Code" (not to be resuscitated if heart or respiration fails).[4]

Some terminally ill patients will welcome a focused commitment to use all extreme measures. However, this orientation can lead to problems. Another study suggests that the number of visits by, and the attention of, hospital staff members toward patients tends to taper off as soon as those patients are labeled terminal.[5]

Hospitals are bureaucratic settings in which efficiency is a key goal. In many hospitals today there is no institutionalized routine for easing death. In other words, when they can't do anything more to cure you, they have no plan.

Control, Schedules, and Privacy

Hospitals with hundreds, even thousands, of inpatients maintain schedules aimed at ensuring that every patient receives essential care, and the staff must fit the needs and daily activities of dying patients into the hospital's schedule. They tend to require all patients, whether terminal or not, to give up virtually all personal control over the little things that make up their day-to-day lives. The kinds of personal items that can make a big difference, such as your own pillow from home, are often not allowed. Visits by children may be curtailed, and having a pet stay with a dying person is prohibited. Activities such as waking, eating, bathing, and any physical exercise will proceed according to an established routine.

You might welcome the opportunity to relinquish decision making regarding these matters. It can be very helpful and very reassuring to have basic requirements fulfilled without question. But for some people this loss of autonomy exacerbates their fears about dying and can leave them feeling helpless and disoriented. In addition, it can add to the anxiety of families and friends if they have little or no control over the particulars of visitation or care.

One of the most common complaints about hospitals voiced by terminal patients and their families is the lack of privacy. Under most policies, private rooms are not covered by medical insurance. Families sometimes feel as if they are intruding on the hospital staff, or vice versa, when they visit the patient.

If you wish to discuss personal or legal matters and are bothered by the lack of privacy, it may be possible to use a conference room or make an arrangement with the staff that allows a brief period of time in private.

At the Moment of Death

Assuring privacy at the moment of death or finding a private place in which to mourn or express grief can be difficult in the hospital setting. Margaret Gold, in a special report on terminal care in hospitals and at home (written for the Institute for Consumer Policy Research), found the following: "In many hospitals, the patient's death and the family's response are seen as disruptive to hospital routines and to the care of recovering patients. Death is often treated as an event to be handled quietly and smoothly, with as little interference from the family as possible."[6]

If being together at the moment of death is important to you, you should know that it is much more likely to occur in a home setting than it is at a hospital. Often in hospitals the family is asked to leave the room soon after the death in order to allow the staff to prepare the body for disposition. This can be very difficult and painful for survivors.

Institutional procedures are not designed to encourage attendance at death or the practice of sitting with the body for a period immediately after death. If it is a priority, you should make your wishes known to your doctor and/or to hospital personnel.

Communication with Staff

Visiting hours and physicians' regularly scheduled rounds rarely overlap. If you want information about how a patient is doing, try to arrange a meeting with the attending physician. Otherwise, you will need to rely solely on the patient or sympathetic nurses for information. You may find that both patients and their families must be persistent in order to gain access to information about the patient's condition.

If you have any complaints or questions about the care provided, staff support or sympathy, the lack of privacy, the absence of information, or any other problem, consumer advocates recommend that you notify your physician, the hospital's patient representative, the hospital social worker, or hospital clergy.

Winslade and Ross put it this way:

> To balance the power of hospital bureaucracies, patients and their families may need to enlist support from one or more of several sources. (They) may be helped by patient advocates, hospital chaplains, bioethics consultants, hospital ombudsmen, social workers, ethics committees, attorneys, insurance companies or personnel from the

bureaucracy itself, such as a hospital administrator. Hospitals usually will not tell patients as a routine matter whether they have people on staff to assist with patient care problems. Patients should be specific about the type of assistance they need.[7]

Hospital Care for the Dying Child

Most hospitals have pediatrics wards, units for children under sixteen or eighteen years of age. If the hospital is part of a large medical center, it may have a pediatrics intensive care unit as well.

Pediatrics wards are usually designed to be appropriate for children. The staff may wear colorful uniforms instead of the more intimidating all-white, and there will be flexible visiting hours and a generally looser routine. Most pediatrics wards utilize volunteers who spend time with the kids telling stories, playing music, etc., and a number of hospitals have play therapists who specialize in working with seriously ill children.

When a child is dying in the hospital, many of the same issues are raised: How can the setting be made more personalized and comfortable? How can the family and the child have some control over the daily routine? When should aggressive treatment be reconsidered? How can the family have privacy for intimate time together with the child?

However, there are a number of additional issues when the patient is a child. The hospital setting is almost always more frightening for a child than it is for an adult. And because children don't generally participate in decisions about their treatment and care, the questions surrounding informed consent and treatment cessation are made even more complex as parents, guardians, and medical professionals try to make decisions on behalf of the patient. (See chapter 4 for more on this.)

For parents, all the usual problems surrounding any loved one's dying in a hospital are exacerbated by the fear and guilt they often feel at not being able to protect their child. It is quite common for parents to feel great anger at the loss of control they experience when a diagnosis is terminal. For some, this loss of control is heightened by the practices and procedures common to the hospital setting.

For others, a hospital setting can help by reinforcing the sense that they are "doing everything possible." The idea of taking care of a dying child at home may be intimidating; many parents worry about doing the wrong thing or somehow hurting the child. Indeed, a dying person of any age may suffer acute symptoms—vomiting, hemorrhaging, convulsions, gagging, etc.—that require expert care. This care can be arranged either through a home care service (see later discussion in this chapter) or a hospice program (see chapter 7), but for many parents the perceived security of the hospital environment outweighs the impersonal or regulated aspects of hospital care.

If your child is facing death in a hospital setting, it would be a good idea to find out how flexible and sensitive the pediatrics staff will be to you and to your child's special needs. The staff member most likely to be able to answer your questions is the *nursing manager of the unit.* The kinds of questions you might ask include:

Are there twenty-four-hour visitation rights (will you be able to stay overnight with your child)?

Will you be allowed to help your child with basic personal care (brushing teeth, washing up, combing hair, etc.)?

Will the staff teach you to provide other primary care (administering medication)?

You will also want to clarify the staff policy on palliative (pain control) versus curative treatment and to discuss the point at which you may wish to consider discontinuing aggressive efforts and ensure that your child will be comfortable and as pain-free as possible.

For some parents this experience is simply overwhelming and they are not able to effectively communicate or advocate on behalf of their child. In their informative book *Making Medical Decisions,* Thomas and Celia Scully recommend asking another family member, friend, or spokesperson to be with you when you talk to the doctor or hospital staff. They also advise:

Some doctors will talk to family members in the waiting room; others will find a quiet room or office where you can discuss your child's condition. If the waiting room is filled with visitors who are "all ears," ask if there is some other place you can talk.[8]

Death in a Hospital Emergency Room

The emergency room epitomizes the constructive role of the hospital institution—an acute-care center with the goal of stabilizing a medical crisis and controlling physical deterioration. The staff focuses on lifesaving efforts, and the setting is designed specifically toward that end. Unfortunately, this does not create the best environment for families and friends trying to cope with the sudden loss of a loved one.

While an emergency-room staff is expert at maintaining a human being's vital signs during physical trauma, they are not necessarily expert at helping survivors with the emotional trauma of sudden death. Sometimes they may appear cold or indifferent to suffering. It has been pointed out that "the staff behaviors that appear to be 'callous' to the outside observer (can) be understood as necessary 'coping mechanisms' for dealing with difficult choices, decisions, and patient situations."[9] In other words, the staff may be unable to provide much comfort.

If a friend or relative dies in a hospital emergency room, you can expect to go through some version of the following process:

- Arriving and seeking information
- Waiting
- Being notified of the death
- Viewing the body
- Signing necessary papers and forms
- Concluding the process (depending on the policies of the hospital)

An emergency room is a legal exception to the principle of informed consent (an individual's right to refuse treatment). When a dying person is brought to an emergency room, s/he will be given every life-support treatment and life-prolonging measure available. If the patient is at the end stage of a terminal illness and would prefer to die peacefully, a hospital emergency room is not the best place to be.

Death in the Intensive Care Unit

A hospital intensive care unit is a very specialized environment designed to maintain vital functions in patients that are unstable or in danger of suddenly worsening. Again, the staff and setting are focused exclusively on life-sustaining efforts, the environment is usually depersonalizing, and there is little or no privacy available to the patient or the family. It is not a great setting in which to die.

When it is clear that an ICU patient is dying, the staff may encourage moving the patient to a regular ward. This trend is increasing as a result of ICU overcrowding and a growing concern about the inappropriate use of life-support equipment on the terminally ill.

In their engrossing book *Intensive Care: Facing the Critical Choices,* Thomas Raffin, Joel Shurkin, and Wharton Sinkler III describe the particular concerns that arise when a patient is dying in the ICU and offer advice for families and friends.*

Some hospitals are developing programs to help families and friends deal with the frightening and confusing environment of an ICU. The programs are made up of a corps of social workers and trained volunteers who give advice, offer support, and answer questions about medical procedures, hospital policy, or other concerns. Such programs are mostly in the pilot stage, but many hospitals are beginning to see the need to address the anxiety and disorientation that can accompany death in the ICU.

ORGAN DONATION

If a member of your family is dying in a hospital, there is the possibility that someone on the hospital staff will approach you at or near the time of death regarding the potential donation of organs and tissue. The staff is most likely to make this inquiry if the patient is comparatively young and dying of an injury in an ICU.

The medical industry needs healthy organs, bone, and tissue for transplantation. When someone who is otherwise fit dies suddenly, especially as the result of neurological trauma, leaving the heart, liver, kidneys, and pancreas otherwise unharmed, s/he is a candidate for organ harvesting.

In addition, medical researchers use organs and tissues from donors with illnesses such as Alzheimer's disease, cystic fibrosis, and rheumatoid arthritis, which can be helpful in research and experimentation. However, a direct request from medical staff at the hospital is more likely to come in a trauma-care situation.

An article in *The Journal of the American Medical Association* states:

---

*Another resource is Frederick Wiseman's documentary film entitled *Near Death,* which records the experiences of several patients and their caregivers in the ICU of a major urban hospital.

Approximately 98 percent of all actual organ donors originate from intensive care units. . . . Severe head injury is the cause of death in 56 to 77 percent of actual organ donors; central nervous system catastrophes and brain tumors account for the second most common cause of death in the donor population. A small percentage of donors die of cardiopulmonary arrest, anoxia, and drug overdose.[10]

The Request

Most large hospitals in major urban areas have a standard procedure for soliciting organ donation. This procedure includes a search for family members, any one of whom may veto the donation.

Although technically it is legal for a surgeon to harvest organs from anyone carrying a Uniform Donor Card without asking the permission of relatives, and although the Uniform Anatomical Gift Act states that "no willed donation may be revoked by relatives," doctors do not go against the wishes of the next of kin.

As pointed out by Mark Dowie in his fascinating book on organ transplantation, *"We Have A Donor": The Bold New World of Organ Transplanting*:

> The sanctity of family and medical tradition, which regards the living as more important (and powerful) than the dead, still prompts doctors and hospitals to ask the next of kin for permission to harvest organs. . . . If a spouse, parent, or sibling of a patient is found and says no, the hospital will abide by the family's request, even if the patient carries a signed donor card.[11]

It is the family that decides. A parent or guardian, for example, will have the responsibility of deciding whether a dying child will make a donation of organs and tissue. Similarly, when adults are incapacitated, their spouse or adult children will need to make the choice.

The Legal Side of It

As stated in *The Rights of the Critically Ill* by attorney John A. Robertson, "In the United States, organ donation is not compulsory, and there is no routine salvaging of organs from dead persons."[12] You do not have to say yes.

All states and the District of Columbia now have what are called "routine inquiry" or "required request" laws that mandate hospital staff (if a dying patient is a potential donor) to ask the patient's family whether they would be willing to donate the organs and tissues of the deceased. This inquiry generally takes the form of telling families about the "option" of organ donation.

In a number of countries it works the other way around. Some nations have responded to the organ shortage by enacting a Universal Donor Principle, which considers everyone an organ donor unless an individual has specified otherwise. Mark Dowie writes:

> Following an example set by France, Israel, Greece, Norway, Italy, Switzerland, Finland, Sweden and Denmark passed laws mandating the right of a hospital or transplant surgeon to remove organs from the body of anyone who hasn't written a will or declaration to the contrary. Under presumed-consent, or implied-consent laws, instead of voluntarily "opting in" to organ donation, people have to actively "opt out" or their organs can be harvested without anyone's permission. Poland, Czechoslovakia, and Austria have passed even more authoritarian statutes which say that organs, at the moment of death, become the property of the state.[13]

There is controversy, even within the transplantation field itself, over the efficacy of "implied consent" versus voluntary donation. Some professionals say the critical shortage of organs demands a compulsory policy or a more aggressive approach, and others feel that procuring organs from a family in shock over the sudden death of a loved one is inappropriate, if not unethical. Many medical professionals are not entirely at ease with the protocol of organ solicitation. As a result, even routine inquiry is not always practiced.

Specifics

If the patient is under the age of sixty, free of cancer, AIDS, hepatitis, venereal disease, and other infectious or communicable diseases, s/he can be considered a potential donor. Of course, the organs themselves must be free of disease or injury.

Organs must be harvested from a "beating heart" cadaver—a patient who has been declared brain-dead but is being maintained on a respirator. Retrieval of the organs will take place as soon as possible after the declaration of brain death. Once the decision is made, time is of the essence. However, bone and most nonvascular tissues can be removed from a cadaver any time within the first twenty-four hours after death.

Questions and Concerns

MEDICAL CARE   Agreeing to allow surgeons to take a patient's organs will not adversely affect the care the patient receives before death. A hospital staff must make every effort to save a potential organ donor's life, and the patient must be declared brain-dead before any organs can be removed. State law forbids the physician who certified death to remove organs from a donor.

COMPENSATION   Organ removal is performed at no charge to the donor. Neither the family nor the estate of the deceased will incur any of the additional expenses involved in removing organs for donation. The agency that procures the organ(s) must take care of the costs involved. Conversely, it is illegal to sell human organs. You cannot reduce hospitalization costs through organ donation.

DISPOSITION   Organ, tissue, and/or bone donation, even the removal of the major organs, will not interfere with customary funeral arrangements. Family members retain custody of the body after the organs are removed, allowing them to proceed with their plans for disposition. Donation does not rule out an open-casket funeral.

If you would like to know what happens to the organs after they have been removed, request this information from the agency that procures them. (Ask the hospital staff to provide you with the names and phone numbers of the agencies involved.) Many agencies will write donor families to inform them which tissues and organs were successfully used for transplantation. Although they will not release the names of recipients, you can learn such particulars as the age, sex, and diagnosis of the recipient if you so request. For further information, contact the United Network for Organ Sharing (UNOS) in Richmond, Virginia. (See listings at the end of this chapter.)

EFFORTS TO IMPROVE
INSTITUTIONAL DYING

If you or someone you care for is facing death in a hospital setting, you may find that the situation has improved over the last few years.

Recently there has been an increase in the number of medical professionals with an awareness of the special needs of the dying. Health care administrator Jeanne Benoliel points out that over the last decade a general move toward death awareness has

> legitimized medical care of the dying patient and permitted the introduction of palliative care services and hospice units into established hospitals. It stimulated a variety of workshops and other educational activities to prepare physicians, nurses, and other health care providers for work that involved them with dying patients and their families.[14]

Benoliel goes on to say that while the goals of the health care system have not changed from curing to caring, still these teaching efforts "did sensitize a number of providers to the complexities of interpersonal collaboration in death work." In other words, today's hospital staff may be more attentive and helpful toward a patient who is dying, even though they are not trained to provide death care.

In today's hospital you are much more likely to find what is called a "palliative care" or "comfort care" unit where patients at the end stages of terminal disease can receive pain management and emotional support instead of curative treatment. Many medical professionals are truly interested in trying to assist, rather than deny or ignore, the dying process. Their experiences have sensitized them to the need for providing comfort and care rather than inappropriately aggressive treatment.

If you are responsible for a loved one who is dying in a hospital, you may wish to inquire if there is a palliative-care unit and how to facilitate a transfer. You should be able to get help and advice from nurses, administrators, social workers, or clergy on the hospital staff.

The Patient Self-Determination Act, a federally legislated measure due to take effect in November 1992, requires any health care institution participating in Medicare or Medicaid (or receiving any government support) to inform patients of their right to refuse treatment. It also requires them to record if a patient has a written directive regarding life-support treatment decisions.

MONEY

Dying in a hospital can cost an awful lot of money. For the very affluent, who are usually fully insured, and the very poor, who are protected by government-sponsored insurance and health assistance programs, coverage is fairly adequate. Being in the middle, however (neither rich nor poor), can be difficult.

The average cost of room, board, and ancillary hospital services varies widely from city to city, county to county, and state to state. In some areas it can run as little as $200 to $500 per day; in others, as high as $1,200 or more. These are *daily* charges for *routine* services and do not include intensive care, emergency, or other out-of-the-ordinary procedures that often accompany end-of-life hospital costs. Intensive care costs run considerably higher. The average figure is estimated at between $2,000 and $3,000 per day.

A number of private insurance companies have begun to develop plans that allow for terminally ill patients to cash in their life insurance benefits for use in paying terminal-care costs. These policies provide a payout of insurance benefits if a doctor certifies the policyholder has less than six months to live or has been a resident in a nursing home for at least six months with no hope of leaving. At this writing, this type of plan is in effect in ten states. As the insurance industry is pressed to address ways of paying the "high cost of dying," it is assumed there will be increased policy options of this sort. If you are interested in finding out more about this kind of payout, you might try calling your insurance agent, the American Council of Life Insurance in Washington, D.C., or your state's Department of Insurance.

Diseases like AIDS and some cancers have highlighted the systemic difficulties in supporting the high costs of lingering terminal illness. Taking advantage of these difficulties, a few entrepreneurs have begun purchasing life insurance policies from terminally ill individuals. The entrepreneur gives the dying person 50 to 80 percent of the value of his or her life insurance policy and is then made the beneficiary of the policy. When the patient dies, the entrepreneur makes his profit. There are many questions and some serious concerns about this practice, which, to date, is totally unregulated.

Financial Assistance

Many hospitals have patient advocates or social workers on staff who can help identify entitlement programs and tell you if you are eligible for any financial assistance. Or check with your state Human Resources Department.

The Hill-Burton Act, which became law in 1946, ensures that any hospital that has received certain types of federal loans must provide medical services to anyone living or working in the area served by that hospital. Although the hospitals need not provide these services for free, they are forbidden to employ admission policies that would exclude patients based on their ability to pay. For additional information on the Hill-Burton Act, contact: U.S. Public Health and Human Services, Washington, DC 20201.

Dying Where It's Paid For

Health insurance and the method in which medical care is financed play a significant part in determining where Americans die. We tend to die where insurance will pay for it. Although the number of deaths occurring in hospitals steadily increased from 1949 to 1983, a study published in the *New England Journal of Medicine* describes a slight shift *away* from this trend in the years since 1983.[15] The article identifies the reason for that shift as a change in the reimbursement policies of Medicare. In 1983, Medicare began to pay hospitals according to a system known as DRGs (diagnostic related groupings)—fixed rates for each admission, determined according to the patient's diagnosis—rather than paying for the actual cost of patient care. Unable to recover the costs incurred by many terminal patients remaining for lengthy periods, some hospitals began to discharge these patients "quicker and sicker" than before.

As a result, the percentage of deaths in hospitals has declined slightly since 1983, while the percentage of deaths occurring in nursing homes and private homes has risen. (The data suggest that most of the discharged patients were moved to nursing homes.) If this trend continues in the 1990s, nursing homes will have an even greater responsibility of caring for the terminally ill.

NURSING HOMES

A nursing home can provide the level of attendance and services that may overwhelm the family or friends of a dying patient. A good home can relieve the exhausting burden on those who are unable or unwilling to supply twenty-four-hour-a-day terminal care.

There are different types of nursing homes offering different levels of service. Some are more rightly called "retirement homes," or "rest homes," and are a kind of communal housing for elderly people who either can't or prefer not to live alone. Others are skilled nursing facilities and provide a high degree of medical service and round-the-clock attention. It is in these latter institutions, or in what are called intermediate-care facilities (offering nursing and personal services), where terminal care is an issue.

While most nursing homes tend to advertise or present themselves as "convalescent care" institutions where residents stay until they are well enough to leave, in fact "only one nursing home resident in five will return to their home; some will be transferred to a hospital, but most of them will die in the nursing home."[16]

The Dreaded Nursing Home Scandal

Despite the negative stories about nursing homes that hit the evening news—frightening tales of physical, emotional, or drug abuse, theft, or fraud—many do provide competent and secure environments in which a patient/resident can receive good medical and custodial care. To find a good one, however, you will need to do your homework. Ask for references from friends, relatives, doctor, or clergy.

Some organizations such as the AARP publish helpful material on nursing home selection, care, and related issues. Another resource is *How to Evaluate and Select a Nursing Home,* published by the People's Medical Society. (See listings at the end of this chapter.)

If you are considering nursing homes, you can often tell a lot about an institution simply by using your own senses. Talk to the residents to find out how they feel about the place. See whether they tend to appear clean, alert, and reasonably content or whether they seem to be underfed, dirty, and/or overmedicated.

Many problems in nursing homes spring from an overworked or underqualified staff. Since many of these organizations tend to pay low wages, some aides regard their work—and the residents—with indifference, and turnover is high. Check to see whether attrition has caused the nursing home to become understaffed or staffed with unlicensed or uncertified employees.

As with hospitals, many nursing homes tend to remove an individual's personal control over the details of daily life. This delegation of control may comfort some patients, providing a sense of secure routine to their lives; others respond with feelings of confusion and helplessness. In contrast to most hospitals, however, many nursing homes do allow patients to decorate their rooms, or the area around their beds, with various personal possessions, which can help them to retain a sense of individual identity.

Patient Advocacy
To ensure that someone is receiving good care in a nursing home can require watchful attention. In *The Age Care Sourcebook,* a very useful and informative guide for families of the elderly, author Jean Crichton says:

> . . . organizations that act as advocates for nursing home residents say that well-informed family members can be very effective in improving conditions. One such organization is Friends and Relatives of the Institutionalized Aged (FRIA), a New York City-based group working to assure quality care for nursing home residents. FRIA officials say patients whose relatives act as their advocate tend to receive better care than those without active relatives.[17]

Crichton also points out that "in some areas, private groups like FRIA have been organized to defend the rights of nursing home residents. To find out if such a group exists in your locality, contact: the National Citizens Coalition for Nursing Home Reform (a coalition of nursing home advocacy groups)." Or contact your state's Office for the Aging or your local-area agency on aging.

Dying in a Nursing Home
As noted above, most people who enter nursing homes die there. In fact, 25 percent of *all* elderly people die in nursing homes, and this number is increasing at a time when the fastest-growing segment of the population is over eighty-five years old. The truth of the matter is, when you are looking for nursing home care, you are quite often looking for terminal care.

Unfortunately, in many nursing homes, large patient populations, low staff-to-patient ratios, and little outside involvement either by families or by volunteers lead to a regimented program of treatment and a tendency to "objectify patients." For the staff, the patients become problems or obstacles in the way of getting their work done. This can create seriously dehumanizing conditions. In the nursing home setting it can be very difficult to receive good death care.

Of course not all homes are terrible places to die. A good example is described in *The Last Dance,* an excellent educational text by Lynne DeSpelder and Albert Strickland:

> In one nursing home, staff members' schedules are rotated so that as death nears, someone is with the patient almost constantly. The patient's family is notified and, if desired, a member of the clergy is called to the patient's bedside. If no relatives live nearby, the nursing home's staff assist in making arrangements for the funeral or disposition of the body. Staff members who had developed a close relationship with the patient are given time off to attend funeral services if they wish. Other patients who express an interest are informed of the death.[18]

It is possible to find good death care in a nursing home, but you have to look for it. *Ask specifically about terminal care.* What is the policy on advance directives? Find out if dying patients are transferred to a different room or a separate wing of the institution. Do they work with a local hospice program or provide any special hospice-type care? (See chapter 7 for an explanation of hospice.)

Nursing Homes and Advance Directives

The same conditions that make it difficult to provide compassionate, personal care also make it difficult for homes to honor individual preferences regarding life-support or treatment cessation.

Do Not Resuscitate orders are the most commonly used directive, but whether it will be honored or ignored or even misunderstood depends entirely on the nursing home. More complete directives such as a Medical Durable Power of Attorney should be filed with the home and brought to the attention of the staff. Not many nursing homes have ethics committees.

Some authorities point out that nursing homes are caught in a bind. For instance, government regulations require nursing homes to "nourish" all residents, and such regulations can cause confusion regarding treatment choices. If a patient stops eating, a feeding tube will probably be inserted even if the family, the advance directive, or the patient has requested otherwise.

These situations can create tremendous ambiguity and complexity. In some cases, the right-to-die issue would never come up if there was better death care in the first place. For instance, when a feeding tube is inserted because the staff doesn't have time to spoon-feed a dying patient whose arthritic condition doesn't allow her to feed herself, that is a death-care issue. In one case, the patient in question pulled at the tube and tried to remove it. (The intubation process is extremely uncomfortable, and many patients make an effort to resist it.) Her action was in danger of being interpreted as a desire to end treatment, while in reality the problem was not an individual's right to die but an individual's right to decent care.

MONEY

The average cost of nursing home care is around $30,000–$40,000 annually. A nursing home in a large urban area can easily cost twice as much or more. Some homes are privately owned and run for profit; others are nonprofit organizations operated by religious or other service groups, and still others are public agencies supported by government funds. Costs and reimbursement options vary from one type of facility to another.

Private Insurance
Unfortunately, nursing home care (long-term care) for the chronically or terminally ill is not often covered by standard medical insurance policies. Some companies are beginning to make long-term-care coverage available, but these policies are prohibitively expensive and contain so many restrictions that it is estimated you have only a four in ten chance of collecting on your coverage. A number of studies have shown widespread abuses by insurance companies in dealing with the elderly or chronically ill who have purchased nursing home coverage.[19]

Some insurance analysts say that improved policies will be available in the future as the industry learns how to estimate costs of nursing home claims. Others say this problem is just part of the whole tangled mess of medical-care financing in the United States and it won't get better until major changes are made in the system itself.

As described previously, some insurance companies are beginning to offer policyholders the option of selling their life insurance policies to pay for long-term health care. If you are interested in learning more about this option, call your insurance agent, the American Council of Life Insurance, or your state's Department of Insurance.

Medicare/Medicaid

Medicare and Medicaid coverage varies with the type of home and level of care. The variance can be significant, depending on whether it is a skilled nursing facility or the intermediate-care type. Speaking generally, Medicare does not cover long-term care.

The Medicare catastrophic and long-term coverage bill was designed to help address this need. However, in 1989, for a number of reasons, this legislation was repealed shortly after taking effect. At this writing, Congress has not yet designed a new bill.

Medicaid (the government program providing health care for the poor) *does* cover custodial care in a nursing home, but you must be impoverished to be eligible. To qualify, those elderly without other resources routinely pay out all their assets for care and then turn to Medicaid. This practice can create a serious problem if there is a surviving spouse who becomes impoverished as well.

The regulations and qualifications governing Medicaid coverage vary greatly from state to state. In New York, for instance, the spousal impoverishment rules are fairly liberal, and an individual can get Medicaid without totally bankrupting himself or herself. In other states, that is not the case. For more information, check with your Medicare or Medicaid representative (at the Social Security Administration), your state Office on Aging, or a local-area agency on aging.

There are legal maneuvers around these legislative catch-22s, maneuvers that are routinely employed by people who can afford to hire a lawyer specializing in "spending down for Medicaid." As described by Jean Crichton, the practice is common but controversial. Many consumer advocates and others point out that the law as it stands creates hardships for the elderly, the ill, and their families and that we as a society have not addressed these needs satisfactorily. This is most certainly true.

The National Citizen's Coalition for Nursing Home Reform (see listings following this chapter) can refer you to whatever state or local group can give advice. Some advocacy groups provide lists of lawyers who are experienced in this area.

HOME CARE

As we have seen, dying at home used to be the way everybody did it. Today the option of dying at home is just that, an option, not the norm. However, in recent years there has been a slow but steady increase in the number of people who die at home. That's because there's been an increase in home care of all kinds, including care for recovery, chronic illness, and/or infirmity.

This trend is a direct result of several factors: The development of home medical technology previously available only in the hospital setting (portable kidney dialysis machines, ventilators, etc); an aging population that prefers to remain at home as long as feasible; efforts of third-party payers (private insurance and government) to contain medical costs (home care is generally cheaper than institutional care); and, as mentioned above, a new Medicare reimbursement system that encourages hospitals to discharge patients earlier than in the past. For all these reasons, more health care happens at home; thus, more death care happens there, too.

Although some terminally ill patients do feel more comfortable with the security afforded by round-the-clock institutional care, dying people often want to be at home. Given the choice, most people prefer to end their lives in the same familiar surroundings in which they have lived.

The fear of death is often greatly intensified by the fear of isolation, separation, and loneliness; the fear of being taken from home, family, and friends. The atmosphere at home can permit more openness and relaxation in the dying person's communication and encourage more warmth and greater closeness than the usually impersonal atmosphere of institutions.

Ideally, most of us would prefer to die in a place where we feel comfortable, surrounded by the people who have meant the most to us. Realistically, however, we may fall short of achieving this ideal. For some people, the problems of dying at home can outweigh the advantages. If you are considering caring for someone who wants to die at home, you will need to evaluate the disadvantages very clearly and realistically to ensure that it is indeed the best solution. Questions you will need to ask include:

- What is the patient's condition?
- Is there medical support?
- Can the patient be made comfortable?
- Who will provide primary care?
- Do others in the family support the decision?
- Are the necessary resources available?
- How much will it cost?[20]

Requirements of Home Care

The most serious drawback to home death care is the substantial burden placed on the primary caregiver and the patient's family. Caring for the terminally ill is a lot of work and can drain family members both physically and emotionally.

Home care may require specialized equipment. Primary caregivers will probably need some special preparation and instruction, especially regarding home-nursing skills. Although home health care agencies can offer assistance, the main responsibility for tending to the patient is in the hands of family and friends, who will need to deal with feeding, bathing, nursing, and pain control.

The pressure and stress that come with taking twenty-four-hour-a-day responsibility for a dying person may produce serious emotional consequences. Anger, resentment, frustration, and depression are not uncommon reactions among both patient and caregivers. Also, people often feel inadequate to the task or frightened that they may in some way "hurt" the patient. Some families may find, through no failure of their own, that they simply cannot physically, financially, or emotionally handle the demands of nursing a terminally ill patient.

On the other hand, many people have reported the experience to be tremendously "important," "beautiful," and "profound." Some studies show that mourning periods are often shorter, grief more reasonably handled, and feelings of guilt comparatively lessened for survivors who cared for or were with their loved ones when they died.

Home Care for the Dying Child

Recent studies and reevaluations have shown that often terminally ill children do much better at home than in a hospital setting.[21] Once the decision has been made to stop curative treatment and to employ comfort measures, the child's needs can often be readily met in the home environment.

In an essay entitled "Helping the Dying Child," sociologist David Adams points out that

> care at home is less disruptive to the child, provides the comfort of familiar surroundings, enables interaction with the whole family, including pets, allows access to the child's friends, makes parents feel their inadequacies are less visible and enables even brief escapes to pleasant places more readily than the hospital.[22]

In *Making Medical Decisions,* authors Thomas and Celia Scully put it this way:

> Children who are dying need a place to die that's warm, caring, and comfortable, and where their medical needs can be met. And most parents of dying children want to be involved in their child's care and have some control over it. In a hospital setting, doctors are in control; in your own home, you are. Your child's doctor may suggest that you take him home and let him do as much as he wants to do or feels like doing. Or you may bring up the subject yourself. Many times, it's the child who says, "No more of this—I want to go home."[23]

If you or your child feels that home care may be the best alternative, there are a number of resources upon which you can rely for assistance, including community home care services, children's hospice services (see chapter 7), and hospital home care assistance. A very good guide is *Home Care for Seriously Ill Children: A Manual for Parents,* published by Children's Hospice International. (See listings at the end of this chapter.)

Help with Home Care

Getting help can be as informal a process as asking friends and relatives to give assistance, or as formal as hiring professional, medical, or housekeeping aid from a commercial home health care provider.

A wide range of services are available from a variety of private organizations and public agencies. The primary services are:

- Medical and skilled nursing care

- Respiratory, speech, physical, or other kinds of therapy, chemotherapy, or intravenous drug therapy

- Nutrition or dietary services

- Personal care (assistance with bathing, dressing, feeding, and toileting)

The kinds of professionals providing this care are nurses, home health aides, therapists, dietitians, and/or social workers.[24]

Who's Good and Who Isn't

While there are a number of community and public agencies that have long provided home health care, the recent trend back home has spurred a lot of growth in the field. This growth is seen primarily in the for-profit sector, with an increase in commercial agencies and a general shift in the ownership of smaller community and volunteer-based groups as they merge with larger, often profit-based organizations.

The oldest home health care service in this country is the Visiting Nurse Association (VNA). The VNA (also called the Visiting Nurse Service, or VNS) is a collection of organizations numbering more than five hundred, with local agencies throughout most states in the United States. These groups operate independently, but the history of the VNA overall is indicative of changes in the field. In some large urban areas the VNA is now a sizable corporate entity operating a wide variety of home health care programs and even related commercial interests. In other locations the VNA may still be a small direct-care provider. Visiting Nurse Associations offer health care, personal care, physical, speech, and occupational therapy, social service, nutritional counseling, and specialized nursing services. In some locations they also operate adult day care centers, wellness clinics, hospices, and Meals on Wheels programs.

Licensing, Certification, and Accreditation

Home health care groups can be licensed, certified, and/or accredited. Accrediting agencies are the Joint Commission on the Accreditation of Health Care Organizations (JCAHCO) and the National League for Nursing. Two additional accrediting agencies for paraprofessional services (for instance, homemaker and home-health aides providing personal care) are the National HomeCaring Council and the Council on Accreditation of Services for Families and Children.

Although it is possible to find a good home care agency that is not accredited or licensed, you are more likely to avoid problems if you seek out one that is. Home care is one of the least regulated fields around. Virtually anyone can set up a home care service. You want to be sure you're hiring competent people backed by a legitimate agency.

Legislative regulation varies significantly from state to state. While many, if not most, agencies are aboveboard and reliable, the field is vulnerable to fraud and abuse, and there is little consumer advocacy in place.

For referrals you can call the National League for Nursing, the JCAHCO, or to help specifically with terminal care, the National Hospice Organization (NHO) or Hospice Link.

One of the best resources in this field is a book entitled *The Home Health Care Solution: A Complete Consumer Guide* by Janet Zhun Nassif. It provides information on home care, including helpful advice on how to find, evaluate, and choose an agency and how to cover the costs of home care.

Another publication that presents a brief overview of what's available and gives you information on how to protect yourself is *A Consumer Guide to Home Health Care,* available through the National Consumers League. (See listings following this chapter as well as chapter 7 for further information on these resources.)

How to Find Help

If you have been in the hospital and are being discharged to return home for terminal care, you should be able to get advice on home care from the hospital staff. Social workers, nurses, or "discharge planners" will refer patients and families to available community resources.

In fact, you may find the hospital has its own home care service.

Hospitals are getting into the home health care business with both feet. (More than one-third of hospitals in the United States now offer home care.) One advantage of a hospital-based agency is that it usually has been surveyed by the JCAHCO.

Also various community agencies can provide information on what's available and how to find the help you need. The National Consumers League recommends the following:

- Area agencies on aging

- Family service agencies

- Religious organizations, such as Catholic Charities or Jewish community centers

- The social services or health departments of the city or county in which you live

If there is a VNA near you, they can offer guidance and information on the cost of the home care services available in your community. If you can marshal these resources, you can significantly reduce the emotional and physical stress that comes with home death care.

As the population of frail elderly continues to grow and more people look for an alternative to institutionalization, there are a number of programs being developed by the government and by private foundations to help with respite care (to spell home caregivers for brief periods). Such adult day care programs can also provide help for the terminally ill (if the patient is mobile or during a mobile period in the course of a disease). One of these programs may provide the kind of assistance you need. To learn more, inquire through your state's equivalent of the Health and Human Services Agency (in some states called the Department of Social Services and in others called the Department of Human Services.)

Another major resource is a hospice program. A concept designed specifically to improve care of the dying and to help and support their caregivers for the dying, hospice is becoming more widely known and available. It may be the answer to your needs. Chapter 7 explores the hospice idea and describes how it works.

MONEY

In addition to the emotional and physical strains placed on family members, home death care can create financial burdens as well. Specialized equipment (a hospital bed, a wheelchair, a bath rail, oxygen, and various medications and lotions) can be costly. Many insurance policies, however, *do* cover the costs of essential home medical expenses, such as rental of a wheelchair or a hospital bed, especially if the equipment is prescribed by a physician.

Of the proliferating home health agencies in this country, some, but not all, are Medicare certified. Check with an insurance agent or Medicare or Medicaid representative to see what equipment and other costs will be covered. In some cases, you may be eligible for more reimbursement in the hospital than you are at home. In other cases, home care will offer the more reasonable financial solution.

More and more third-party payers (insurance companies or the government) are allowing for home care coverage as a solution to the high costs of institutional care of the terminally ill elderly. Despite the costs of purchasing or renting home equipment, under most medical insurance plans home care often proves less expensive than either hospitalization or placement in a nursing home. Statistics compiled by the National Association for Home Care make the following comparisons:

> . . . between $300 and $500 a day in a hospital. At home, the same treatment would cost between $25 and $200 a day. Daily hospital care for an AIDS patient averages $773; home care for the same patient comes to $94 a day. Care for patient with neurological disorder and respiratory problems (excluding cost of equipment), is $196 per month at home versus $17,783 in hospital.[25]

Even allowing for additional costs of equipment, this is still a substantial savings.

In his book *Dealing Creatively with Death,* Ernest Morgan suggests approaching your insurer directly if you would prefer home care to traditional hospital or nursing home care. "Some insurance companies will cover home care services not mentioned in the policy—if you can demonstrate that they will save money by avoiding hospital or nursing home care." Morgan goes on to say, "It is reasonable to ask one's insurance company, preferably in advance of need, whether and under what conditions their coverage will apply to home care."[26]

In deciding whether to choose home death care, you may need to balance this lower outlay of costs with the strong possibility of a lower income as well. Few insurers cover the cost of private home care services, making the expense prohibitive to many. If there is no one at home to provide round-the-clock care, someone in the household may be required to take a leave of absence from work. To date, very few businesses have instituted such an enlightened employee benefit as death-care leave.

AN IMPORTANT NOTE

When someone dies outside the auspices of a hospital or other medical or long-term-care institution, legal regulations require that the local coroner or medical examiner investigate the death. Such an investigation can involve the police taking custody of the body, among other undesirable complications.

To avoid this eventuality, when an individual dies at home without an attending physician, you need to make arrangements for providing the funeral home with a signed death certificate. A medical professional (a home care nurse or the patient's physician) can make these arrangements for you. If you are in a hospice program, a member of the hospice staff will do so.

HEALTH CARE VERSUS DEATH CARE

Today, in the United States, the face of medical care is changing significantly. The way in which we have financed and delivered medical services has come to create as many problems as it solves. For the reasons we have seen—an aging society, more expensive technology, too many people needing limited resources, etc.—the shortcomings in the current system are growing worse.

Unfortunately, nobody has a master plan for real change. At present, it all happens by default. Insurance companies change the criteria for reimbursement, and doctors do less diagnostic testing; the government revises Medicare policies, and hospitals release patients quicker and sicker. These shifts occur piecemeal, creating a fluctuation here, a displacement there, and slowly, over time, the whole landscape changes. But the changes are reactionary, occasioned by short-term need and unguided by any overall vision, creating unforeseen and unwanted circumstances (such as the current moral crisis in treatment cessation). Meanwhile, the problems continue.

Within this amalgam of difficulties sits the question of death care. Where *can* people die? Where *should* people die? We wind up in hospitals as the result of big science; we wind up in nursing homes when hospitals change policies. We try to go home to die, and the burden of care falls on family or friends who are already overwhelmed. Where do we go for good death care?

Should there be "terminal care facilities"? Places where people go to die? How would they be financed? Regulated? Run? Maybe this isn't a good idea at all. Such places could easily become death houses for the shunned and impoverished, a horrific end instead of a comforting haven.

Between now and the year 2050 the number of people in this country age eighty-five and over will have increased from 3 million to almost 20 million. This "aging of America" is already beginning to create a health care crisis. Soon it will be a death-care crisis. Where are we going to do all this dying? And how are we going to pay for it? One attempt to address these questions is "hospice," the first new conceptual approach to death care since the Middle Ages. Chapter 7 describes the hospice answer to care for the dying.

RESOURCES AND SUPPORT

Books

Evelyn M. Baulch. *Extended Health Care at Home: A Complete and Practical Guide.* Berkeley, Calif.: Celestial Arts, 1989.

Deborah Duda. *Coming Home: A Guide to Dying at Home with Dignity.* New York: Aurora Press, 1987. Available in bookstores or through Aurora Press, P.O. Box 573, Santa Fe, NM 87504; (505) 989-9804. [Recounts the author's experiences, presenting her personal opinions and beliefs. It also includes helpful practical information on many aspects of home care for the terminally ill.]

Margaret Gold. *Life Support: Families Speak About Hospital, Hospice and Home Care for the Fatally Ill.* Mount Vernon, N.Y.: Institute for

Consumer Policy Research, 1983. Full Report, 200 pp.; Summary
Report, 40 pp. Available from The Institute for Policy Research,
Consumers Union Foundation, 256 Washington Street, Mount Vernon, NY 10553; (914) 667-9400.
[A study based on interviews with forty families, comparing their
experiences with terminal care in hospitals, at home, and with hospice
programs. Summary report describes the experiences of the families
and the study's conclusion that there are advantages to hospice care
for both families and patients.]

Thomas Andrew Gonda and John Ruark. *Dying Dignified: The Health
Professional's Guide to Care.* Reading, Mass.: Addison-Wesley, 1984.
[Although aimed at the medical professional and clinician, this book
is appropriate for laypeople. Covering a broad spectrum of subjects,
including terminal care, psychological, emotional, and social aspects
of hospice, institutional death, cultural factors, and more.]

Deborah Whiting Little. *Home Care for the Dying: A Reassuring, Comprehensive Guide to Physical and Emotional Care.* New York: Doubleday, Dial Press, 1985.
[A very helpful book for those considering home care for the terminally ill. Currently out of print but worth looking for; check your
local library or used-book store.]

D. Gay Moldow and Ida M. Martinson. *Home Care for Seriously Ill
Children: A Manual for Parents.* 2nd ed. Arlington, Va.: Children's
Hospice International, 1984. Available from Children's Hospice International, 700 Princess Street, Suite 3, Alexandria, VA 22314;
1-800-24-CHILD; (703) 684-0330 (in Virginia).
[An excellent manual offering practical advice on home care of the
terminally ill child. Tells how to decide if home care is appropriate;
advice on medications, pain control, emotional concerns, and more.]

Janet Z. Nassif. *The Home Health Care Solution: A Complete Consumer
Guide.* New York: Harper & Row, Perennial Library, 1985.
[A comprehensive guide for consumers. Includes advice on choosing
a home health care agency, financial aspects, special services such as
emergency-response systems. Provides checklists for self-assessment of
home care services; choosing an agency; insurance; and choosing a
medical-equipment dealer. Although slightly outdated on a few spe-
cifics (addresses and phone numbers), this book still offers some of the
best advice for home care consumers.]

National Consumers League. *A Consumer Guide to Home Health Care.*
Washington, D.C.: National Consumers League, 1986. Available

from the National Consumers League, 815 15th Street NW, Suite 516, Washington, DC 20005; (202) 639-8140.
[A book describing home health care services; includes a checklist for consumers.]

Cicely Saunders and Mary Baines. *Living with Dying: The Management of Terminal Disease.* 2nd ed. Oxford and New York: Oxford University Press, 1989.
[A slim text written for health care professionals detailing both the physical and psychological aspects of terminal pain and its management. Based on practice and research at St. Christopher's Hospice.]

Paula White. *Home Care of the Hospice Patient: An Information/Instructional Booklet for Caregivers in the Home.* Norwalk, Conn.: Purdue Frederick Company, 1986. Available at no charge by written request only: Janet Barsa, Purdue Frederick Company, 100 Connecticut Avenue, Norwalk, CT 06856; (202) 853-0123.
[A thorough booklet covering such topics as family support systems, daily care, nutrition, breathing care, pain management, and the death experience in the home.]

Books Containing Related Information

George J. Annas. *The Rights of Patients: The Basic ACLU Guide to Patients' Rights.* 2nd ed. Completely revised and up-to-date. American Civil Liberties Union Handbooks. Carbondale, Ill.: Southern University Press, 1989.
[Contains chapters on how hospitals are organized; rules hospitals must follow; and death, organ donation, and autopsy.]

R. Barker Bausell, Michael A. Rooney, and Charles B. Inlander. *How to Evaluate and Select a Nursing Home.* People's Medical Society Books. Reading, Mass.: Addison-Wesley Publishing, 1988. Available in bookstores or from the People's Medical Society, 462 Walnut Street, Lower Level, Allentown, PA 18102; (215) 770-1670.

Robert N. Brown, with Legal Counsel for the Elderly. *The Rights of Older Persons.* 2nd ed. Completely revised and up-to-date. American Civil Liberties Union Handbooks. Carbondale, Ill.: Southern University Press, 1989.
[Includes discussion of Medicare and Medicaid coverage for home care and nursing homes. Also includes a chapter on the rights of nursing home residents.]

Jean Crichton. *The Age Care Sourcebook: A Resource Guide for the Aging and Their Families.* New York: Simon & Schuster, Fireside Books, 1987.
[Contains advice on home care and nursing homes. Also offers a clear explanation of Medicare and Medicaid programs and reimbursements and other helpful information.]

Paula Brown Doress, Diana Laskin Siegal, and the Midlife and Older Women Book Project. *Ourselves, Growing Older: Women Aging with Knowledge and Power.* New York: Simon & Schuster, Touchstone Books, 1987.
[Includes discussion on nursing homes.]

Mark Dowie. *"We Have a Donor": The Bold New World of Organ Transplants.* New York: St. Martin's Press, 1988.
[A most readable account of the science (and politics) of organ transplantation. Includes descriptions of the procedures involved.]

Thomas T. Frantz. *When Your Child Has a Life-Threatening Illness.* Rev. ed. Washington, D.C.: Association for the Care of Children's Health, 1988. Available from the Association, 7919 Woodmont Avenue, Suite 300, Bethesda, MD 20814; (301) 654-6549.
[A booklet that discusses some of the emotional and psychological aspects of caring for children with life-threatening diseases.]

Jo Horne. *The Nursing Home Handbook: A Guide for Families.* Washington, D.C.: American Association of Retired Persons; Glenview, Ill.: Scott, Foresman and Company, AARP Books, 1989.

Ernest Morgan. *Dealing Creatively with Death: A Manual of Death Education and Simple Burial.* 11th ed., revised and expanded. Edited by Jennifer Morgan. Burnsville, N.C.: Celo Press, 1988. Available in bookstores or from Celo Press, 1901 Hannah Branch Road, Burnsville, NC 28714; (704) 675-4925.
[Includes a discussion on home care and the right to die.]

Sheila Petersen. *"A Special Way to Care": A Guide for Neighbors, Friends and Community in Their Efforts to Provide Financial and Emotional Support for Terminally Ill and Catastrophically Ill Children.* Croton Falls, N.Y.: Friends of Karen, 1988. Available from Friends of Karen, Box 217, Croton Falls, NY 10519; (914) 277-4547.
[Written from the author's personal experience. Includes advice on handling problems such as hair loss and feelings of isolation.]

John A. Robertson. *The Rights of the Critically Ill.* Rev. ed. American Civil Liberties Union Handbooks. New York: Bantam, 1983. Avail-

able from the American Civil Liberties Union, 132 West 43rd Street, New York, NY 10036; (212) 944-9800.
[Includes a chapter on the rights of critically ill children.]

Charles E. Rosenberg. *The Care of Strangers: The Rise of America's Hospital System.* New York: Basic Books, 1987.
[A history of the development of the hospital as the major medical-care institution in America.]

Thomas Scully, M.D., and Celia Scully. *Making Medical Decisions: How to Make Difficult Medical and Ethical Choices for Yourself and Your Family* (originally published as *Playing God: The New World of Medical Choices*). New York: Simon & Schuster, Fireside Books, 1989.
[A practical guide to medical ethics for the layperson. Includes section on nursing homes that discusses how to find a nursing home and place a loved one in an institution. Also includes material on terminally ill children and hospital care.]

Paul Starr. *The Social Transformation of American Medicine.* New York: Basic Books, 1984.
[The definitive social history of the American medical profession. A readable and very informative book.]

Norma S. Upson. *When Someone You Love Is Dying.* New York: Simon & Schuster, Fireside Books, 1986.
[Includes advice on home care. This book is currently out of print but worth looking for; check with your local library or used-book store.]

Harry Van Bommel. *Choices: For People Who Have a Terminal Illness, Their Families and Caregivers.* Toronto: NC Press Limited, 1990; distributed in the United States by Seven Hills Book Distributors. Available through Seven Hills Books, 49 Central Avenue, Cincinnati, OH 45202; 1-800-545-2005.
[Contains practical advice on home care and pain and symptom control; covers Canada, the United Kingdom, and the United States.]

Hannelore Wass, Felix M. Berardo, and Robert Neimeyer, eds. *Dying: Facing the Facts.* 2nd ed. Series in Death Education, Aging, and Health Care. Washington, D.C.: Harper & Row, Hemisphere Publishing, 1989.
[This textbook is useful for both professionals and laypeople; includes a discussion on institutional dying.]

William J. Winslade and Judith Wilson Ross. *Choosing Life or Death: A Guide for Patients, Families, and Professionals.* New York: Macmillan, Free Press, 1986.
[Includes information on how to deal with hospital policy and how to enlist support in the hospital setting.]

Agents/Service Organizations

American Health Care Association
1201 L Street, NW
Washington, DC 20005
(202) 842-7424
The nation's largest federation of nursing homes and long-term health care facilities; offers free pamphlet on nursing homes. Can refer people to their state affiliates for assistance.

Association for the Care of Children's Health
7910 Woodmont Avenue
Suite 300
Bethesda, MD 20814
(301) 654-6549
A clearinghouse for information whose concerns include the psychosocial aspects of caring for children with chronic or terminal illnesses. Maintains a national network of parents with children who have special needs (including those with terminal illnesses). Offers publications with practical advice.

Compassion Book Service
216 Via Monte
Walnut Creek, CA 94598
(415) 933-0830
Distributes books concerned with various aspects of death and dying, including home care and hospice. Catalog is available at no charge.

Joint Commission on Accreditation of Healthcare Organizations
Home Care Accreditation Program
One Renaissance Boulevard
Oak Brook Terrace, IL 60181
(708) 916-5600
Accredits both hospital-based and freestanding home health care programs. They have surveyed over 2,000 programs and agencies. Will make referrals and answer questions regarding home care practices by agencies they have accredited.

National HomeCaring Council
519 C Street, NE
Washington, DC 20002
(202) 547-6586
A division of the Foundation for Hospice and Homecare, the Council accredits homemaker-home health aid health agencies. They will make referrals to local health care agencies. A pamphlet "All About Home Care: A Consumer's Guide" is available at no charge from the address above.

National Citizens Coalition on Nursing Home Reform
1424 16th Street, NW
Suite L-2
Washington, DC 20036
(202) 797-0657
A national consumer advocacy group organized around the concerns of relatives and residents of nursing homes. They can refer you to a state or local group that can provide assistance and advice concerning the selection and financing of nursing home care. The coalition also distributes a free guide on choosing a nursing home.

National League for Nursing
Community Health Accreditation Program (CHAP)
350 Hudson Street
New York, NY 10014
1-800-669-1656
(212) 989-9393 ext. 242
The CHAP currently certifies 350 home health agencies, with accreditation pending for another 2,000.

United Network for Organ Sharing
1100 Boulders Parkway
Suite 500
Richmond, VA 23225-8770
800-24-DONOR
This organ-placement network operates a 24-hour telephone service offering information to the public about organ donation.

Visiting Nurse Associations of America
3801 East Florida Avenue
Suite 806
Denver, CO 80210
800-426-2547

The nation's oldest community-based nonprofit home health care providers. VNAs provide home health care services to over 40 percent of all Medicare eligible patients. The national headquarters can refer you to one of the 503 local VNAs in 45 states.

Additional Resources

There are many organizations that provide education, support, and guidance for dealing with a specific chronic or terminal illness.

FOR CHILDREN   Perhaps the best-known support group is the Candlelighters Childhood Cancer Foundation. This and 300 other organizations concerned with children's health can be found in the free book *Reaching Out: A Directory of Voluntary Organizations in Maternal and Child Health* available from the National Maternal and Child Health Clearinghouse, 38th and R Streets, NW, Washington, DC 20057; (202) 625-8410. The National Information Center for Children and Youth with Handicaps, 7926 Jones Branch Drive, Suite 1100, McLean, VA 22102; 1-800-999-5599; (703) 893-6061 is also helpful for parents who need referrals. They provide a free publications list.

FOR ADULTS   You can find referrals to support groups and their hotlines in Jean Carper's *Health Care U.S.A.* (New York: Prentice Hall, 1987) or other references readily available at your local public library. The National Health Information Center, U.S. Department of Human Services, P.O. Box 1133, Washington, DC 20013-1133; 1-800-336-4797; (301) 565-4167 (in Maryland) offers services that include referrals to government agencies, voluntary associations, self-help groups, and support groups.

FOR OLDER ADULTS   Your state Department of Aging and local-area agency on aging offer help around issues of concern to older adults. Every state is required to have a long-term-care ombudsman who oversees the quality of care in nursing homes. Most ombudsmen maintain offices at the state Department of Aging. They can sometimes help with nursing home or long-term-care problems. The American Association of Retired Persons (AARP), 1909 Street, NW, Washington, DC 20049, (203) 872-4700, has available a number of helpful and relevant publications, including *A Handbook About Care in the Home, Before You Buy: A Guide to Long-Term Care Insurance* and *Making Wise Decisions for Long-Term Care.*

Additional sources for information concerning local home care and nursing home facilities are family and children's social service agencies.

7

Hospice

I conceive it the office of the physician not only to restore the health but to mitigate pains and dolours; and not only when such mitigation may conduce to recovery but when it may serve to make a fair and easy passage.

Francis Bacon

To date, the most successful contemporary model for enlightened death care is hospice.

A Kind of Care
Defined by the National Hospice Organization (NHO) as "a medically directed, interdisciplinary program of palliative services for terminally ill people and their families," the hospice vision is, in many ways, the opposite of conventional institutional approaches to care for the dying. The primary goals of a hospice program are comfort and emotional support.

Sometimes there is confusion between the definition of hospice as a place and hospice as a program. Often it is assumed that "a hospice" is a place where people go to die. In some countries, most notably Great Britain, the development of the hospice ideal has been centered in specific institutions, called hospices, designed to care for the terminally ill. But in the United States there are few freestanding hospices. More often, the term *hospice* refers to a program of care rather than a place of care. For the most part, hospice in this country can be defined as a support network for people who are dying at home, with the added provision of inpatient care when needed.

Another confusion can arise between hospice care and home care. Although the two phrases are sometimes used interchangeably, they really mean two different things. *Home care* means caring for someone at home, while *hospice care* is a specialized *program* of support for the dying that is primarily implemented in the home.

The National Consumers League says,

> Although the differences between conventional treatment in a hospital and hospice are clear, it is more difficult for people sometimes to understand the distinction between *home care* in general and *hospice home care*. Many home care agencies, hospitals and other organizations offer home care programs for the terminally ill. These programs provide nurses, therapists and home health aides to help with patient care in the home. These programs do not usually attempt, however, to provide the comprehensive services of a hospice nor are services generally provided for the whole family.[1]

THE HOSPICE IDEAL

Two of the primary principles of the hospice concept are as follows: (1) The terminally ill person's own preference and life-style are key to all decisions about care, and (2) family members and other caregivers also have legitimate needs and interests deserving of consideration.

In their book *The Hospice Experiment,* Vincent Mor, David Greer, and Robert Kastenbaum describe the hospice approach as founded on patient needs:

> Starting from this broad perspective, then, one would not expect patients and their families to accept the treatment styles and preferences of the medical establishment. On the contrary, it is the "system" that must find ways to respect the distinctive circumstances and needs

of every individual facing death. . . . Simple though these principles may appear, they signaled a revolutionary approach in terminal care. Fulfillment of the hospice vision would preclude depersonalizing a person as a "colon," "head-neck," or "lung" to be managed according to local protocol. Each patient would be appreciated instead as a total person who had vital connections to other people and who should not be expected to surrender values and preferences developed over a lifetime in order to die in a manner convenient to the system.[2]

While most terminal patient care in the United States still happens in what might be called the "institutional" manner, the hospice model is increasingly utilized, and the vision of compassionate care offered by the hospice concept has now gained a secure foothold.

The History of Hospice
The word *hospice* comes from the same Latin root (*hospes,* meaning both guest and host) as does hospital and hospitality. The antecedents of the modern hospice can be found as long ago as 238 B.C., when, in India, dying pilgrims traveling to the Ganges were given shelter in the homes of families living near the sacred river. In Europe, during the Middle Ages, hospices run by religious orders of monks and nuns offered comfort and shelter to the sick traveler.

The modern hospice movement developed in the 1950s and 1960s. The first international model was St. Christopher's Hospice, established in a suburb of London under the leadership of Dr. Cicely Saunders in 1967. In the United States, the Hospice of New Haven in Connecticut (now known as Connecticut Hospice, Inc.) was founded in 1974 by a coalition of professionals from Yale University, local hospitals, and the New Haven community. By 1979 there were over 200 hospice programs in the United States. Today there are about 1,700.

These programs share the general methodology and philosophy of the hospice approach but vary as to their structure and affiliation. (Some are affiliated with hospitals, some with community health care agencies; a few are freestanding organizations.)

In 1978 the National Hospice Organization was founded as a clearinghouse for information and education on hospice, devising standards and principles of practice for national hospice certification. The NHO is the predominant national association representing hospice programs, but there are others, including the Hospice

Association of America, Children's Hospice International (CHI), and the National Institute for Jewish Hospice. (See listings at the end of this chapter.)

In 1982 the federal government passed legislation providing benefits for hospice care under Medicare and Medicaid coverage, and private insurers began to cover hospice costs as well.

THE HOSPICE PROGRAM

Hospice emphasizes caring rather than curing. In its pamphlet "The Basics of Hospice," the NHO makes this commitment clear.

> The purpose of hospice is to provide support and care for people in the final phase of a terminal disease so that they can live as fully and comfortably as possible. Hospice affirms life and regards dying as a normal process. Hospice neither hastens nor postpones death. Hospice believes that through personalized services and a caring community, patients and families can attain the necessary preparation for a death that is satisfactory to them.[3]

As described by the noted clinical administrator Glen Davidson, editor of the book *The Hospice, Development and Administration*, "Different groups have articulated the hospice philosophy in various ways. Generally, however, all such statements address the following five principles:"

- Dying is a normal part of living.

- Control of pain and distressing symptoms is the goal of treatment.

- Both patients and their closest companions—family and friends—need care.

- Care should include support for survivors throughout their bereavement.

- An interdisciplinary team, including volunteers, is best able to provide the necessary care.[4]

The hospice concept implies that death is not a terror against which we must fight desperately and at all costs. Rather, death is seen as an inevitable event requiring and deserving of significant attention and respect.

In order to even begin to consider the possibility of death as an interesting experience, it is necessary to believe that it will not be an experience suffused with pain. Whatever conscious or unexamined fear we may have of death itself, it is compounded by our fear of the pain and suffering that we associate with dying. If we were confident that our suffering could be assuaged, it could change the nature of our apprehension.

Pain, Suffering, and the Way We Die

Describing the development of hospice, Mor, Greer, and Kastenbaum state: "The hospice vision centered on a person who was not distracted by suffering and the fear of suffering and therefore could still think clearly and maintain significant interpersonal relationships."[5]

Very often our assumption is that terminal illness (especially cancer) is pain filled, and sometimes it is, but even when that is the case, pain can almost always be controlled if treated properly and attentively. In her book *The Hospice Alternative: A New Context for Death and Dying,* Anne Munley points out that there is

> a widespread cultural fear that a death due to cancer is a death riddled with agonizing physical pain. In reality, pain studies of terminal patients refute this notion. As many as 50 percent of those dying from all malignancies have no physical pain at all; another 10 percent have mild pain; and the remaining 40 percent experience severe or intractable pain. Many effective techniques have been developed to alleviate mild and even intractable pain; but analgesics must be artfully tailored to the needs of the individual patient.[6]

In an article entitled "Control of Pain in Terminal Cancer," the noted expert Dr. Cicely Saunders said:

> It must not be forgotten that "intractable" does not mean "impossible to relieve"; its meaning is "not easily treated." Successful treatment may call for much imagination and persistence but pain can be abolished while the patient still remains alert, able to enjoy the company of those around him and often able to be up and about until his death.[7]

You might expect the most effective pain control to be available in hospitals or specialized medical institutions. The truth of the matter is that the acute-care hospital is not very practiced in the more discriminating aspects of modern pain management and can be inadequate in providing *terminal* pain and symptom control.

Why? There are a number of reasons, not the least of which is that pain is a rather complicated phenomenon. Controlling pain demands very particular attention to subtle factors. Speaking generally, pain can be divided into two categories: (1) the acute pain of trauma or the "resolving" pain after surgery, which may be intense but has a limited duration, and (2) the long-term, chronic, or "terminal" pain that is the result of the deterioration of organs or bodily functions or other conditions that will not improve.

The management of terminal pain is a special science. But unfortunately, many physicians do not know the latest techniques of this specialty. Doctors and nurses accustomed to dealing with standard remedies for acute pain may not know enough about different types of medication and how to assess and prescribe them as pain changes during the progression of disease. According to Harry van Bommel, the author of *Choices: For People Who Have a Terminal Illness, Their Families and Their Caregivers,* "Pain and symptom control is a relatively new field requiring specialized training. A family physician, or a specialist in cancer or heart diseases, while knowledgeable, may not know the latest techniques of pain and symptom control."[8]

Studies have shown that common assumptions about addiction and tolerance of opiate or other pain-relieving drugs do not apply in terminal or chronic pain cases, especially if drugs are administered in the proper dosage at the proper time. And yet these assumptions are still widely held among many health care professionals.

In addition, the effective management of terminal pain requires, as Dr. Saunders puts it, imagination and persistence. The priorities of many institutions demand systematic routines and procedures that tend to work against assessment of an individual's particular pattern of pain. Drugs are given at standardized intervals that do not necessarily correspond to need. Harry van Bommel puts it succinctly: "The secret to pain control is giving the right drug, in the right amount, in the right way and at the right time."[9] This demands a degree of individuation that is hard to maintain in the average medical facility.

Sandol Stoddard (author of *The Hospice Movement, A Better Way of Caring for the Dying*) writes about pain management in large medical institutions:

> Morphine shots and heavy doses of tranquilizers, administered in a clockwork pattern in an automatic and impersonal atmosphere, tend to make screaming addicts or deeply depressed or helpless "vegetable" cases out of dying people who, with the right kind of care and medication, might otherwise be quite serene, clear-headed and comfortable.[10]

In some hospice programs patients keep their own "pain charts," also known as "comfort charts," and dispense their own medicine. This allows for a great sense of personal control over pain. Such an approach is amazingly effective in providing relief not only from pain but from the fear that comes from lack of control as well. Experience has shown conclusively that when you allay the fear of pain, you reduce the amount of drugs necessary to control it.

The hospice approach to pain management can significantly change the experience of terminal illness. In fact, the development over the last twenty years of the specialized field of pain management and symptom control is a direct result of the work of hospice professionals in this area.

In addition to pain management, hospice gives priority to the control and management of "distressing" symptoms, such as nausea, vomiting, diarrhea, bleeding, coughing, etc. Much of the physical suffering that comes with terminal illness stems from discomfort secondary to the primary disease, such as muscle spasms, headaches, difficulty with digestion or elimination, or side effects from medications. Because nutritional and digestive problems are often intrinsic to illness, some hospices offer dietary counseling to family members, instructing them on how to keep the patient appropriately nourished. Hospice care includes special attention to the relief of such problems.

Comfort is a primary goal. Hospice care doesn't try to keep you from dying, but it does try to keep you from doing so in terrible pain or in a humiliating condition. The idea is to make dying less horrific in its particulars so that each individual can approach the inevitable as they find it in themselves to do so.

Who's Involved in Hospice Care?

Another principle of hospice care involves the family, along with the patient, as a single unit of concern to the professional staff. It is assumed that the well-being of the patient is most likely achieved in cooperation with the family, friends, or loved ones who are looking after the patient. At the very least, hospice can ensure that those who care will not be shut out of the process or relegated to a role of background handwringing or helplessness. The standards and principles of hospice as defined by the NHO state: "The family members are seen both as primary caregivers and as needing care and support so that their own stresses and concerns may be addressed."[11]

A hospice interdisciplinary team offers encouragement, advice, support, assistance, and an opportunity to rest. Support is provided by groups of professionals and volunteers comprising what is called an "interdisciplinary team." These teams include doctors, nurses, social workers, psychiatrists or psychological counselors, physical therapists, music and art therapists, home health aides, clergy members, and volunteers.

Generally, the hospice team works with the "primary caregiver" (the individual predominantly responsible for caring for the patient), in the home, to coordinate assistance as it is needed and requested. In cases in which there is no primary caregiver, the hospice program may be able to help find some support, but this depends on the size, resources, and policy of the particular program. Some hospice groups cannot take on a patient unless there is a primary caregiver available.

The hospice team *physician* shifts the focus of medical care from treatments aimed at cure to treatments aimed at relieving pain and other distressing symptoms. The hospice *nurse* makes regular visits to monitor the patient's physical condition, provides instruction and expertise in symptom management, supervises home health aides, and provides emotional support. *Physical, speech, art, and music therapists* assist patients as is appropiate. These other team members visit the patient on an as-needed basis.

In addition to these regularly scheduled visits, most hospice programs have a nurse on call twenty-four hours a day, seven days a week. As described in *A Consumer Guide to Hospice Care,*

> It is important to remember that 24-hour *availability* does not mean 24-hour *presence.* Hospice physicians and nurses direct and coordinate

health care, assisting and supporting whoever is taking care of the patient. But hospices rarely routinely have the resources to offer around-the-clock direct care. On the other hand, not many hospice patients require around-the-clock skilled medical care. The hospice doctors and nurses are available by telephone and, when necessary, someone will come out to the house.[12]

This permits family members to phone for advice or assistance whenever an emergency arises or the patient's symptoms intensify. A nurse may go to the patient's home, if necessary, or may arrange admission to an inpatient unit.

Important to the team is a good *home health aide* (what is called a "nurse's aide" in the hospital setting), who can help with a range of activities, such as basic physical care, bathing or moving the patient, shopping, running errands, or staying with the patient to spell the primary caregiver.

Social workers help families plan for terminal care and find financial assistance, if needed. These professionals are experienced in the sometimes dismayingly complex world of entitlements and can help guide the patient or family to monetary aid, if appropriate. They also provide supportive counseling to families facing death, helping them negotiate the many emotional problems, conflicts, and fears that arise. *Clergy members* also provide emotional and spiritual support.

Complementing the team are *volunteers*. Volunteers can play a critical part in hospice care. After undergoing extensive training, volunteers supplement the efforts of family members or the primary caregiver, often furnishing an invaluable respite. Volunteers may assist family members in providing personal care and companionship to the patient and in doing small household chores. They may, for example, attend to a patient's cleaning or grooming needs, give haircuts or shaves, shop or cook a meal, or help with light housekeeping. Volunteers may also run errands, provide transportation, read to patients, etc.

Hospice services generally extend beyond the death of the patient. Social workers can help a family with funeral arrangements and offer comfort and support during the bereavement period. The counselors identify those at risk in bereavement and maintain contact after the patient's death. Some hospice programs offer bereavement support groups. During the first year of mourning, mailings are sent, offering information on programs, books, and other resources to assist survivors.

How and Where Does Hospice Work?

Hospice programs can be put into effect in any of a number of settings. In describing different types of hospice care, Glen W. Davidson says: "As with other European ideas and institutions adopted in North America, the hospice has been reshaped, reorganized, and reapplied according to the unique needs and values of a specific locale."[13]

Hospice programs share a common philosophy and set of standards but otherwise can vary significantly in their structure, organization, and the way in which services are provided. The different types of hospice programs follow:[14]

FREESTANDING   Freestanding hospice programs are not owned by another institution or agency and are organized solely to offer hospice services. They have their own administration and staff, and inpatient care is provided in the hospice's own unit or through arrangements with a hospital or nursing home. There are few freestanding hospices in the United States.

HOSPITAL BASED   A hospital or nursing home may provide hospice care to patients wherever they are in the facility. Home care can be made available through either the hospital's own home health care unit or through arrangements with community-based home health agencies.

HOME HEALTH AGENCY BASED   Hospice care is one of many services that may be provided by a home health agency. Such organizations include visiting nurse services, for-profit home care agencies, and public agencies such as county home care services.

COMMUNITY BASED   These groups are not part of other agencies, have no building, and contract for services from the community. They are often made up primarily of professional and lay volunteer workers.

ALL-VOLUNTEER ORGANIZATIONS   Professional staff are all volunteers, with only one or a few paid staff to coordinate patient care and volunteers. The hospice program may be carried out in conjunction with local home health agencies and hospitals. These kinds of groups were the backbone of hospice care when it began in the United States; now there are fewer of them.

In addition, hospice programs may be found in nursing homes, in "group homes," and through coalitions of health care agencies.

Inpatient Care
Supplementing these home services, most hospices also offer short-term inpatient care. Depending on the type of hospice, its inpatient facilities might be located in a building or wing of an affiliated hospital, an owner hospital, or a nursing home or other extended-care facility.

There are several reasons for moving a patient to the inpatient setting: Pain and symptoms may require special treatment only available in a hospital (the palliative use of radiotherapy, chemotherapy, or nerve blocks to treat some types of terminal pain). Patients in an acute stage of a progressive illness, suffering from severe pain or nausea or other symptoms, would be encouraged to turn to a hospice's short-term inpatient services.

Another reason to use inpatient care is respite; the primary caretaker needs a rest. Respite care is a temporary stay giving the family a break from the pressures of continuously providing for the needs of the dying person.

Hospices generally try to maintain a homelike atmosphere in their permanent facilities. If you visit a hospice unit housed within a hospital, you will be struck by how it differs from the rest of the hospital. It is less hectic, more to a human scale, less intimidating. Many units have more liberal visiting policies than the hospital proper and allow both children and pets to spend time with the dying person, if that is desired.

Who Is Eligible for Hospice Care?
There are, generally speaking, four criteria for acceptance in a hospice program. You must be terminally ill, with a life expectancy of six months or less (most programs require that a physician or the hospice medical director establish a prognosis); be unable to benefit from further aggressive (curative) treatment; be interested in receiving care at home; and have a primary caregiver (relative or friend) who will assume the responsibility for custodial care of the patient and be the decision maker in the event the patient becomes no longer competent to make decisions.

By definition, participation in a hospice program demands recognition of terminal illness. *A Consumer Guide to Hospice* states: "Hospice is called 'palliative' care which means that the care is intended to ease pain without curing. It also means that no attempt is made to prolong life beyond its natural end. On the other hand, hospice does nothing to hasten death."[15]

Those who are actively seeking a cure for their illness do not belong in a hospice program. This is not to say that you are required to make a formal declaration. In some instances, patients and families don't wish to speak openly about death. Those wishes are honored. However, in order to take advantage of the program, the goal must be comfort rather than cure.

For hospice care to be most effective, it needs to be in place over a period of time. Sometimes a family will call a hospice program at the point where death is immediately imminent (within a day or two), but by then it is almost impossible to provide meaningful assistance, and some programs have a policy against accepting patients at the very last minute.

If you aren't sure whether you (or your relative or friend) are eligible, contact a hospice program. Many of them offer free family consultations to help determine whether a patient's condition is appropriate for the program.

CHILDREN'S HOSPICE

The hospice ideal very purposefully includes the family and loved ones of the dying person in the plan of care. It assumes that support for the dying person will be greater if the caregivers are also aided in their efforts to deal with the difficulties and trauma of dying. This can be especially critical in the care of a dying child.

A conventional wisdom of terminal-care education says that when a child is diagnosed terminal, the entire family becomes the patient. Health care professionals are encouraged to keep this in mind and to treat "the whole family." Since hospice is designed to do this anyway, it is a particularly good program of death care for children. The extended services of a hospice program—family counseling and bereavement follow-up—are especially pertinent when the patient is a child.

However, for much of their history in this country most programs didn't accept children. In 1983 only 18 of the 1,400 hospice programs then in operation accepted children. In that year, Ann Armstrong Daily founded Children's Hospice International to encourage the establishment of children's hospices. Now there are over 200 hospice programs that include children, and many more institutions are making plans to provide pediatric hospice care.

There are a number of reasons it has taken longer to begin to provide hospice care for children. When the patient is a child, there is an overwhelming emphasis on curative treatment (as opposed to when the patient is an elderly adult). The death of a child is so comparatively uncommon that it can take a long time before parents are able to accept that aggressive care aimed at cure is no longer appropriate, and move to palliative care or support the dying process. Also, initially there was little pediatric expertise in the professional hospice community. Today there is expertise and interest.

Children's Hospice International

Children's Hospice International is a nonprofit organization serving as a clearinghouse for research programs, support groups, and education and training programs for the care of terminally ill children and adolescents.

The goals of the group are to "promote hospice support through pediatric care facilities, encourage the inclusion of children in existing and developing hospices and home care programs, and include the hospice perspectives in all areas of pediatric care, education and the public arena." They "provide medical, psychological, social and spiritual support to terminally ill children and their families."[16]

To find a children's hospice, call CHI at their toll-free number: 1-800-24-CHILD (and see the listings at the end of this chapter for further information).

MONEY

Many hospice programs are initially supported through contributions and grants from foundations and individual contributors, memorial gifts, fund-raisers, and local gifts. Reimbursement for services comes from Medicare, Medicaid, and private insurance carriers. This reimbursement does not cover actual costs, however. Most programs run at a deficit, which makes them very dependent on donations and other types of assistance. They are always in need of financial contributions.

Although, at first, hospice programs encountered legal and financial difficulties as well as powerful resistance from traditional health care providers in this country, they have gradually gained acceptance in the world of health care financing.

Over the past decade, insurance companies as well as the federal government have increasingly accepted the concept of hospice—especially after discovering that hospice care could significantly cut costs when compared to traditional treatment of the terminally ill. Today more than sixty national health insurance companies offer hospice benefits, although availability and levels of coverage still vary greatly.

Corporations, too, have begun to establish hospice care as an employee benefit. A 1987 survey of 1,500 corporations revealed that 64 percent offered a hospice benefit.[17]

Hospice and Medicare

Although the government resisted the concept in the 1970s, hospice programs for the dying became an acceptable form of reimbursable care under the Medicare system when it was shown to significantly lower the cost of end-of-life care. (Medicare is the federal health insurance program offered as an option to all recipients of Social Security.)

Half the total of all standard Medicare payments are for the treatment of patients in the last year of their lives. Hospice, however, eliminates expensive, life-prolonging treatment efforts to patients with a terminal illness—the most costly aspect of death care. Motivated as much by economics as humane concerns, the government gradually realized the cost benefits of financing hospice care and began viewing it as an acceptable alternative to standard care.

Hospice and Medicaid

In 1986, hospice coverage became a permanent benefit of Medicaid. (Medicaid is the governmental health program for the poor.) Those ineligible for Medicare coverage may need to turn to Medicaid in order to meet the costs of hospice care. Once an eligible recipient of Medicaid has satisfied an annual deductible amount. Medicaid will usually cover 100 percent of the cost of a physician's care, skilled nursing care, medical supplies and equipment, and prescription medications.

You needn't be totally destitute in order to qualify for Medicaid. You may not be required to sell your house or your car and empty your small savings account. If you own nothing more than these and you have an income at or near the poverty level, you may be eligible for Medicaid. Different states have established different requirements. Check with your county's Department of Social Services.

Medicare Certification

Medicare now covers virtually the entire cost of hospice care to terminally ill beneficiaries *if you use a Medicare-certified hospice program.* Some hospice programs are Medicare certified, and some are not. Medicare standards determine certification. Some hospice programs do not meet all the criteria for certification, which does not mean that they may not provide good-quality services. It can mean that they simply do not have the administrative staff available to deal with the Medicare reimbursement process. Others avoid seeking certification because the reimbursement rates paid by Medicare do not adequately cover the actual costs of patient care. For these and other reasons, not all hospice programs choose to become Medicare certified.

An Additional Note

If you cannot finance hospice care through either public or private health insurance and you cannot afford to pay for hospice care without help, try to get financial assistance directly from a local hospice program. Many will accept patients regardless of their ability to pay. Most will try to help you find assistance.

HOW AND WHERE TO FIND A
HOSPICE PROGRAM

In selecting a hospice program for yourself or for a terminally ill relative, location is key. Since hospice is primarily a type of home care, your choices will depend on what is available near your home. The NHO or Hospice Link can provide you with information on programs in your area. (See listings at the end of this chapter.)

If you plan to use Medicare to finance or help pay for the cost of hospice care, you will need to make sure that the program you choose is Medicare certified. Keep in mind that a lack of Medicare certification does not necessarily indicate a lack of quality care for terminally ill patients.

THE HOPE OF HOSPICE

When we are dying we need support, warmth and compassion, surcease from pain, and help with distressing symptoms. Our families and loved ones need understanding, assistance, and a break. The purpose of hospice is to fill those needs. Hospice professionals are dedicated to practicing medicine in a way that gives comfort and a good quality of life for patients who are dying (while including the family in the circle of caregiving). Hospice is the single most encouraging response to the problems of dying in America today. For many it has already answered a tremendous need.

RESOURCES AND SUPPORT

Books

Margaret Gold. *Life Support: Families Speak About Hospital, Hospice and Home Care for the Fatally Ill.* Mount Vernon, N.Y.: Institute for Consumer Policy Research, 1983. Full report, 200 pp.; Summary Report, 40 pp. Available from Institute for Policy Research, 256 Washington Street, Mount Vernon, NY 10553; (914) 667-9400.
[A study based on interviews with 40 families, comparing their experiences with terminal care in hospitals, at home, and with hospice programs. Summary Report describes the experiences of the families and the study's conclusion that there are advantages to hospice care for both families and patients.]

Thomas Andrew Gonda and John Ruark. *Dying Dignified: The Health Professional's Guide to Care.* Reading, Mass.: Addison-Wesley, 1984.
[Although aimed at the medical professional and clinician, this book is appropriate for laypeople. It covers a broad spectrum of subjects, including terminal care, psychological, emotional, and social aspects of hospice, institutional death, cultural factors, and more.]

Vincent Mor, David S. Greer, and Robert Kastenbaum, eds. *The Hospice Experiment.* Johns Hopkins Series in Contemporary Medicine and Public Health. Baltimore: Johns Hopkins University Press, 1988.
[An analysis of the National Hospice Study (1978–85), which examined hospice as an alternative in terminal care. Includes essays on the impact of hospice care on health care costs, the final weeks of life, and where patients die.]

Anne Munley. *The Hospice Alternative: A New Context for Death and Dying.* New York: Basic Books, 1986.
[An examination of the hospice experience written by a sociologist.]

National Consumers League. *A Consumer Guide to Hospice Care.* Washington, D.C.: National Consumers League, 1986. Available from the National Consumers League, 815 15th Street NW, Suite 516, Washington, DC 20005; (202) 639-8140.
[A booklet for families thinking about hospice care that includes a discussion of when to decide upon hospice and a checklist for consumers.]

Cicely Saunders and Mary Baines. *Living with Dying: The Management of Terminal Disease.* 2nd ed. New York: Oxford University Press, 1989.
[A slim text written for health care professionals detailing both the physical and psychological aspects of terminal pain and its management. Based on practice and research at St. Christopher's Hospice.]

Sandol Stoddard. *The Hospice Movement: A Better Way of Caring for the Dying.* Chelsea, Minn.: Scarborough House, 1977.
[One of the first books written for laypeople about the hospice approach toward care of the terminally ill; includes discussion of St. Christopher's Hospice in London and methods used for pain and symptom control.]

Paula White. *Home Care of the Hospice Patient: An Information/Instructional Booklet for Caregivers in the Home.* Norwalk, Conn.: Purdue Frederick Company, 1986. Available at no charge by written request only: Janet Barsa, Purdue Frederick Company, 100 Connecticut Avenue, Norwalk, CT 06856; (203) 853-0123.
[A thorough booklet covering such topics as family support systems, daily care, nutrition, breathing care, pain management, and the death experience in the home.]

Jack M. Zimmerman, M.D. *Hospice: Complete Care for the Terminally Ill.* 2nd ed. Baltimore: Urban and Schwartzberg, 1986.
[Written for caregivers in a question-and-answer format.]

Books Containing Related Information

Robert N. Brown, with Legal Counsel for the Elderly. *The Rights of Older Persons.* 2nd ed., American Civil Liberties Union Handbooks. Carbondale, Ill.: Southern University Press, 1989.
[Includes discussion of Medicare coverage for hospices and home care.]

Jean Crichton. *The Age Care Sourcebook: A Resource Guide for the Aging and Their Families.* New York: Simon & Schuster, Fireside Books, 1987.
[Contains a clear explanation of Medicare and Medicaid programs and reimbursements. Also includes a discussion of hospice and advice on how to choose a hospice program.]

James Halpern. *Helping Your Aging Parents: A Practical Guide for Adult Children.* New York: Fawcett Crest, 1988.
[Includes a brief discussion of hospice care for a dying parent.]

Ernest Morgan. *Dealing Creatively with Death: A Manual of Death Education and Simple Burial.* 11th ed., rev. and expanded. Edited by Jennifer Morgan. Burnsville, N.C.: Celo Press, 1988. Available in bookstores or from Celo Press, 1901 Hannah Branch Road, Burnsville, NC 28714; (704) 675-4925.
[Includes a discussion of hospice.]

John A. Robertson. *The Rights of the Critically Ill.* Rev. ed. American Civil Liberties Union Handbooks. New York: Bantam, 1983. Available from the American Civil Liberties Union, 132 West 43rd Street, New York, NY 10036; (212) 944-9800.
[Includes a chapter on the rights of those in hospice programs.]

Harry Van Bommel. *Choices: For People Who Have a Terminal Illness, Their Families and Caregivers.* Toronto: NC Press Limited, 1990; distributed in the United States by Seven Hills Book Distributors. Available through Seven Hills Books, 49 Central Avenue, Cincinnati, OH 45202; 1-800-545-2005.
[Includes practical advice on hospice. Covers Canada, the United Kingdom, and the United States.]

Hannelore Wass, Felix M. Berardo, and Robert Neimeyer, eds. *Dying: Facing the Facts.* 2nd ed. Series in Death Education, Aging, and Health Care. Washington: Harper & Taylor, Hemisphere Publishing, 1988.
[This textbook is useful for both professionals and laypeople; includes hospice care and an analysis of institutional dying.]

Agencies/Service Organizations
Children's Hospice International
700 Princess Street
Suite 3
Alexandria, VA 22314
800-24-CHILD
(703) 684-0330 (in Virginia)

An information clearinghouse for health care professionals, support groups, and families involved with care of the terminally ill child. They will respond to telephone inquiries and make referrals during business hours. Offers many publications and audiovisual aids on topics such as hospice care, home health care, and pain management. One such is D. Gay Moldow and Ida M. Martinson's "Home Care for Seriously Ill Children: A Manual for Parents," a very helpful manual.

Compassion Book Service
216 Via Monte
Walnut Creek, CA 94598
(415) 933-0830
Distributes books concerned with various aspects of death and dying, including home care and hospice. Their catalog is available at no charge.

Hospice Association of America
519 C Street, NE
Washington, DC 20002
(202) 547-7424
A trade association affiliated with the National Association for Home Care. Publishes a directory of hospice programs.

Hospice Education Institute
5 Essex Square
P.O. Box 713
Essex, CT 06426
1-800-331-1620
(203) 767-1620 (in Connecticut and Alaska)
Organization whose services include offering advice and assistance to educators and those involved with hospice care. Also operates Hospice Link (see below).

Hospice Link
5 Essex Square
P.O. Box 713
Essex, CT 06426
1-800-331-1620
(203) 767-1620 (in Connecticut and Alaska)
A toll-free referral service offering information about hospice care and local hospice programs. They do not offer medical advice or psychological counseling; however, their staff will provide limited informal support to callers with difficulties related to terminal illness. A program of the Hospice Education Institute (see above).

National Hospice Organization
1901 North Moore Street
Suite 901
Arlington, VA 22209
(703) 243-5900
The predominant national organization serving as an advocacy group and clearinghouse for information on hospice and hospice care for both health care professionals and laypeople. They can answer questions and make local referrals from their comprehensive "Guide to the Nation's Hospices" (also available in many libraries), which lists hospice programs and health care professionals. The NHO also provides a publications list and free literature on hospice care, including the Health Care Financing Administration's booklet "Hospice Benefits Under Medicare."

National Institute for Jewish Hospice
P.O. Box 48025
Los Angeles, CA 90048
(213) 467-7423
Offers toll-free referral and guidance concerning the availability of hospice, hospital, and home care services (1-800-446-4448 outside of California; 213-HOSPICE in California). Other services include publications, research, and education programs.

In the Aftermath

III

8

Taking Care of the Dead

Let your eye go to the sun; your life to the wind; by the meritorious acts that
you have done, go to heaven, and then to the earth again; or, resort to the
waters, if you feel at home there; remain in the herbs with the bodies you
propose to take.

Ancient Vedic funeral chant

Before the turn of the century, when someone died, their family and
friends were often directly involved in the entire process. They were
usually present at the time of death, they stayed with the body while
other family members gathered, they moved the body when it was
time to do so, and frequently they prepared the body for burial.

Those most incapacitated by the death were supported in their
grief, while extended family and community members handled the
tasks of disposition—building a coffin, digging a grave, transporting
the body. Thus, most adults had had some indirect experience of
death by the time they were required to cope with it directly. They
had seen someone die, perhaps even buried the body; they knew
what needed to be done in the wake of death and had probably
helped to do it at one time or another.

Today we do not learn about this tangible aspect of death as we grow up within the family circle. We are unfamiliar with basic disposition procedures and are even less equipped to deal with them.

Today, when we die in a hospital (as most people do), orderlies or nursing attendants will remove the tubes, catheters, and soiled dressings (as well as jewelry, a wedding ring, or religious items), bathe the body, wrap it in a mortuary gown (crossing the arms and loosely pinning the sleeves of the gown together to hold them in place), attach an ID tag at the wrists, and fold a mortuary sheet diagonally around the body, "snug but not too tightly."

The body is then lifted onto a false-bottom gurney with a shelf that hides the body. When draped with a sheet, the gurney looks empty. Thus camouflaged, the cart is wheeled through the back halls of the hospital to an inconspicuous door, usually in the basement.

Some hospitals have small morgues; others have holding rooms— empty but for the stainless-steel lockers in the wall. The body is placed in a refrigerated locker drawer, headfirst. Another ID tag is then attached to the ankle or toe. The drawer is closed, and a third ID tag is slipped into the nameplate on the door of the unit. The body will remain there until it is picked up by the funeral provider to be prepared for disposition.

THE GIFT OF PREPLANNING

The period immediately following death will be considerably easier for you if the deceased preplanned* for disposition and/or commemoration. If a Letter of Instruction (or other communication) was prepared, find it and follow the directions to the best of your ability.

Find out whether the deceased prepaid for disposition, a funeral, or both—in part or in full. If the deceased purchased a burial plot or membership in a memorial society or direct-disposition firm, the letter should include the name and location of the provider, any contracts or signed agreements, and in the case of a burial plot, the plot number and the deed.

Call the firm identified by the deceased. The provider should have

---

*The word *preplanned* is used here to mean directions left by the deceased for either bodily disposition, commemoration, or both.

a record of the plans made for both disposition and services. If the deceased discussed these plans with you, you'll have a real sense of what was wanted and will be able to guide the funeral director or provider.

WHEN THERE IS NO PLAN

When there is no plan, we tend to rely on the funeral industry. This is not surprising. The funeral industry is prepared to handle every aspect of disposition and commemoration. In many ways, this is helpful. Since we don't know what to do and we don't know how to do it, we are grateful to find someone who will "take care of everything."

However, if we totally relinquish our options, we can wind up paying a lot of money for services that do not fill our needs. All too often this approach can result in an artificial experience that does little to commemorate the deceased or acknowledge the survivors. It can remove all sense of control, reinforcing a feeling of helplessness in the face of death. And it can cost a bundle. (The standard adult funeral averages between $3,000 and $5,000.)

In most cultures throughout history, the function of disposition and commemoration has been performed by the family, the community, the clan or tribe, the church or religious institution, or the government or the state. In our culture it is performed by profit-making businesses. This makes for a delicate situation. As described by one writer on the subject,

> . . . rarely do the emotional conditions in which funeral services are purchased allow for such coolheadedness or presence of mind that the bereaved can simply walk away and go elsewhere to compare prices. In some localities, there may be only one mortician to serve the entire community. Even in the best of circumstances, the customer may be hard put to find suitable alternatives. When a death has already occurred, it can be too late to start investigating the options.[1]

This, of course, is the problem. In the aftermath of death, few people are ready to go out and comparison shop. However, even at this point, there *are* some things you can do that will make a big difference. Although you may have just a few days, you *can* choose rather than simply acquiesce. This chapter covers the information you will need to make good decisions about disposition and commemoration after a death has occurred.

IMMEDIATE REQUIREMENTS

Generally speaking, the tasks requiring attention after a death can be divided chronologically between what must be done immediately or very soon after death and what can be done as the weeks unfold. Of immediate concern are matters of disposition, anatomical gifts, and commemoration. Then, as time goes on, the business side of things will need to be managed—including claiming benefits, settling the estate, and dealing with banks, insurance companies, government agencies, and the like. (See chapter 9.)

Most immediately, if you are responsible for someone who has died, you will need to answer two questions:

1. How do you wish to dispose of the body?
2. What kind of commemoration will be most appropriate for the deceased and most meaningful to the survivors?

In Most Cases
If death has occurred in a hospital or nursing home, you will be asked to provide the name of a funeral parlor, direct-disposition firm, or someone with authority to transfer the body for disposition. A staff member will call the provider you select, who in turn will pick up the body and arrange for final disposition.

Most health care institutions are not equipped to store a body for any length of time. They will expect you to make arrangements promptly. If you are unsure about how you want to handle disposition, you may feel pressured to make decisions hastily. Try to avoid being rushed. It is not unreasonable to demand a few extra hours in which to make arrangements. (No institution is permitted to release or dispose of a body without the consent of the next of kin.)

If you need more time, one option may be to find a funeral director who will transfer and hold the body temporarily, allowing you to talk with family and friends and come to a considered decision. If you do this, be sure the funeral director understands that at least for the time being you are paying only to have the body stored in the mortuary.

If the individual died at home, chances are you will have given some thought to the whole idea of options and may even have made some decisions or arrangements. In any event, the first order of business will be to move the body from the place of death to the place of disposition. The arrangements you make will depend on your choice for disposition.

IMMEDIATE CHOICES

Ernest Morgan, author of *Dealing Creatively with Death,* one of the most respected books on this subject, has set forth a list of options for body disposition. He places the alternatives in order of approximate cost, starting with the least expensive and ending with the most expensive.

1. Immediate removal to a medical school, followed by a memorial service. (Since the body must have been bequeathed to, and accepted by, a medical school, this option usually requires planning ahead.)
2. Immediate cremation (also called direct disposition), followed by a memorial service. There may also be a commitment service (a brief ceremony accompanying final disposition) at the crematory chapel, if desired.
3. Immediate earth burial (also called direct disposition), followed by a memorial service. There may also be a graveside commitment service, if desired.
4. A funeral service in the presence of the body, followed by removal to a medical school.
5. A funeral service in the presence of the body, followed by cremation.
6. A funeral service in the presence of the body, followed by earth burial.[2]

Burial at sea is an option if circumstances permit, as is burial by the family, a special nonprofessional group, or a religious organization. (See "Caring for Your Own" in this chapter.)

FINDING A PROVIDER

Arrangements for disposition and commemoration can be made through a direct-disposition company, a nonprofit memorial or funeral society, a commercial funeral home, or on your own. Most people choose funeral providers on the basis of proximity, religious or ethnic affiliation, and recommendations from others. There is a substantial difference in cost from one type of disposition to another and from one provider to another.

Direct-Disposition Firm

A direct-disposition firm provides immediate burial or cremation, eliminating embalming, viewing, and other features of the conventional funeral. They will transfer the body from the place of death directly to the place of burial or cremation. Most will handle the paperwork needed to obtain and file death certificates and cremation permits. Many are membership organizations providing the least expensive fees to those who join before need; they also make services available to nonmembers at higher rates.

Sometimes direct-disposition groups will advertise on the obituary pages of the newspaper or in the yellow pages of the telephone book. The oldest of these companies are The Telophase Society and The Neptune Society. You may try calling them to see if they have any chapters or affiliations near you.

Membership fees are usually nominal (around $25 or so). Costs for services at death range from about $200 to under $1,000. (For more information on direct disposition see chapter 2.)

Memorial Society

Memorial societies are cooperatively run membership organizations. They are also called funeral societies in some parts of the country. These nonprofit consumer groups provide information and advice on how best to deal with disposition in your city, town, or area. They do what most people don't have the time or the inclination to do themselves: They compare prices and services and determine the most economical and efficient means of managing both disposition and memorial commemoration. In some regions, memorial societies have negotiated contracts or agreements with local funeral directors on behalf of their members, providing group rates and other special benefits.

Some memorial societies will allow immediate posthumous memberships to those acting on behalf of a recently deceased person. At the very least, they can provide advice and information on making local funeral arrangements or recommend one of the mortuaries with which they do business. In all likelihood, a funeral home recommended by a local memorial society will afford reasonable prices and fair practices.

Check the yellow pages under "Memorial Societies" or "Funeral Services" or contact the Continental Association of Funeral and Memorial Societies for the name of a group near you. (See listings at the end of this chapter.)

Prices obtained through a memorial society can be as much as 50 percent or 75 percent less than the cost of dealing directly with a conventional funeral home. (For more information on memorial societies, see chapter 2.)

Funeral Home or Mortuary
A commercial business selling services and products for disposition and commemoration, the funeral home (or mortuary or funeral parlor) is today's most commonly used provider. Operated by a funeral director, the home may or may not be associated with a cemetery. (A cemetery is often an autonomous business requiring a separate transaction for burial.)

A funeral director is licensed and equipped to provide everything from simple direct disposition to a complete funeral ceremony, procession, and interment.

When you need a funeral home, ask for recommendations from friends, family, or clergy. Funeral homes advertise in the yellow pages and sometimes in the newspapers.

Costs vary greatly depending on region, types of services and products chosen, and whether or not there is any local competition. Average cost for services ranges from about $2,000 to $10,000.

THE TRADITIONAL FUNERAL

The word *funeral* is used to denote a ceremony that takes place with the body present, in either an open or closed coffin (as opposed to a *memorial service,* which is a commemorative gathering in which the body is not present). A funeral, followed by earth burial, is the customary commemoration and disposition practiced in the United States today.

The traditional funeral is the hallmark of the professional funeral home, which will:

Embalm the body and prepare it for viewing (makeup, clothing, etc.).

Provide the casket of your choice.

Provide facilities for funeral or memorial services (or viewing room).

Coordinate the service (with clergy, musicians, florists, pallbearers, and any other assistance you may require).

Provide a hearse, limousines, and any other transportation necessary.

Provide memorial cards, register books, etc.

Refer you to a cemetery (if one is not associated directly with the funeral home) and advise you on purchasing a cemetery plot, vault or liner, headstone, and other cemetery services.

Provide a funeral procession to the cemetery and a committal service at the grave site.

The funeral director can also help in preparing or placing death notices and obituaries.

Placing the entire undertaking in the hands of a competent, sensitive professional funeral director can be the most convenient way to handle the needs of disposition. Another option is working with a funeral director and choosing some of the services offered and eliminating others. Items and procedures you may wish to consider separately include:

EMBALMING Embalming is a process whereby preservative and disinfectant solution (formaldehyde) is injected into the arteries and body cavities, replacing blood and body fluids. This procedure preserves the body long enough to allow for open-casket viewing, if that is desired. It does not preserve the body indefinitely.

Despite common assumptions, embalming is not required by law except in certain special circumstances—if the body is to be transported long distance by common carrier, stored for a length of time, or, in some states, if death was due to a communicable disease. Some traditions (including orthodox Judaism, where earth burial is usually carried out within twenty-four hours) oppose embalming on religious grounds.

Refrigeration can often be used as an acceptable and legal substitute for maintaining a body over a period of days, although some funeral directors will not arrange a viewing without first embalming the body.

An open-casket viewing may be encouraged by a funeral director on the premise that it helps to advance the mourning process. While some bereavement specialists agree, others argue otherwise. The decision to view the body (and to embalm) should be based on the personal wishes of the survivors.

Embalming is one of the most expensive procedures provided by funeral homes. If state law, or any other circumstance, mandates embalming (or the purchase of any other funeral item or service), the funeral director must inform you and attach a written statement to this effect on your itemized bill.

The Federal Trade Commission Funeral Rule requires funeral providers to "seek to obtain express approval before embalming the deceased for a fee." However, if you do not wish the body to be embalmed, you should make a point of informing the funeral director immediately.

CASKETS   Most funeral homes have a wide variety of caskets available, ranging from deluxe models of mahogany, copper, or bronze, lined with plush velvet or satin material, which can cost as much as $10,000 or more, to a simple pine coffin for $250.

Choosing a casket is a personal matter based on such variables as individual taste, tradition, beliefs, and budget considerations. The manner in which the casket will be displayed, if at all, may also be a factor. For instance, if, during a service, it will be covered by a flag or a pall (a cloth covering used in some funeral ceremonies), it may hardly be seen.

The casket is often the most expensive item purchased in a traditional funeral. Since funeral directors rely on the sale of caskets to pay a large part of their overhead expenses, most would understandably prefer to sell a higher-priced model than an inexpensive box. You can, however, obtain a plain wooden casket for hundreds rather than thousands of dollars. If you set a firm limit, most funeral directors will try to accommodate you.

Although the FTC's Funeral Rule requires funeral providers to display their least expensive caskets just as prominently as those in the higher range, you may need to be persistent if you want to purchase an inexpensive casket. If the funeral director appears reluctant to show you the economical models or does not have them on display, ask to see the manufacturer's catalog. This catalog will have a complete listing of all available models—expensive, moderate, and inexpensive.

A casket, no matter how durable or costly, will not preserve or protect the body. If the body is to be directly cremated, no casket is required. By law you have the option of purchasing an unfinished wooden box or an "alternative container" (made of heavy cardboard or composition materials). (See "Cremation" section in this chapter.)

Additional Services Provided by Funeral Homes

PALLBEARERS   Many funeral homes provide staff to serve as pallbearers (people who carry the casket from the chapel or funeral home to the hearse and from the hearse to the grave site or crematory). However, families often prefer to name pallbearers from among relatives and friends as a designation of honor. (In some locations, such as New York City, paid professional pallbearers are required by the pallbearers union unless you can obtain a waiver. If this is a problem in your area, check with the funeral director for alternatives.)

HONORARIA AND OTHER PROFESSIONAL FEES   You can pay honoraria to the clergy or other officiants directly or through the funeral director. If you don't know how much to give, the funeral director can help you determine an appropriate amount. If you have engaged the funeral home to hire musicians or other professionals, they usually add a surcharge to the cost of any cash fees or payments made on your behalf. The FTC's Funeral Rule requires that you be informed of this fact.

ADDITIONAL CASH-ADVANCE ITEMS   The funeral director may also advance payment on items such as flowers, memorial cards, signature books, or other memorabilia. These should be listed and agreed to before arrangements are finalized. If a surcharge is added for this service, it must be disclosed.

A NOTE ABOUT FLOWERS   Many people prefer that the money that is often spent on floral gifts and tributes be contributed to a particular charity, church, or nonprofit organization instead. If this is your preference, you should make it known in any printed death notice or funeral announcement.

CEMETERIES AND MEMORIAL PARKS

Earth Burial

Interment in the earth is the most common form of disposition in the United States today. The cost of a cemetery plot can average from $500 to $5,000 or more, depending on the particular cemetery and the region of the country. There are small rural communities in which a plot in the town graveyard costs as little as $25 for residents, while exclusive metropolitan cemeteries may charge five figures.

If the deceased is a military veteran, free burial in a national cemetery is an entitled benefit. Call the Veterans Administration for further information. (See listings at the end of this chapter.)

In addition to the plot itself, you will also probably need to purchase a grave liner or burial vault, required by many cemeteries on the premise that it maintains the grounds and keeps the earth from sinking around the grave. Grave liners are generally cheaper than burial vaults, and both are usually less expensive when purchased directly from the cemetery rather than through a funeral director. (This is also true of other purchases, such as memorial stones or monuments, which tend to cost less when you buy them directly from the monument dealer or the cemetery rather than through the funeral home.) Cost of liners and vaults may range from $200 to $500. (Some vaults, supposedly designed to provide more protection, can cost considerably more.)

Additional cemetery charges include fees for opening and closing the grave and the "setting" or installation of a memorial marker. Many cemeteries charge for what is called a "perpetual care fund" to maintain the grounds. This usually means mowing the lawn and does not include specific maintenance for particular memorials.

Total costs of earth burial generally range from $900 to $10,000, once again depending on the region, the cemetery, and the nature of the services provided.

Important Note: A cemetery plot—whether for an individual, a couple, or a family—is one of the most commonly *pre*purchased items in the funeral industry. If the deceased was a widow, for instance, she might have bought a plot next to the one where her husband had been interred. Be sure to find out if a burial plot has already been purchased.

Entombment
Another option is entombment, aboveground burial in a tomb or mausoleum. In some parts of the country this is done out of necessity because the ground-water level is too high to allow for routine earth burial. Usually, however, a mausoleum is the less customary choice, selected by families wishing to establish a significant and visible monument to the deceased or to the family name.

Most cemeteries sell mausoleums. The cost of aboveground burial is substantial, with mausoleum space beginning at $1,500 and going as high as the client will pay, depending on the materials chosen and the complexity of the design.

Monuments and Memorial Markers
Generally speaking, there are two types of graveyards: a *cemetery*—which usually permits the installation of upright memorial stones and statues; and a *memorial park*—which usually allows only flush markers or those that lay flat in the ground.

If it is important to you to erect an upright monument, check with the cemetery to be sure you'll be allowed to do so. You may also want to know if there are any restrictions on personal memorials, such as the placement of flowers or the lighting of candles at graveside. The cemetery should provide a printed information sheet describing their decoration policy and any other pertinent restrictions.

If the deceased was a veteran, the federal government will provide a free bronze or granite memorial marker. Contact your local Veterans Administration or ask your funeral director to obtain the marker for you.

CREMATION

Cremation is the most common form of disposition in a number of countries, including England, India, and Japan. In the United States the practice has increased steadily, and it is estimated that by the year 2000, nearly one-quarter of all disposition will be by means of cremation.

There are over 900 crematories in the United States. You can find one near you by asking a local funeral director or by looking in the yellow pages. As noted in the section on providers, direct-disposition firms offer cremation services at reasonable rates. These companies pick up the body, acquire permits and complete paperwork, cremate the body, and scatter the ashes (or return the ashes to the survivors, whichever you prefer).

In some states, 48 hours must pass between the time of death and the time of cremation to confirm that no autopsy need be performed. A cremation permit may be required. The funeral director or direct-disposition firm will take care of this for you.

If you plan to hold a memorial service at a later time, direct disposition can be a practical and economical choice. If you wish to have a funeral service with the body present, you will probably want to arrange for cremation through a funeral home or memorial society.

If you have chosen direct cremation, no casket is required. By law you have the option of purchasing an unfinished wooden box or an "alternative container" (made of heavy cardboard or composition materials). This is most appropriate if you are planning a memorial service at a later date. If, however, you wish to have a funeral with the body present, you will want to purchase a casket. Some providers offer rental caskets for this purpose, but you may find it is less expensive to purchase a simple coffin. (Some caskets, with vinyl or other plastic ingredients, are not accepted by crematories because they give off lethal gases when burned. A funeral director will help you ensure that the casket you choose is suitable for cremation.)

In the crematory, the body is placed in a retort, where extremely high temperatures reduce it to a few pounds of ash and bone fragments called cremains.

The cost of cremation itself is generally between $50 and $200. However, if arranged through a funeral home, total costs can range from about $800 to several thousand dollars, depending on the nature of all services purchased (transporting the body, casket, funeral service, etc.). Direct-disposition firms generally charge anywhere from $250 to $900, again depending on the region and the services provided.

Urns and Ashes

The ashes can be kept by the family, buried in a cemetery or an urn garden, placed in a columbarium (a building with walls of recessed niches for storing urns), or scattered on land or at sea.

It is common to have cremains placed in an urn, to keep or to bury, or to transport before scattering. Urns come in a variety of materials, styles, and sizes and vary greatly in price, costing anywhere from $25 to thousands of dollars.

Some states have laws governing where cremains can be scattered, but they are difficult to enforce. If you are concerned, you might ask the funeral director or direct-disposition firm to provide you with information about your local laws and any permits required.

Some people prefer to scatter ashes at sea or to the wind. For others it is important to place the ashes in a particular spot to which they can return. The funeral industry has developed what are called "scattering gardens" for this purpose, usually located in or near a cemetery or crematorium. Another alternative is to store the urn in a columbarium niche. Most crematoria offer this option.

There are those who prefer to bury the urn in a cemetery or other burial plot, which allows for the survivors to return to a grave site where they can leave personal memorials or spend commemorative time. Of course, this adds the expense of the plot and attendant costs, including opening and closing the grave, the purchase of a vaultlike container in which the urn will be placed, and a memorial marker.

SPECIAL CIRCUMSTANCES

In the Case of Anatomical Donations

If permission has been granted for organ donation, the harvesting procedure begins immediately after death is pronounced. The operation may take anywhere from two to ten hours, depending on the particular techniques used and the organs involved. After the procedure is completed, the body will be sutured, washed, and prepared for disposition, as above.

If the body has been donated to a medical school, your responsibilities are limited and fairly straightforward. Find the certificate or form verifying the gift, call the institution (which may or may not provide transportation), and confirm the donation. If the body is to be sent by common carrier or if you wish to have a funeral service with the body present, a funeral director should be informed immediately and put in touch with the school for instructions. (Special embalming procedures are necessary, as ordinary embalming makes a body unsuitable for donation.)

In the case of anatomical gifts (either organs or whole body), action must be taken expeditiously. Delay can disqualify the donation. (For more on anatomical donation, see chapter 2.)

In the Case of Autopsy

An autopsy is the examination and dissection of a dead body. It is done to determine how and why a person died. The word *autopsy* comes from the Greek word that means "to see for oneself." During an autopsy, the body is dissected, the organs are removed, weighed, and examined, and various chemical and microscopic analyses are made of tissues and body fluids.

The procedure has its antecedents in the earliest history of Western medicine, dissection being a primary means of learning about the body and disease. It has been used regularly since the nineteenth century as a diagnostic tool, a teaching process, and a method of testing and research. In the mid-1940s, autopsies were performed in 50 percent of all deaths. However, as a result of changes in the way in which medicine is taught and practiced, along with the development of technologies such as magnetic resonance imaging, fiberoptic endoscopes, ultrasound, and nuclear medicine (which allow direct viewing of internal organs), the number of autopsies routinely performed has declined considerably over the last few decades. In 1989, the Joint Commission on Accreditation of Hospitals adopted a policy encouraging health care institutions to increase the number of autopsies performed as a way of assessing quality of care.

In some cases, a physician may approach a family to ask to have a postmortem autopsy performed as a way of providing specific answers about the death of a patient or to learn more about a disease or the treatments attempted. In the past, patterns detected through autopsies have helped establish connections between cancer and cigarette smoking and have advanced the understanding of the multitude of complications produced by AIDS.

Unless required by law, autopsies are performed almost always at the discretion of the family. You can deny authorization entirely if the prospect of an autopsy disturbs or offends you, or you can place conditions on your permission. You may choose to grant permission for a limited autopsy, in which you authorize the removal and study only of certain organs (for instance, those most likely to have been affected by disease).

Sometimes an autopsy is required by law. The types of deaths that come under this jurisdiction include the following:*

1. Deaths resulting from criminal violence or casualty
2. Deaths due to suicide
3. Persons dying suddenly when in apparent health
4. Unattended deaths
5. Deaths occurring in a correctional facility
6. Deaths occurring in any other suspicious or unusual manner

In some situations, you might want to consider taking the initiative to ask for an autopsy yourself. A committee of the College of American Pathologists recommended that families should consider having an autopsy performed whenever someone dies in the following circumstances:

- When doctors have not made a firm diagnosis

- When there are concerns about a hereditary disease that might affect other members of the family

- When there are concerns about the possible spread of a contagious disease

- When the cause of death could affect insurance settlements, such as policies that cover cancer or that grant double indemnity for accidental death

- When environmental or workplace hazards are suspected

- When the death follows use of an experimental drug or device, new procedure, or unusual therapy

- When the death occurs in a nursing home and the quality of care is questioned

- When the death is during or after childbirth

*As listed in *Autopsy Manual,* New York Academy of Medicine, Office of Public Health, New York, 5th ed., 1988, p. 12.

- When death follows a dental or surgical procedure done for diagnostic purposes and the case does not come under the jurisdiction of a medical examiner or coroner

- When death comes suddenly or under mysterious circumstances from apparently natural causes but the case does not come under the jurisdiction of a medical examiner or coroner[3]

If you decide to request an autopsy, check with the hospital or physician to find out what procedures you will need to follow. If the patient dies at home or in a nursing home, for example, you may need to arrange for transportation to the hospital or county morgue, where the autopsy will be performed.

When an autopsy is mandated by law or requested by a physician or a medical institution, there is no charge to the family of the deceased.

TRANSPORTING THE BODY LONG DISTANCE

If someone dies in one place and is to be buried a long distance away, there are additional complications and expenses. If the body is to be shipped by sea, air, or rail, a funeral director will invariably be needed. (See the following section for information on transporting a body across international boundaries.)

Embalming is mandatory if a body is to be transported by common carrier (airlines, railroads, ships). If cremation is an option, it should be seriously considered, as it is both cheaper and easier to transport cremains.

If the deceased belonged to a memorial or funeral society but died away from home, check first with the local society to which s/he belonged. They can connect you with a memorial society near the place of death that will provide you with assistance and low-cost services.

You will probably need to employ the services of two separate funeral directors: one at the place of death to prepare the body for transport and one at the destination to receive the body and arrange for disposition. (Most airlines will release a body only to a licensed funeral director.) Be sure you aren't charged twice for the same services or talked into buying two caskets—one for shipping and one for the funeral ceremony—unless, of course, you *want* two caskets.

The cost of sending a body by air freight varies from one region to another. Delta Airlines, for example, charged a $262.50 flat fee for shipping a coffin (price quoted in 1990). Some airlines offer a discount fare to a passenger traveling with the deceased. (By law, no one needs to accompany the body.)

Altogether, the costs of preparing the body, shipping, services, and handling fees for long-distance funeral arrangements can run upward of $2,000.

WHEN DEATH HAPPENS IN A FOREIGN COUNTRY

If a U.S. citizen has died in a foreign country, contact the U.S. consulate. If the deceased was carrying detailed disposition instructions with his or her passport at the time of death (a rare but not unwise precaution), the consul will carry out those wishes as closely as local law and custom allow. If there were no instructions, the consul can help arrange for disposition of the body according to the survivors' wishes. They will provide a "report of death," which is the equivalent of a death certificate, and can act as the "provisional conservator" of any property involved.

If you wish to bring the deceased home, transcontinental shipping requires that the body be embalmed (a procedure not readily available in many countries) and that it be packed in a hermetically sealed coffin with an additional outside shipping case. This costs a great deal—several thousand dollars at minimum. Cremation is an alternative (if facilities are available), and shipping the ashes home is much less expensive.

Or you might choose to have the deceased buried according to local practices in the country where s/he died. The options that will be open to you will not be entirely under your control. Many countries, for instance, do not practice any embalming of bodies, while others—chiefly Islamic countries—do not have cremation facilities.

COMMEMORATION

Human beings have always marked death with ceremony as a means of honoring the dead, respecting the grief-stricken, and acknowledging the loss of a community member. Today social psychologists see commemorative ceremony as necessary to the healing process after loss has occurred.

Different cultures and traditions mark death in widely varying ways. Some people party (the New Orleans jazz funeral, the Irish wake); some set aside a defined period of time in which to mourn (the Jewish custom of sitting shiva) or to observe ceremony (the Buddhist practice of forty-nine days of prayer between death and rebirth).

The inclination of our culture toward a more secular approach to ritual and ceremony has led to a decrease in some of the more traditional orthodox practices of mourning. However, grief and bereavement counselors, and those professionals who deal with death and dying, find that the lack of any ceremony can have detrimental effects on those left behind. It is clearly very important and helpful to survivors to have some form of commemoration or ritual that marks the fact of the death, publicly acknowledges their loss, and provides the opportunity for support and comfort.

Choices

The three most common types of ceremony are:

1. *A funeral*—a ceremony held in the presence of the body
2. *A memorial service*—a ceremony held without the body present
3. *A committal service*—a brief ceremony accompanying final disposition, either at graveside or in a crematory chapel (generally reserved for family and close friends)

Personal, cultural, and religious beliefs will, of course, play a large part in making commemoration or memorial choices. All of the above ceremonies can be as religious or secular in tone and content as is desired. Other considerations include the needs of the survivors. Is a large public ceremony appropriate? Or is an intimate gathering of family and close friends preferred? It can be possible to accommodate both needs by holding a private funeral followed by a more public memorial service or, alternatively, through a public funeral, followed by a private committal service.

Traditional Funeral

In the course of the traditional funeral, a member of the clergy or a family representative will usually give a eulogy or speak about the life of the deceased. If it is a religious ceremony, the accustomed rituals and observances can be followed or adapted to personal preference. Even the most traditional religious ceremonies, although they involve well-established protocol, generally afford some room to add personal touches (choosing music and readings that reflect your own tastes and the deceased's values).

Planned in conjunction with disposition, the funeral is usually arranged by a funeral director.

Memorial Service

A memorial service differs from a traditional funeral in that it tends to focus more on the personality, character, spirit, values, and social relationships of the deceased. It is also significantly less expensive.

Usually more informal than a funeral, a memorial service can afford family members and friends the opportunity to get together and share thoughts and memories about the deceased. It can include organized testimony, spontaneous reminiscences, or both. (And since the body will not be present, you can plan a memorial service at a time and place convenient to most mourners.)

Memorial services are frequently planned by someone close to the deceased but not necessarily in the immediate family. They are often arranged without the assistance of a funeral director, but if you need some guidance, a funeral director can be helpful.

In *Dealing Creatively with Death*, Ernest Morgan includes advice for making a service personally meaningful. He suggests including any or all of the following in the memorial service you are planning: religious ritual, instrumental music, singing, prayers, readings, formal biographical remarks and informal reminiscences about the deceased, films, slides, and pictures, a moment of silence, and personal contributions from any mourners who wish to share thoughts or memories.

Other books with good information, advice, and examples include *The Wheel of Life and Death* by Philip Kapleau and *Giving Sorrow Words* by Candy Lightner and Nancy Hathaway. (See listings at the end of this chapter.)

Other Kinds of Commemoration
Ultimately, commemoration can be anything that you want it to be. Sometimes the most meaningful memorial is something simple and unconventional, such as planting flowers or a tree in honor of the deceased or giving a dinner party, accomplishing a goal, or dedicating work in his or her name.

Such gestures can be made at any time. It may be more likely that a truly significant commemoration will take place a substantial period of time after the death, after the initial period of shock, confusion, or sadness. There is no time limit on acknowledging your feelings. Your options for memorial or commemoration, for gathering together to mark the death and to receive and give emotional support, may be as personalized or as unique as you would want it to be.

MONEY

In arranging for disposition and commemoration through a funeral professional, you can spend a very substantial amount of money, or you can achieve a dignified disposition and memorial for as little as several hundred dollars.

It is often helpful to have a limit in mind as to how much you can spend. Avoid trying to overcompensate for the grief you feel by spending more money than you can afford on a funeral you don't really want. You can express your love for the deceased just as well— and often even more powerfully—through a thoughtful eulogy or a moving memorial service.

Help with Funeral Expenses
Some government benefit programs, such as Social Security and the Veterans Administration, offer funeral benefits as may some insurance policies provided through the workplace or a union or fraternal organization. The amount of these benefits is usually fairly small (several hundred dollars in the case of government), but they can be paid directly to the funeral provider and help offset disposition costs.

Survivors must take the initiative and apply for these benefits. They are not automatically forthcoming, nor will the agency paying the benefit notify you that it exists unless you inquire. Most funeral directors will handle the paperwork involved in applying for death benefits if payment is made directly to them. (See chapter 9 for further information on death benefits.)

Who Pays?

In most cases, when the cost of a funeral exceeds the available benefits or if there are no benefits, the balance will be charged to the estate of the deceased or to the survivor responsible for making funeral and disposition arrangements. A funeral director, unless known to the family, may ask you to guarantee payment by cosigning the funeral bill. If you do sign, you are accepting responsibility for any costs that exceed the financial resources of the estate.

THE FTC FUNERAL RULE

In 1984 the Federal Trade Commission adopted what has become known as the Funeral Rule, which regulates methods of pricing and disclosure. (Although called the "funeral" rule, it applies to burial and cremation as well as to the funeral ceremony itself and is intended to regulate the entire funeral industry.) The FTC Rule requires funeral providers to give you any price information you request over the telephone. This can be very helpful if you are trying to get an idea of the range of prices charged by several different providers.

The Funeral Rule also requires providers to give you a copy of a complete price list, including the funeral home's entire range of caskets offered, before you make any arrangement. When you have made your choices, the funeral director is supposed to give you an itemized statement showing the price on each service. Thus, you can see how much everything will cost altogether before committing yourself to any single purchase. You can then delete or add goods or services as you wish, and before signing an agreement.

If you are told that a particular item (such as a vault or liner) must be purchased because of a legal, cemetery, or crematory requirement, you are entitled to a written statement citing the requirement that compels that purchase.

Dealing with Funeral Directors

Many people, especially when beset by severe grief, are extremely grateful for the kind of professional help offered by a funeral director. And there is no question that this help can be essential at the time it's needed. But sometimes a funeral director will try to persuade you that a certain item or service is a basic necessity when, in fact, for you it is not. The funeral business is, after all, a business.

Don't let a funeral director manipulate you into spending more than you want to spend—or even worse, more than you can afford to spend. Don't be talked into staging an elaborate funeral if you find it distasteful or unnecessary.

Complaints

If you have any problem in dealing with a member of the funeral industry, you do have some means of recourse. First, try to talk with the funeral director, explain your concern, and see if you can reach an amicable resolution. If this strategy fails to yield satisfactory results, you can call on other agencies for help.

If you believe a funeral director has behaved unethically, failed to fulfill professional responsibilities, misrepresented the value of merchandise, failed to inform you fully of the costs involved in a funeral, or violated the FTC's Funeral Rule, contact the Funeral Service Consumer Assistance Program (FSCAP). FSCAP is an independent arbitration board made up of consumer advocates who will hold an impartial hearing reviewing your complaint or dispute with any funeral provider. If the board decides in your favor, your concerns will be redressed. (See listings at the end of this chapter for further information.)

In most states there is an agency called the state funeral board that oversees the industry and consumer interests. Try contacting them. If you are unable to resolve your complaint, try sending a letter to your state's attorney general, the local Better Business Bureau, or to local, state, or national consumer protection agencies. Lisa Carlson's book, *Caring for Your Own Dead,* includes helpful advice on protecting your interests.

PRACTICAL HELP FROM FRIENDS AND FAMILY

Even when death is not a surprise or comes as a welcome relief, it is difficult to deal with the demanding tasks of disposition, funerals, and memorial arrangements. If death is sudden, these demands may seem overwhelming. This is a time when assistance from family members and close friends can be a real blessing.

If you can, get help in making disposition decisions from someone who is not so immediately affected by the death and is more likely to see the practical side of the matter. A friend may provide a more detached point of view and less clouded judgment. S/he can help you to consider your choices among various funeral providers and will probably feel less awkward than you might in comparing prices and asking pertinent questions. In addition to the emotional support a good friend or relative can provide, s/he can help you to make prudent financial decisions at a time when that may be difficult to do on your own. Don't be afraid to ask for help directly. Most people are eager to do something concrete and really mean it when they say, "Let me know if there is anything I can do." Let them know.

When Survivors Disagree

Sometimes disagreements over disposition preferences arise, or over the question of who has the right, or responsibility, to make decisions and arrangements. Legally the next of kin (usually defined in order as the legal spouse, adult children, both parents, adult siblings, and then, in lieu of kin, a guardian or medical authorities) has control over disposition.

If possible, talk over decisions with members of the family by telephone or in person in an attempt to arrive at a consensus about disposition and commemoration. If arguments arise *before* finalizing funeral arrangements, they can often be settled by mutual compromise.

If the deceased left written instructions, there is usually less room for argument. The purpose of a Letter of Instruction or of directions left in a will is to inform survivors about any contracts, agreements, and prepaid arrangements that have been made and/or to serve as a guide to funeral preferences. In most cases, survivors will be grateful to have this guidance. Occasionally, questions or challenges may arise.

In some states, disposition instructions are legally binding on survivors. In others, they are not. Survivors are free to disregard directions if they are deemed unreasonable, excessively burdensome, or financially unrealistic. (Instructions left by the deceased, even if they are bequest conditions written into a will, cannot be carried out if they are illegal or go against "public policy.") If you are in a situation where this is an issue, you may wish to consult an attorney.

CARING FOR YOUR OWN

Some religious and ethnic groups regularly handle their own funeral and disposition arrangements. The Amish, the Mennonites, and many small Native American tribes, for example, often care for their own dead without professional assistance. In *Dealing Creatively with Death,* Ernest Morgan describes situations in which burial by the family or by a committee or a religious organization is an option. His book is based on experience gained in developing a burial committee in a Quaker community. In traditional Judaism, the Hevra Kadisha is a special committee of experienced volunteers who prepare the body for burial. It is considered a privilege to be a member of this group.

If you are interested in handling disposition personally or with the assistance of friends and family, you should read *Caring for Your Own Dead,* by Lisa Carlson. This book tells you how to go about getting the proper permits and making arrangements yourself. It is filled with practical information and helpful advice.

Although possible, handling arrangements on your own is not easy and therefore not for everyone. Because this kind of involvement is rare, you can expect to meet with some resistance from medical personnel, municipal officials, and cemetery or crematory owners. Carlson describes these potential obstacles and suggests ways to deal with them. She proposes that for some people handling death arrangements personally will not only save a considerable amount of money but might also provide a sense of control and connection that can help you through the grieving process.

If you live in a rural or semirural area, you may be able to bury the deceased on private property owned by you or the deceased. If you choose a home burial, however, you should check local zoning ordinances to find out what restrictions exist in your area. You will also need to notify municipal, county, or state health officials and, in most states, obtain a burial permit prior to interment. Carlson's book includes a state-by-state directory of laws and regulations regarding disposition. (See listings at the end of this chapter.)

RESOURCES AND SUPPORT

Books

Lisa Carlson. *Caring for Your Own Dead: A Complete Guide for Those Who Wish to Handle Funeral Arrangements Themselves . . . as a Final Act of Love.* Hinesburg, Vt.: Upper Access Publishers, 1987. Available in bookstores or from Upper Access Publishers, One Upper Access Road, Hinesburg, VT 05461; (802) 482-2988.
[This unique book furnishes detailed information for those who desire to make their own funeral arrangements and provide for body disposition without a funeral director. Includes explanation and discussion of cremations, embalming, and body and organ donation; a listing of crematories willing to deal directly with families; and a breakdown of cremation costs. Includes a directory of laws, regulations, and services for each state in the United States. A valuable directory of hard-to-find information.]

Sara Engram. *Mortal Matters: When a Loved One Dies.* Kansas City, Mo.: Andrews and McMeel, 1990.
[Includes useful step-by-step advice about practical requirements. Based on letters and inquiries sent to the author, who writes a syndicated column.]

Katie Maxwell. *No Lifetime Guarantee: Dealing with the Details of Death.* Crozet, Va.: Betterway Publications, 1988. Available in bookstores and from Betterway Publications, P.O. Box 219, Crozet, VA 22932; (804) 823-5661.
[Maxwell offers practical information for survivors of a death in the family. Includes information on claiming survivor's benefits, making disposition arrangements, autopsy, anatomical gifts, and more.]

Ernest Morgan. *Dealing Creatively with Death: A Manual of Death Education and Simple Burial.* 11th ed., revised and expanded. Edited by Jennifer Morgan. Burnsville, N.C.: Celo Press, 1988. Available in bookstores or from Celo Press, 1901 Hannah Branch Road, Burnsville, NC 28714; (704) 675-4925.
[This book is the classic in the field. It includes discussions of simple burials and cremations, memorial societies, and commemorations. Contains helpful appendices.]

Thomas C. Nelson. *It's Your Choice: The Practical Guide to Planning a Funeral.* Washington, D.C.: American Association of Retired Persons; Glenview, Ill.: Scott, Foresman and Co., AARP Books, 1987. Available in bookstores or through the American Association of Retired Persons. For complete information, write AARP Books, 2720

Des Plaines Avenue, Suite 113, Des Plaines, IL 60018; (708) 298-2852.
[Discusses options and offers advice on disposition and funerals. Appendixes include a checklist for survivors, price-comparison forms, and personal-planning forms.]

Books Containing Related Information

Lynne Ann DeSpelder and Albert Lee Strickland. *The Last Dance: Encountering Death and Dying.* 2nd ed. Mountain View, Calif.: Mayfield Publishing Company, 1987.
[A comprehensive text on the subject of death and dying, with chapters on last rites, funerals, and body disposition.]

Theodore E. Hughes and David Klein. *A Family Guide to Wills, Funerals & Probate: How to Protect Yourself and Your Survivors.* New York: Charles Scribner's Sons, 1987.
[Section on coping with death in the family includes discussion of body disposal, funeral rites, and negotiating with funeral directors.]

Philip Kapleau. *The Wheel of Life and Death: A Practical and Spiritual Guide.* New York: Doubleday, 1989.
[An exploration and meditation on death in Eastern and Western religious traditions, including sections on cremation and burial, funeral services, and anatomical donations.]

Candy Lightner and Nancy Hathaway. *Giving Sorrow Words: How to Cope with Grief and Get On with Your Life.* New York: Warner Books, 1990.
[Primarily about the grieving process, this book includes a chapter on funerals and mourning customs that provides interesting examples of cultural practices and memorial ceremonies.]

Harry Van Bommel. *Choices: For People Who Have a Terminal Illness, Their Families and Caregivers.* Toronto: NC Press Limited, 1990; distributed in the United States by Seven Hills Book Distributors. Available through Seven Hills Books, 49 Central Ave., Cincinnati, OH 45202; 1-800-545-2005.

Agencies/Service Organizations

American Cemetery Association
Three Skyline Place
Suite 1111
5201 Leesburg Pike
Falls Church, VA 22041
(703) 379-5838

The major cemetery and memorial-park trade association. They can answer questions regarding cemetery rules and practices in addition to making referrals. The ACA will help arbitrate complaints concerning their own members or refer you to an appropriate agency or organization.

Cemetery Consumer Service Council
P.O. Box 3574
Washington, DC 20007
(202) 379-6426
Sponsored by four of the major industry groups to resolve consumer complaints. Provides free pamphlet explaining services.

Conference of Funeral Service Examining Boards
P.O. Box 497
15 N.E. Third Street
Washington, IN 47501
(812) 254-7887
The association representing licensing boards in both Canada and the United States. They can refer you to the licensing board in your state in addition to responding to complaints about funeral directors.

Continental Association of Funeral and Memorial Societies
7910 Woodmont Avenue
Suite 1208
Bethesda, MD 20814
(301) 913-0030
Consumer membership organizations advocating memorial societies as a means of ensuring dignity, simplicity, and economy in funeral arrangements. Each local society is independent, and the level of service provided may vary. The national office of CAFMS can refer you to a local society in the United States or help you establish one if none exists where you live. The CAFMS also has available anatomical donor cards and information concerning anatomical gifts. Pamphlets listing the societies throughout the United States are provided at no charge. In Canada, memorial associations are a confederation, the Memorial Association of Canada, but have no national office. Check your local telephone directory for a memorial association in your area.

Cremation Association of North America
111 East Wacker Drive
Suite 600
Chicago, IL 60601
(312) 644-6610

A national trade association with free pamphlets discussing cremation. They can also make referrals.

FSCAP (Funeral Service Consumer Assistance Program)
National Research and Information Center
1614 Central Street
Evanston, IL 60201
800-662-7666
An independent organization that arbitrates consumer complaints concerning funeral-related purchases. They will handle prelitigation or postlitigation complaints. Write an initial letter describing the complaint to the FSCAP; their staff will respond and follow up.

Jewish Funeral Directors of America
250 West 57th Street
New York, NY 10107
(212) 757-0578
A national trade association of funeral directors serving the Jewish community. Has free pamphlets available and can make referrals over the telephone.

National Funeral Director's Association
11121 West Oklahoma Avenue
Milwaukee, WI 53227
(414) 541-2500
The largest educational and professional association of funeral directors. Provides a number of free pamphlets available to consumers, including: "A Way to Remember: Choosing a Funeral Ceremony"; "Death Away from Home"; "Embalming"; "Funeral Etiquette"; "The Traditional Funeral"; "What Are My Options? A Guide to Final Disposition"; and "Yes, Funerals Are for the Living." The NFDA represents the funeral industry, and they definitely have something to sell. This material can be a helpful source of information, but remember, it is written from their point of view.

National Funeral Directors and Morticians Association
P.O. Box 377993
Chicago, IL 60637
(312) 752-7419
A national association primarily of African-American funeral providers. Will make referrals by telephone.

U.S. Federal Trade Commission
Public Reference Section
6th and Pennsylvania, NW
Washington, DC 20580
(202) 326-2222
Oversees the enforcement of the Funeral Industry Rule. Will answer consumer questions over the telephone; however, complaints must be made in
writing and sent to the FTC's Correspondence Branch, Washington, DC
20580. Copies of public documents, such as the pamphlet "Consumer
Guide to the FTC Funeral Rule," are available at no charge.

Social Security
Find the local or toll-free (800) telephone number listed for Social Security
offices under "Department of Health and Human Services" in the U.S.
Government Agencies and Offices section of your telephone book. There
should be a local or toll-free (800) telephone number listed.

Veterans Administration
Find the local or toll-free (800) telephone number listed for "Veterans
Administration" in the U.S. Government Agencies and Offices section of
your telephone book. The local VA will have staff and publications helpful
to your filing for veteran's survivors benefits. Two publications available are
"A Summary of Veterans Administration Benefits" and "Federal Benefits
for Veterans and Dependents."

9

Taking Care of
Final Business

Chances are, once you've gone through this, you'll never again watch Greta
Garbo's death scene in *Camille* without wondering if Robert Taylor had joint
tenancy with right of survivorship.

Emily Brennen, widow

We have seen how the experience of death has changed dramatically
over the last half century. At the same time, the experience of
surviving a death has also changed. In the past, survivors received
emotional comfort and material support in a large, extended family
that provided a way to grieve and a place to be cared for. While it
may not have been as ideal as it seems in nostalgic hindsight, life and
death on the old family farm had its advantages, and the extended
domestic structure definitely helped absorb the shocks and solve
many of the practical problems that emerge in death's wake.

As families grew smaller and more widely dispersed and death itself
moved out of the family circle, those support systems disappeared.
For the survivor in the aftermath of death today, finding both solace
and practical assistance has become more complicated. Theodore E.

229

Hughes and David Klein, in their useful book *A Family Guide to Wills, Funerals, & Probate,* put it this way:

> . . . the normal process of our survivors' grief and bereavement is interrupted by their need to deal with a number of bureaucracies—banks and brokers, probate courts, federal and state tax authorities and other government agencies—many of which did not exist or played no part in deaths that occurred a few decades ago.[1]

As with most of our experiences concerning death, this one is made more disconcerting by its being unfamiliar. This chapter describes the business and paperwork required following a death and offers some resources to help you cope.

THE PRACTICAL CONSEQUENCES

The amount and complexity of the paperwork surrounding a death is dependent on the complexity of the deceased's business affairs and the preplanning s/he did or didn't do. An additional factor is the nature of the death. If death comes at the end of a long illness and the deceased and survivors had talked and planned together, dealing with such details can be fairly rudimentary. However, if death is sudden or, for whatever reasons, a devastating experience for the survivors, the practical aftermath can be very difficult indeed.

If you've never done this before, you will be surprised at how many details will require your attention. Blessed are the survivors of those who planned ahead. The entire process will be much easier if the person who died prepared properly or even if s/he prepared at all.

NOTIFICATION

When someone has died, there are a number of different ways to let people know. Generally, we telephone family and close friends immediately. Newspaper announcements notify a larger range of acquaintances as well as the general public. Formal printed announcements, usually used by businesses to inform colleagues or clients, are sometimes sent after the initial period following the death.

The Need to Know

In addition to immediately notifying friends and relatives who will want to know, there will be others who will need to be informed about the death fairly promptly, including business partners or clients regularly dependent on the deceased. If the executor of the will is not immediately aware of the death, s/he should be informed straightaway. If the person who died had children of school age, someone should notify their teachers and the parents of their close friends in order to explain absences and ensure understanding and support for the child at school.

It is recommended that after telling the immediate family, you wait to call others until funeral arrangements have been made in order to avoid having to call a second time with the additional information. If you wish to notify a number of people by telephone, it can be a good idea to enlist help or to ask a relative or friend to contact others in his or her same geographic vicinity.

The identity of the individual from whom you receive the news of a death may be very important. (If you were especially close to the deceased, it can be disconcerting to learn of the death in an informal way or from someone you don't know.) Within the intimate circle of family and friends this may be a significant factor. However, for the more routine telephone calls, such as those to a school principal or to business associates, it doesn't matter so much who is doing the calling as long as he or she communicates the information clearly and in a seemly manner. If making these calls is particularly difficult for you, this job may best be turned over to others. People are usually willing to help in this way. In fact, the word of a death spreads quite rapidly.

Death Notices and Obituaries

There are two types of public announcements published in newspapers—death notices and obituaries. These notices inform those outside the immediate circle or those whom survivors don't contact by phone. A *death notice* is a paid announcement briefly listing a few basic details submitted by the family or friends of the deceased. The cost is usually determined by the length or number of words in the notice. An *obituary* is a news story written by the paper's staff and printed, at no cost, as a standard news item.

In smaller communities the local paper will often routinely give obituary coverage to the death of local citizens, especially those who have had some prominence in the vicinity. In large metropolitan areas, however, only very well known individuals are regularly given obituary notices. If the deceased was quite famous or widely known, the national media will also cover the death. In fact, most news organizations keep "obit" files, with pertinent background information on the life and accomplishments of people who are going to "die big" so that they are prepared ahead of time and can produce a news story immediately.

For most of us, however, family or friends must promptly pull together the necessary information if a death notice is desired. Paid announcements usually include the date of death, names of survivors, important accomplishments, and the date and location of the funeral or memorial service, if any.

If you are responsible for placing a death notice, you should call the obituary department of the local newspaper office, determine the cost and the deadlines for submission, and ask if the paper has an obituary form you can fill out. Or read through the announcements in a past edition of the paper to get an idea of what the notice should look like.

If the survivors want to encourage obituary coverage, they can notify the paper and provide relevant biographical information and a list of significant career accomplishments, etc. Estates attorney Denis Clifford says: "In my experience, if a family submits a well-written, factual obituary immediately after a person's death, a local newspaper is likely to use a good part of it, or at least echo its major themes."[2] Providing this information to the paper does two things: It increases the possibility of obituary coverage as well as the likelihood that coverage will be accurate.

Printed Announcements

Sometimes businesses and corporations will mail a card announcing the death of a partner or esteemed colleague. These are usually engraved and fairly straightforward. For example: "We announce with sorrow the death of our partner Mary M. Doe on January 18, 1991." This is most often done in the case of law firms and other organizations dealing with a wide range of clients or those needing to inform people who would not otherwise know about the death.

Places to Notify

As the days and weeks go by, you will need to notify banks, credit-card and other charge-account companies, and if appropriate, such agencies as utilities companies and the Department of Motor Vehicles. Then, depending on the deceased's commitments, you may need to maintain or terminate agreements with rental or leasing agencies, subscriptions, book clubs, or other membership plans, such as health clubs, or groups such as lodges or fraternal organizations.

In her book *No Lifetime Guarantee,* a practical guide for dealing with these details, Katie Maxwell gives comprehensive advice on how to handle notification as well as many other necessary tasks. (See listings at the end of this chapter for further information.)

THE DEATH CERTIFICATE

The first piece of paper you will need is a death certificate. No matter what decisions you make regarding disposition and funeral or memorial services, a death certificate will be necessary in order to proceed. The law requires that a doctor, coroner, or health officer prepare and sign a death certificate, and in most states you can't even move a body without this document.

If death occurs in a hospital or other institutional setting (nursing home, long-term-care facility, etc.), the death certificate will be provided and signed by the attending physician. Customarily, it is then turned over to a funeral director, who fills in additional information and files the certificate reporting the death with the county health department.

If death occurs at home, the attending physician, the county coroner, or a medical examiner will need to complete the document before the body can be moved. In some states, when death has long been expected, a registered nurse can sign a certificate that has been completed ahead of time. If the deceased has been under the care of a hospice program, the hospice staff will help arrange to provide the death certificate.

An Official Record of Our Existence

In conjunction with a birth certificate, a death certificate provides a public record of our existence. Before the twentieth century this

record was kept by church sextons, and burial counts were enumer-
ated by cemetery caretakers. Today statistics drawn from the U.S.
Standard Certificate of Death are used to calculate national death
and disease rates, which in turn are used to determine the allocation
of government health funds.

In 1989 the national death certificate model was revised to encourage more complete reporting as to the cause of death and more
specific information regarding ancestry, descent, and education. The
new model allows for two physicians to contribute to filling out the
form so that a pronouncing physician can record the time of death
and sign the certificate and, after the body has been removed, another doctor can check through records and write a more informed
description. Several states have modified the death certificate to
include specific questions about alcohol and tobacco use as factors
contributing to death. For instance, Utah's certificate includes a box
to indicate whether tobacco contributed to the death, and in the
state of Washington the doctor is asked whether the decedent
smoked in the fifteen years before death.

While the form varies slightly from state to state, most require the
following biographical information: name, sex, age, occupation,
date of birth and date and hour of death, place of birth, residence,
and death, country of citizenship, social security number, marital
status, name of surviving spouse, names and birthplaces of both
parents, and the name of the individual furnishing the personal
information.

In addition, the certificate must describe both the immediate and
underlying cause of death and whether any surgery or an autopsy has
been performed. Also required is the type and place of disposition
and the signature of the funeral director or person in charge of
disposition.

Except for the required medical information, which is provided by
the physician or coroner, the person handling funeral arrangements
fills in the rest of the form. In most cases, this is done by a licensed
funeral director, who may or may not charge a fee for the service.
The signature of a licensed funeral director is mandatory in some
states. The certificate is then filed with the county or municipal
registrar of health within a specified period of time, which varies
from state to state.

It's a good idea to check the death certificate to make sure that
everything has been correctly entered. A mistake as simple as a

signature in the wrong place can cause a delay in filing, which in turn will delay everything else.

You'll Need More Than One Death Certificate

The death certificate is required for more than moving the body. It is also necessary to present a copy of the death certificate in many of the transactions that will follow, including obtaining death benefits, applying for life insurance and/or pension benefits, closing bank accounts, transferring ownership of real estate, motor vehicles, or stock certificates, and gaining access to a safe-deposit box.

As with a will, the word *copy,* when applied to a death certificate, usually means an official certified copy as opposed to a photocopy. Official certified copies can be purchased for under $10 apiece from the local or state health department or your county clerk's office. Often a funeral director obtains these copies (and may or may not add a surcharge for each), or it can be done by your lawyer or by yourself.

Although it is usually cheaper to buy all the copies you need at one time, you may not know exactly what that number will be until you begin to settle the deceased's estate. It is recommended that you purchase the minimum number you anticipate needing and then buy additional copies later on.

HOW A FUNERAL DIRECTOR CAN HELP

If you are trying to keep costs down to a minimum; if you have the time and energy to do it yourself; if there is someone who wants to help and is capable; or if, for whatever reason, you want to have personal control over such details as notification, you can do much of this yourself. However, most people turn many of these tasks over to a funeral director, who, in addition to the primary function of furnishing disposition and funeral rites, often provides the following assistance:

1. *Notification.* A funeral director can help with the wording of a death notice or an obituary and will submit the notice to the

newspaper of your choice. If you provide a list of clubs, church groups, lodges, or other membership organizations you wish to have notified, the funeral director can do this on your behalf.

2. *Death certificate.*   As described, a funeral director can complete the death certificate, file it with the county health department, fulfill any local requirement for recording the death, and procure the certified copies of the death certificate necessary to complete the business of the estate. If the death was unattended (no physician treated the deceased) or if death occurred unnaturally, the funeral director can contact the county coroner or medical examiner and arrange for an autopsy if necessary or help arrange and explain the required official procedure.

3. *Death benefits.*   In addition to these services, a funeral director can help you file for and claim any funds available for disposition to which you may be entitled. Veterans' benefits, social security benefits, union or fraternal benefits, and other types of insurance packages sometimes contain a burial or funeral allotment—a sum of money to be applied toward disposition. The funeral director may arrange to have this money paid directly to himself or herself. (Also see "Death Benefits" section later in this chapter.)

LOCATING IMPORTANT PAPERS

In addition to the death certificate, there are a number of papers and documents that you will need in the course of settling business and financial matters after a death. If the person who died planned ahead, now is when you are really going to appreciate it. You will have a Letter of Instruction or an envelope containing directions for disposition, the will (or instructions on how to find the will), and the papers and documentation needed to settle the estate.

However, since most people don't prepare in this way, you'll probably have to spend some time looking for all the stuff you are going to need, which can include:

The will and estate plan
Safe-deposit box and key

A record of all bank accounts (checking, savings, etc.)
Checkbooks and passbooks
Insurance policies (life, property, auto, medical, etc.)
Pension plans
A record of all loans
Real estate
   deeds
   title policies
   closing statements
   mortgages
   record of mortgage payments
   tax receipts
   leases
Stock certificates and bonds (plus records of cost and date of
   purchase; name and address of stockbroker)
Income tax returns (plus name and number of preparer)
Birth certificate
Marriage certificate (record of divorce)
Social Security number
Automobile registration and proof of ownership
Contracts (including installment-purchase agreements)
Business records
Receipts or appraisals of valuables
Credit cards
A record of all charge accounts
Veteran service record and discharge

THE WILL

Although statistics show that most people do not prepare wills,
many do, and if a will does exist, you certainly want to take advantage of having it to guide you through the business ahead. Hughes
and Klein note that "although detective novels may have left you
with the impression that an urgent search for the will immediately
after a death is a mark of villainous greed, the fact is that a will should
be located and read promptly. . . ."[3] They also point out that while
movies and books usually depict the reading of a will as a legal ritual
with everyone gathered together in a lawyer's office, "no formalities
whatever are specified by law." Thus, you needn't worry that it is in
any way improper to find and read a will as soon as is possible. On

the contrary, the will may include instructions for disposition and/or anatomical gifts, in which case it must be found posthaste if you are to follow those wishes. (If you are unable to find the will in time and must make disposition decisions without these instructions, you are not under any legal or moral obligation. Just do the best you can.)

If the deceased took the advice given in this book and prepared separate instructions for disposition, making them readily available to survivors, the time factor would not be quite so critical. Still, it is important to find the will as soon after the death as can be managed. It will designate an executor who should take over the administration of the estate and may name guardians for minor children.

Where to Look
If no one knows for sure where the will might be located, the best places to begin to look are in personal files or records in the home (or in a house safe if there is one). If you have no luck at home, check with the deceased's attorney, banker, or with the probate registrar at the county courthouse to see if a will was filed there.

Often people leave their will in a safe-deposit box. If the box is held in the name of the deceased alone, you'll need permission to open it according to state law and bank regulations. Even if the box is held jointly, it may still be sealed and you will be required to apply to the state tax authority in order to open it. In most states you can gain access to a safe-deposit box to look for a will, but this usually necessitates filing a petition with the court and takes too much time to make anatomical gifts possible.

When the will is found it must then be registered with the probate court.

IF THERE IS NO WILL

If no will exists or you can't find one anywhere, someone must take the responsibility of petitioning the probate court and requesting the appointment of an administrator over the estate. Usually this will be the spouse or an adult child or other close relative, although it can be anyone with an interest in the estate (including creditors with claims against it). The appropriate court office may be called Probate

Registrar, Register of Wills, or Surrogate Court Clerk. If you don't know where to go, check with the county clerk's office in the county in which the deceased was resident. They will provide the necessary forms and information.

After you file your petition, the probate court will then appoint a representative to fulfill the role of executor (the administrator of the estate). If there is no appropriate next of kin, the court can appoint a lawyer, a creditor to the estate, or an officer of the court as the administrator. The court will then supervise the distribution of the property and assets in accordance with that state's intestacy laws.

Intestacy laws and procedures vary somewhat from state to state. Generally speaking, an inheritance will be divided between the spouse, children, parents, siblings, or other relatives as directed by law.

If the estate consists simply of personal property and belongings and there is no titled real estate or property requiring an official title transfer, this procedure should be fairly routine.

If there are considerable assets involved, and especially if the estate comes in over the $600,000 Federal Estate Tax Exemption level, the complications incurred in probate can be considerable. You will almost certainly need an attorney with experience in this area, and legal costs, not to mention additional expenses (court costs, appraiser's fees, etc.), can mount quickly.

If someone with a lot of property and/or a complicated business situation dies without leaving a will, your requirements as a survivor will be commensurately complicated. If you are appointed executor, you will take over, in essence, the job the deceased didn't do, but with fewer options than s/he would have had in planning ahead. If you are dealing with this situation, it is important to find a lawyer you can trust to protect the interests of the estate.

APPOINTING A GUARDIAN FOR MINOR CHILDREN

The court also appoints a personal guardian for any minor children (under eighteen or, in some states, under twenty-one years of age). If the will has nominated a guardian, the court will almost always abide by that nomination (so long as the individual agrees to take on the responsibility and is not proved to be grossly unfit). The court issues Letters of Guardianship that give that individual the right to act *in loco parentis,* in the place of the deceased parent or parents. If the deceased left money in trust for the child, the guardian may or may not also be the Trustee or Conservator of the trust (the person who controls the money in the interest of the child). In any case, there are many legal restrictions on the use of such funds.

If the parent(s) die without naming a guardian, the court will do so. The law does not consider children to be property, and they are not treated as such; however, courts do tend to be most inclined to name the next of kin as guardian. If that individual is not willing to take on the guardian role, an orphaned minor child will often be placed with whoever volunteers for the job. If no one offers to take care of the child, state or county social service agencies take over until some kind of arrangement can be made or foster care can be provided.

PROBATE

As described in chapter 1, the word *probate* comes from a Latin root meaning "to prove." The probate process is the process whereby the law confirms that a will is legitimate, and oversees its administration. This process takes place through a county court that is usually called probate court (in some states, surrogate, chancery, or orphan's court).

As we have seen, the probate court has other functions as well. If there is a will, it's filed there; if not, the court names an administrator for the estate. The court appoints guardians for minor children. It also, and primarily, supervises the distribution of estate property.

The probate procedure can be as simple as filing with the court and receiving the proper certification to administer the will (called Letters of Administration or Letters Testamentary). Or it can be so complicated as to involve the court in every aspect of estate administration. Indeed, if there is no will and the estate is sizable and complex, formal probate administration can become a complicated, costly, and lengthy process.

Probate and Nonprobate Assets

The degree to which you will need to deal with probate will depend primarily on the *types* of assets to be distributed. Some categories of assets are required to go through probate, and others are not. Probatable assets include titled property solely owned by the deceased. Nonprobatable assets include jointly owned property, life insurance policies with the beneficiary named directly, and certain kinds of trusts. If the deceased planned ahead, his or her assets were probably placed in nonprobate form. For example, a house owned jointly by married partners, each with the "right of survivorship," does not have to go through probate in order to be transferred. In this case, if a person dies and leaves a $100,000 house, jointly owned, plus $10,000 worth of additional cash or property, the entire estate will be valued at $110,000. However, the *probatable* assets will be only $10,000, allowing the estate (in most states) to be settled through a simplified probate process.

Small Estates Settlement

Sometimes an estate can be settled under what is called "small estates administration." This is a simpler and easier process than formal probate. In order to qualify, an estate must be worth less than a maximum dollar amount, which varies from state to state but is generally somewhere between $10,000 and $50,000. Check with your county court or with a lawyer to find the cutoff point in your state. As we have seen from the previous example, even a sizable estate can qualify if it consists primarily of nonprobatable assets.

Formal Probate Administration

If probate assets exceed the maximum allowed for small estates settlement and you are required to undergo formal probate administration, the estate will probably need to hire an experienced lawyer specializing in the field. This can be expensive. (Most states have regulations setting limits on attorneys' fees for probating an estate, but they are not necessarily low limits.) And formal probate administration involves many other charges (court costs and filing fees, appraisers' fees, brokers' fees, and more). All of these expenses come out of the estate's assets.

If you have just lost a loved one, are unsure about the status of the property and assets involved, don't know anything about the law in these matters, and aren't feeling so hot anyhow, you will need someone who cares about you and your interests to guide you through this process. The impersonal probate court system is not designed to do this. You will need a good lawyer.

There are some useful books that describe the probate system in easy-to-understand language, giving an overview of the process, a summary of your options, and advice about how to protect yourself and the estate. They include the aforementioned *A Family Guide to Wills, Funerals, & Probate* by Hughes and Klein, *Probate, Settling an Estate: A Step-by-Step Guide* by Kay Ostberg, as well as other books in the resource listings at the end of this chapter.

In the aftermath of a death one may be quite vulnerable. When issues concerning property, money, probate, and the law become complicated or confusing, the desire to turn everything over to someone else can be almost irresistible. If you do this, be sure you turn everything over to someone you can trust. Ask friends and family for recommendations before turning to an anonymous legal referral agency or state bar association. Do not be afraid to say no if you have any reason to feel uncertain about whom you are hiring or what they are doing.

Avoiding Probate

The probate system was originally set up to protect people from fraud in the distribution of their property after they were dead and could no longer do anything about it. However, many think the probate process has developed into a kind of costly watchdog taking an interest in, and a piece of, simple business that could be conducted more quickly, efficiently, and economically without it.

Because the probate system has gained a rather bad reputation as an expensive and lengthy procedure, many people plan ahead to avoid probate. This can be done in a number of ways, all perfectly legal, but *must be done before you die, when you write your will and prepare your estate plan.*

You may wonder, Why doesn't a family simply give one another what there is to give and be done with it? Why bother with all this court stuff, lawyers, hearings, and the like? Attorney Denis Clifford, who has written several very helpful books on preparing wills and estate plans, explains it this way:

> Some small estates are undoubtedly disposed of . . . directly and informally by family members. The people involved may not think of

such an arrangement as avoiding probate, but that's what occurs. For example, an older man lives his last few years in a nursing home. After his death, his children meet and divide the personal items their father had kept over the years. What little savings he has have long since been put into a joint account with the children anyway, so there's no need for formalities there. If the father owned no other property, the children have, in effect, "probated" his estate.[4]

Clifford goes on to say that this will only work if the family can gain possession of all the property, agree on the distribution, and pay all the creditors. If there is any real estate, stocks and bonds, bank accounts, or other property requiring the transfer of a title, this method won't work because transferring title from one person to another necessitates involving a legal authority. If any member of the family is unhappy with the arrangement or a creditor is concerned about being paid, they can file for a formal probate.

SETTLING AN ESTATE

The Executor
The executor* is the person who will oversee the administration of the estate and carry out the instructions left by the deceased. Also called the Personal Representative, this job can be fairly routine if the will was comprehensive and well planned, or it can be quite intensive and time-consuming if there are conflicts or complications.

Whether you are the executor or you simply wish to be sure the process is being managed correctly, the following brief overview will give you an idea of the various procedures involved in settling an estate.

Identifying Assets and Liabilities
One of the executor's first tasks is to make an inventory of all the assets, holdings, and possessions left by the deceased. This is the point where you determine in detail what is contained in the estate. It is sometimes called "marshaling the estate."

This job will be made very much easier if the deceased left a Letter

---

*The terms *executrix* or *administratrix* are sometimes used to connote a female executor. Herein the term *executor* will refer to either gender.

of Instruction that included a listing of his or her assets and liabilities. However, the Letter is a recent innovation and even a lawyer who is working with a client to prepare a will often fails to recommend writing one.

If you were married to the deceased or were a business partner privy to his or her financial affairs or an adult child who had an active interest in the business transactions of your parent, you are likely to have a good idea of what comprises the estate. If you are not familiar with the deceased's affairs, you might start by talking with people who could be, including his or her lawyer, accountant, and other financial advisers, such as stockbrokers and investment counselors. And, of course, you'll want to speak with the surviving spouse, children, and other close relatives and friends and/or business partners.

The most likely sources of information will be checkbooks, bank statements and canceled checks, safe-deposit boxes, the deceased's mail, the bank, insurance companies, and other financial institutions.

You are looking for all real estate, stocks, bonds, savings accounts, and personal property owned wholly or in part by the deceased or in which s/he had an interest. You are also looking for debts and liabilities against the estate, bills, notices of payments and premiums due, mortgage payments, liens, and outstanding balances owed.

An inventory will allow you to get a handle on what you're dealing with, to differentiate between probate assets and nonprobate assets, and to judge whether the estate qualifies for small estates administration or will require a more complex probate procedure. Either you, acting as executor, or your attorney will be required to file this list with the court.

Paying Claims, Debts, and Taxes

When someone dies, they may leave debts as well as assets. Obligations may be in the form of ongoing expenses, such as utility bills, car or mortgage payments (which are carried over to the inheritor of the property), or charge-account balances due. Often medical bills are incurred during a last illness, along with funeral or other disposition expenses. Various types of taxes will be due and assessed against the estate. It is the responsibility of the executor to manage liabilities as well as assets.

DEBTS   If debts were incurred jointly, they remain the responsibility of the cosigner (unless covered by an insurance policy that pays the obligation upon death). Debts incurred solely by the deceased become the responsibility of the estate.

If there are significant debts against an estate, it is usually a good idea to go through a more formal probate because the probate process includes a standard procedure for dealing with such claims. This procedure involves notifying creditors and sets a deadline for claimants to come forward. When an estate does not have enough assets to cover liabilities against it, the bills must be paid according to a prioritized list of preferred claims that are determined by state law. (It will come as no surprise that legal fees and court costs are among the first on the list.) If this procedure is necessary in your case, the probate registrar will explain the process, or your attorney will advise you or handle it on your behalf.

Unless you have cosigned a loan or jointly incurred a liability, no one is legally obligated to pay another's debts. For most people, dealing with an estate's creditors will be a pretty routine proposition. As pointed out by Kay Ostberg, "More typically, the estate will be confronted only with routine monthly billings and established debts that are familiar to the deceased person's family."[5]

TAXES   When someone dies, they owe taxes on whatever income they earned during the taxable year in which they died. The executor of an estate is responsible for filing an individual tax return for the deceased. If the deceased customarily filed a joint return, the surviving spouse can choose to file a joint return or not, whichever is preferred. If the estate has income (from investments or a business operation, for instance), it must pay a separate income tax. An estate is a taxable entity until it is settled and closed.

Gift taxes can be levied on both the estate and the inheritance itself. In other words, there can be a tax on the right to transfer assets and a tax on the right to receive assets. Most states have one or the other or both. The tax schedules and exemptions vary from state to state.

If the estate is sizable, the deceased probably worked with an estate planner and structured methods to minimize taxes. If not and the estate is over the $600,000 Federal Estate Tax Exemption level, you should definitely work with a good tax consultant, accountant, or attorney to help you through the labyrinth of tax options and requirements.

If the estate is relatively small, filing the appropriate tax forms is usually routine. The books recommended at the end of this chapter include clear descriptions of death-tax requirements and helpful advice on how to proceed, including tax schedules and particulars for each state.

If, for whatever reason, you prefer not to handle the tax requirements by yourself, there are good professional specialists who can help. An estate-tax lawyer or a CPA with experience in estate-tax matters can save you a lot of headaches. Although it may be expensive, this is one area where securing professional help can really pay off in the long run. Once again, ask friends and family for reliable recommendations.

Distributing the Assets and Closing the Estate

After everything has been assessed and debts, claims, and taxes have been paid, the executor can distribute the assets according to the will (or according to intestacy laws if there is no will). If you are serving as executor, you will want to get receipts from everyone to whom you dispense gifts. Most advisers recommend that you keep these records for several years after the estate has been closed on the highly unlikely chance that there should be any challenges later on. In order to protect heirs from mistakes or fraud the Uniform Probate Code provides that assets that have been improperly disbursed may be redistributed up to one year after the date of distribution or three years after the person died, whichever is later.

Closing the estate involves preparing a final accounting showing total assets, expenses and taxes paid, debts paid, fees paid, etc., and certifying that the assets have been (or are being) distributed according to the will or to law. A Closing Statement is filed with the probate court, and a copy is sent to everyone with an interest in the distribution. Once this form is approved, the estate is closed.

DEATH BENEFITS

Death benefits, also called survivor benefits, are funds or privileges that come to survivors or beneficiaries after a death. Life insurance is the death benefit with which most people are familiar, but there are other types of insurance policies and transaction packages that include special payouts, depending on the nature of the coverage purchased by the deceased (or offered by his or her employer). Groups such as travel organizations, automobile clubs, or credit card companies generally offer policies that include some kind of accidental death benefit.

Death benefits do not come to you automatically; you must make an application and file a claim. Policies often contain time limits for the filing process, so it is important to find out just what benefits you may qualify for and apply as soon as you can.

Life Insurance

A life insurance policy can be the single most significant financial asset left to survivors. If the deceased named one or more living persons as the designated beneficiary, the proceeds do not go through probate and are not liable to any claims against the estate. This money goes directly to the beneficiary. (If the deceased named his or her estate as beneficiary, the proceeds must go through the probate process.)

FINDING THE POLICY   Once again, if there is no Letter of Instruction and the family/friends did not talk together about these matters, it may take some time to find out just what insurance policies are in effect, if any. If you did not find a policy when you looked for the will, you should go through canceled checks to see if a premium was paid to an insurance provider (go back at least twelve months, as some policy payments are annual) or talk with the company or agent providing any other types of insurance to the deceased.

Often life insurance policies are offered through the workplace as part of an employee benefit package or through unions, other professional groups, or credit unions. Sometimes an automobile club or car insurance policy will include death benefits. Be sure to look at all possible sources of funds or privileges for survivors.

If you have reason to believe a policy exists but cannot find a copy of the policy itself, you can write to the insurance company (credit union or whatever), explaining the situation and asking how to proceed. Usually they will provide a "lost policy form" that you complete and return with your claim.

The American Council of Life Insurance, a nonprofit organization located in Washington, D.C., has a free service called Policy Search. They can canvass some 100 life insurance companies to ascertain whether the deceased held a policy with any of them. (See listing at the end of this chapter.)

FILING A CLAIM   If you find a policy, the next step is to file a claim. Insurance proceeds (as well as Social Security, Veterans, or other benefits) will not come to you automatically. It is up to you to ask for your benefits. Obtain a claim form from the company, fill it out, and send it in, along with the necessary attachments, which will probably include a certified copy of the death certificate and perhaps the policy itself. Hughes and Klein point out,

> If the insurance company requires you to surrender the original policy along with the claim form and any supporting documents, be sure to photocopy the face sheet of the policy as well as the application form and your covering letter, which should list and describe all the enclosures.[6]

SUICIDE   Many people think life insurance policies don't pay off if the policyholder commits suicide. Actually, many companies do provide suicide coverage if the policy has been in effect for a minimum period of time (usually about two years).

CONSUMER PROTECTION   If, for whatever reason, you have a problem collecting life insurance benefits, you should consider filing a complaint with your state's regulatory agency (usually called the state insurance board or commission). If the board in your region has a reputation for inaction, you might consider consulting a lawyer. Often, even just the threat of legal action can bring results. In any case, if an insurance company has refused a claim, you should scrutinize the grounds for refusal carefully, as there may be avenues of redress.

Mortgage or Credit Insurance

Often loans, mortgages, or credit card accounts are covered by insurance that pays off the balance due when the borrower dies. The original contract will indicate whether or not this type of insurance was in effect. Write to the company or bank in question, informing them of the death and asking if such insurance existed, and ascertain how to proceed.

Employee, Pension, and Other Benefits

There are a number of other types of benefits available to survivors. Most companies provide fringe benefits, including pension plans, profit-sharing plans, or annuity programs that carry death clauses or survivor payments. The American Association of Retired Persons recommends that you contact all past employers, including federal, state, or local government, to determine if the survivors of the deceased are entitled to any payments from a pension plan or retirement fund.

Earned Income Due

If the deceased was employed at the time s/he died, s/he may have been owed wages, commissions, vacation pay, or sick leave. Some states allow the employer to pay this money directly to the spouse or next of kin. (Otherwise, as income rightfully due the deceased, it becomes a part of his or her estate.) Check with the deceased's employer to determine if such money is due and how to proceed to claim it.

Wrongful Death Benefits

When there is a possibility that death was the result of negligent or criminal behavior on the part of another person or a company, you should consult an experienced lawyer immediately. See Katie Maxwell's *No Lifetime Guarantee* or *Wills, Funerals, & Probate* by Hughes and Klein for more information about how to deal with these special circumstances.

Social Security Benefits

There are two types of benefits that can come from Social Security, if the deceased was covered in the first place. They are: (1) Continuing benefits—you should check with your local Social Security office about continuation of Social Security benefits to a surviving spouse. If there are children under eighteen years of age, benefits may be available for them. If there are minor or disabled children and no surviving spouse, the grandparents and/or guardians may be entitled to increased benefits. (2) Death benefit—Social Security provides a lump-sum payment ($255 at this writing) toward burial expenses.

Many of the books listed at the end of this chapter include information on Social Security benefits and how to apply. Especially complete is Katie Maxwell's *No Lifetime Guarantee*.

Veterans Benefits

If the deceased was a veteran, the survivors may receive a cash payment toward funeral expenses. Veterans have the right to free burial in a military cemetery or a $150 payment toward the cost of a plot in a private cemetery. A headstone or grave marker may be supplied. Another benefit available to veterans is a complimentary American flag that can be draped over the coffin and is then presented to the next of kin. A funeral director can complete the forms necessary to obtain this flag.

When a veteran who had been receiving disability payments dies, dependents are entitled to ongoing benefits.

The VA publishes a pamphlet describing all the benefits available to veterans ("A Summary of Veterans Administration Benefits," VA Pamphlet 27-82-2). Check with your local Veterans Administration office for further information.

If You Don't Know, Ask

If you think you might qualify for a death benefit or payment from an agency of government or a company with which the deceased was associated, it can be a good idea to write a brief letter explaining that you are the spouse, child, or dependent of the deceased and ask if you are entitled to any benefit.

Ernest Morgan's book *Dealing Creatively with Death* includes a helpful section on finding financial assistance for disposition and funeral expenses. (See listings at the end of this chapter.)

ADDITIONAL FINANCIAL MATTERS

Bank Accounts

Almost everybody has a bank account of some sort. They are so much a part of everyday commerce that we tend not to think of them as property. But in fact a bank account is a kind of titled asset and is treated by law as such. Gaining access to the deceased's bank account(s) will depend on the type of accounts held and the way in which the deceased planned ahead.

If an account is held jointly, the survivor can request that the title be transferred solely to his or her name and continue to use the account (or withdraw the funds, if that is preferred). However, individually owned bank accounts (both checking and savings) are treated as property of the estate and as such must go through the probate process before funds can be released.

Some types of accounts, including Keogh plans or Individual Retirement Accounts, may have a "pay on death" agreement that allows a beneficiary to be named. If this is the case, the funds are not part of the estate, do not go through probate, and are payable directly to the beneficiary.

Trust accounts are established specifically to provide the transfer of funds to beneficiaries upon death and are dispensed accordingly.

Credit Cards

As with other debts, credit card balances held in the name of the deceased alone are liabilities of the estate. Cards held jointly with a spouse, or another with the right to charge against the account, remain the obligation of the surviving debtor. To maintain the account, notify the company of the death and request that the card be listed in your name only.

The deceased's solely held credit cards should be canceled and destroyed or returned to the company. If not covered by credit insurance, the balance due is payable by the estate.

Securities and Investments

Speaking very generally, stocks, bonds, and other securities or investments are transferable in the same manner as bank accounts or other titled property. If held individually, they become part of the deceased's estate and pass through the probate process. If held jointly, they pass directly to the survivor, do not become part of the deceased's estate, and do not pass through probate. However, the specific details, features, and qualifications of various securities and investment transfers can vary. Transfers and sales of securities have significant tax consequences as well. Unless you are familiar with these matters, you will probably find it worthwhile to consult with an investment broker, brokerage firm, or other securities specialist.

AS TIME GOES ON

Our lives today are complicated. Our deaths are complicated, too. Many details can continue to require attention over a long period, but with time the more intense demands will lessen, and practical matters will sort themselves out. In chapter 10, we'll look at the most difficult requirement of all—moving through grief.

RESOURCES AND SUPPORT

Books

Alexander Bove, Jr. *The Complete Book of Wills & Estates.* New York: Henry Holt and Co.; Markham, Ont.: Fitzhenry & Whiteside Limited, 1989.
[Includes advice on estate management, will contests, probating a lost will, and hiring an estate-settlement lawyer. Appendixes include an executor's checklist arranged by time periods.]

Charlotte Foehner and Carol Cozart. *The Widow's Handbook: A Guide for Living.* Golden, Colo.: Fulcrum, 1989.
[Offers practical and detailed advice for the first two years of widowhood. Includes information on selecting an attorney, filing claims for life insurance and survivor's benefits, and handling financial matters. Provides checklists and form letters for many situations.]

Theodore E. Hughes and David Klein. *A Family Guide to Wills, Funerals, & Estate Planning: How to Protect Yourself and Your Survivors.* New York: Charles Scribner's Sons, 1987.
[Includes substantial information on handling legal, financial, and other matters after a death.]

Katie Maxwell. *No Lifetime Guarantee: Dealing with the Details of Death.* Crozet, Va.: Betterway Publications, 1988. Available in bookstores and from Betterway Publications, P.O. Box 219, Crozet, VA 22932; (804) 823-5661.
[This book offers practical advice for survivors of a death in the family. It includes information on: claiming survivor's benefits; dealing with obligations, finances, and taxes; and more.]

Julia Nissley. *How to Probate an Estate.* California ed. Berkeley, Calif.: Nolo Press, 1988. Available through Nolo Press, 950 Parker Street, Berkeley, CA 94710 (California edition only).

Kay Ostberg. *Probate: Settling an Estate, A Step-by-Step Guide.* New York: Random House, 1990.
[Concise and readable, with an appendix listing probate rules for all states.]

Charles K. Plotnick and Stephen R. Leimberg. *The Executor's Manual: Everything You Need to Know to Handle an Estate.* New York: Doubleday, 1986.
[Information and advice for executors, including psychological effects of death and dying on survivors; handling insurance claims and government benefits; handling a decedent's debts and taxes; and how to hire an estate team. Extensive appendices include sample forms for applying for Social Security benefits, summaries of state intestacy laws, and tax-planning checklist.]

John Regan, J.S.D., with Legal Counsel for the Elderly. *Your Legal Rights in Later Life.* Washington, D.C.: American Association of Retired Persons; Glenview, Ill.: Scott, Foresman and Company, 1989.
[Includes chapter on probate and administration of an estate.]

Book Containing Related Information
Ernest Morgan. *Dealing Creatively with Death: A Manual of Death Education and Simple Burial.* 11th ed., revised and expanded. Edited by Jennifer Morgan. Burnsville, N.C.: Celo Press, 1988. Available in bookstores or from Celo Press, 1901 Hannah Branch Road, Burnsville, NC 28714; (704) 675-4925.

Agencies/Service Organizations: Legal
American College of Trust and Estate Counsel
2716 Ocean Park Boulevard
Suite 1080
Santa Monica, CA 90405
(213) 450-2033
A membership organization of probate lawyers. Provides a list of probate lawyers in your area upon written request.

American Council of Life Insurance
1001 Pennsylvania Avenue, NW
Washington, DC 20004-2599
(202) 624-2000
Will conduct an insurance policy search free of charge. Send a self-addressed, stamped envelope. They also have a toll-free number (1-800-942-4242) for questions about life, health, property, and casualty insurance.

Commission on Legal Problems of the Elderly
American Bar Association
1800 M Street, NW
Washington, DC 20036

(202) 331-2297
Provides information and guidance in emerging areas of law and generates
pro bono, reduced-fee, and community education programs for senior
citizens. Publishes information on wills as well as other brochures and
books. Call to request a publications list.

HALT—An Organization of Americans for Legal Reform
1319 F Street, NW
Suite 300
Washington, DC 20004
(202) 347-9600
A national public-interest group that advocates reduced probate fees and
simplified probate procedures. They respond to written questions and inquiries; no phone consultations.

Local and Regional Bar Associations
If you use a bar association or lawyer's organization for referrals, always
remember that such referrals are not a seal of approval. The best way to find
a good lawyer is to ask a friend or associate who knows one.

Local and regional *family service associations* or *social service agencies* or *area
agencies on aging* sometimes provide information on how to find low-cost
legal counseling. Your public library can help you find the appropriate
agency.

AARP (American Association of Retired Persons)
1909 K Street, NW
Washington, DC 20049
(202) 872-4700
A large nonprofit membership organization providing a wide range of
educational and community-service programs. The AARP offers a number
of programs and publications that are helpful to widowed persons. Programs and departments include Women's Initiative, Widowed Person's
Service, and Institute of Lifetime Learning. The AARP also has a wide
variety of literature available to the public at no charge. Call to request a
publications catalog.

Social Security
Find the local or toll-free (800) telephone number listed for Social Security
offices under "Department of Health and Human Services" in the U.S.
Government Agencies and Offices section of your telephone book.

Veterans Administration

Find the local or toll-free (800) telephone number listed for "Veterans Administration" in the U.S. Government Agencies and Offices section of your telephone book. The local VA will have staff and publications helpful to your filing for veterans' survivors benefits. Two publications available are "A Summary of Veterans Administration Benefits" and "Federal Benefits for Veterans and Dependents."

Taxes

State

Look in the State Government section of your local telephone book for Department of Taxation and Finance. Many states, such as New York, have separate toll-free (800) telephone numbers to receive estate-tax information and forms.

Federal

Local Internal Revenue Service telephone numbers are usually listed in the U.S. Government Offices section of your local telephone directory under "Treasury Department." The IRS has two publications that include information for people settling estates: "Federal Estate and Gift Taxes" (Publication 448) and "Tax Information for Survivors, Executors, and Administrators" (Publication 559). To order IRS publications, call toll-free 800-424-FORM. The IRS also offers a recorded-information service "Tele-Tax" on a variety of topics, including filing requirements for decedents and estate-tax computation. The local or toll-free (800) "Tele-Tax" telephone number is often listed with other IRS numbers under "Recorded Tax Information."

10

Grief and Bereavement

When we experience grief, we are not just experiencing the loss of our son or daughter, our husband or wife, our parent or loved one. We are dropped into the very pit of despair and longing. We are touching the reservoir of loss itself. We experience the long-held fear and doubt and grief that has always been there.

Stephen Levine, *Who Dies?*

The absolute finality of death creates a kind of loss that is unlike any other. This loss can be the most profound experience of life and also the most painful. Grief, as the expression of that pain, is part of a healing process enabling us to survive loss and to continue to function in the world.

Grief is essentially a private experience. How each of us responds to the death of someone we love is uniquely our own, personal response. However, the way in which we express that private feeling is influenced by what is acceptable in the larger society. Mourning ceremonies (funeral and memorial services) are models for the culturally accepted form of grieving, setting the tone and defining the manner of our expression.

Different societies have radically different approaches: In some cultures in the East, survivors are expected to sob and wail openly, exhibiting their sadness and dismay, while in Japan the bereaved family smiles so as not to burden others. What is considered an appropriate public display in one society is frowned on in another.

Time also influences custom. In Victorian England, death was romanticized and mourning was an elaborate ritual entailing black wreaths, bunting hung on doorways, and "mourning dress" worn for years after the event.

In this country today, however, we have decreased the number and nature of public symbols of mourning and discourage a prolonged expression of grief. We expect feelings to be controlled and mourning to be brief. Open demonstrations of intense grief embarrass us. Survivors are often encouraged to keep a stiff upper lip and disguise their deepest emotions with a display of false reserve. This can cause problems. In trying to measure the results of changes in mourning and bereavement practices, social psychologists are beginning to conclude:

> By giving private sorrow a public face, mourning customs help to confirm social bonds, reorder personal relationships, and establish a new identity for the survivors. Today in the United States, social networks and community ties have become loose; a fourth of the population moves every five years. People die in hospitals and nursing homes, sometimes away from their families. Mourning rituals have lost much of their power; we do not know how to respond to death. This absence of shared rituals and social prescriptions may create special problems for the survivors.[1]

When the funeral or memorial service is over, grief is often just beginning. The disorienting feelings that arise in bereavement can become quite intense and last a long time. If unexpressed and unresolved, they can lead to serious emotional difficulties resulting in, for instance, self-destructive behavior or an impaired ability to function. Thus, it is important to acknowledge bereavement, to experience and resolve grief, and eventually to find a way through the pain.

THE GRIEF PROCESS

Psychologists and psychiatrists have developed a number of theories about how grief works. Although they differ in some respects, many of these theories share common elements, identifying stages or phases of the grief process and agreeing generally about the nature of reactions over time.

Grief is not a static condition, constant and unchanging. It is a process, one that moves from denial and avoidance to recognition and acceptance of loss.

Keeping in mind how widely responses will vary from one person to another, the grief process generally includes the following stages:

- Initial shock and denial
- Yearning or searching for the lost person
- Disorientation and despair
- Adapting, acceptance, and recovery

INITIAL SHOCK   The first reaction to death, especially sudden death, tends to be shock, numbness, and often, denial. It is the psychological equivalent of the kind of physiological reaction we experience when we suffer a serious physical trauma—our body goes into shock, slowing down all nonessential functions until basic equilibrium can be regained.

Emotional shock and numbness allow us to delay the realization of death until we are capable of taking it in. The magnitude of loss inflicted by the death of someone we love is often so great that we cannot comprehend it all at once. Because immediate realization of the totality of the loss would overwhelm us, shock permits the masking of truth, at least in part. It allows us to recognize just a small piece of the truth at a time.

All of the physiological symptoms of shock, fear, and anxiety may show themselves during this initial period. A racing heart, dizziness or even faintness, appetite loss or stomach trouble, restlessness and insomnia, are all common symptoms of this reaction.

Physical shock and psychological denial are also a way of protesting against reality. Denial is our way to try to discredit the information, to cancel the news, to keep it away.

SEARCHING   As the initial shock subsides and the survivor begins to grasp reality, many psychologists have remarked that survivors seek to retrieve or locate the dead person. This searching phase may involve calling out to the deceased, even expecting a response. The bereaved may become preoccupied with thoughts of the loved one or repeatedly recall painful memories. Persistently hoping for the return of the deceased is a common feature of this searching phase.

We search not only for the one who has died but for our role in their absence. During this time, a grieving person may move as if on remote control, retaining the numbness of the initial shock. In the wake of death, survivors frequently feel lost themselves, "abandoned" by the deceased, and confused, insecure, fearful, and alone.

DISORIENTATION AND DESPAIR   As the bereaved begins to accept the fact that the deceased is never coming back, the pain of the loss can really hit hard. Increasing awareness can bring the release of any number of very powerful emotions—anguish, despair, depression, hopelessness, anger, guilt. In many cases, the most powerful and prominent emotions will be anger and guilt. This is a normal reaction.

Feeling that something horrible has happened, we may seek someone to blame. Anger can be directed at anyone—a police officer who informed you of the death, doctors, nurses, family members, or friends. Or it may be directed toward the deceased; you may feel s/he has abandoned you.

But in all likelihood you will serve as the primary target of your own anger. Many people find it much easier to be angry at themselves than at others. In confronting the death of someone they loved, survivors sometimes reproach themselves for their failings in the relationship. You might have thoughts such as "I should have" done this, or "if only" I'd done that s/he would still be alive. This kind of second-guessing guilt can become especially severe in circumstances such as accidental death or suicide. Guilt and self-blame are common reactions and can be the most difficult aspects of grief to overcome.

ADAPTING, ACCEPTANCE, AND RECOVERY   Acceptance of loss comes slowly and inconsistently rather than all at once. The bereaved may feel better for a while and then very much worse. In 1990, the *Harvard Medical School Mental Health Letter* ran a series of articles on bereavement in which the editors state:

> It takes time to accept the reality of the loss emotionally as well as intellectually. Depression and emotional swings may last as long as

several years. A kind of recovery is achieved when the bereaved can finally think of the dead person without overwhelming sadness and invest energy in other thoughts and activities. As the new reality is acknowledged and assimilated, grief fades into treasured memories.[2]

Adapting to a death and being able to function in the world, eventually forming new bonds, is the goal of the grief process. However, as the above article points out, "A new identity and social role are achieved, but recovery is never complete. Some effects last a lifetime, and waves of grief may return for many years on birthdays or the anniversary of the death."

These phases, as defined by mental health professionals, are loose guidelines for discussing the nature of grief. Such a model may or may not describe your particular experience, but most people do find a way through the difficult early disorientation to some form of acceptance or adaptation.

CIRCUMSTANCES THAT
INFLUENCE GRIEF

The way each of us responds to death depends on many factors, including age, gender, maturity, intelligence, cultural conditioning, and ethnic or religious influences. The manner in which someone dies also has a significant impact on the way in which survivors experience grief. Psychologists call this "the death surround." Factors here include the location, the reason and type of death, and the degree of preparation. Sudden or accidental death and suicide generally involve more bereavement complications than a death that had been long expected.

Expected Death
An expected death that follows a lingering terminal illness generally involves a comparatively brief grieving period for one major reason: The forewarning of death encourages what is called "anticipatory grieving." The process of accepting terminal illness can help prepare survivors for loss. In addition, anticipatory grief often gives mourners the chance to improve their relationship with the dying, which may make them feel better about both themselves and the deceased once death has occurred.

As described by the clinical psychologist Therese A. Rando, an expert on loss and grief therapy, "In anticipatory grief, you have the opportunity to say and do things during the illness that may help not only you, your dying loved one, and other family members, but which may create a more positive bereavement experience after the death for those of you left behind."[3]

Clinical research has shown that this advance warning can help the grief process. One study of sixty-eight widows and widowers by the psychiatrist Colin Parkes, a pioneering specialist in the grief and bereavement field, showed that the reaction of those who had at least two weeks' warning before death was less severe and prolonged than those who had little or no advance warning. Even four years later, those who had received an opportunity to prepare themselves were significantly less depressed, anxious, and self-blaming than survivors who had been surprised by death. Those with advance warning had also learned to cope with financial and day-to-day responsibilities more easily.

Of course, a lengthy terminal illness can sometimes *add* complications to the process of grieving. The physical and mental deterioration that accompanies many illnesses may make it difficult for survivors to remember how the deceased looked and behaved before the onset of the disease. In addition, the presence of terminal illness can often provoke emotional responses that sudden death does not prompt. Caregivers may resent the amount of time and attention needed by the terminally ill person or experience relief when s/he finally does die. These feelings can create guilt that complicates the grief process.

Sudden Death
In contrast to anticipated death, sudden death permits no emotional preparation for death whatsoever. The lack of anticipation—and especially the inability to say good-bye or "I'm sorry" or "I love you"—makes sudden death particularly difficult to bear.

As described by Dr. Rando,

> In both sudden death and anticipated death, there is pain. However, while the grief is not greater in sudden death, the capacity to cope is diminished. Grievers are shocked and stunned by the sudden loss of their loved one. The loss is so disruptive that recovery almost always is complicated. This is because the adaptive capacities are so severely

assaulted and the ability to cope is so critically diminished that functioning is seriously impaired. Grievers are overwhelmed.[4]

The lack of preparation in the case of sudden death often results in a score of immediate practical problems demanding time and attention. These details can complicate the mourning process by keeping survivors so busy that they don't have time to grieve over the loss. Overworked survivors tend to remain in shock, numbed by exhaustion as much as by the trauma itself.

Violent Death

Another complicating factor of sudden death is that it often involves violence. A violent death can trigger a similarly violent grieving process, characterized by considerable guilt, rage, or intense despair. Was the death preventable? Did the deceased suffer terribly? Questions of blame and responsibility arise. In such cases Rando says:

> Some people actually assume the blame themselves because they find it easier to deal with a traumatic event's being their responsibility, and thus within their control, than to cope with the fact that it was a truly random event over which no one had any control. They need to maintain a sense that the world is not so random and unpredictable. It is their way of looking for some control. Truly random events are frightening to all of us because we cannot protect ourselves against them.[5]

When death is the result of a random violent or murderous act, the general response may include questions about the behavior of the victim. Statements such as "what was s/he doing in that neighborhood?" or "s/he must have done something to provoke it" are often efforts to find some kind of reason for the event, to find cause and effect and therefore predictability and control.

Suicide

Suicide adds a dimension to grieving that is especially complex and difficult. Because it is a conscious choice by the deceased, suicide appears to be a statement of some kind, a final declaration, or a message. And it is often seen to be a message that reflects upon the survivors, as if they are somehow to blame. Suicide shatters the relationship between deceased and survivor and fuels intense feelings of rejection and abandonment in those left behind. It adds to normal grief a sense of failure, humiliation and betrayal, or a loss of self-esteem. Suicide can be seen as a preventable death. It didn't *have* to happen, and thus the survivor often feels s/he should have prevented it.

Survivors of suicide often react with overwhelming anger or guilt. They may experience anger toward the deceased, but more commonly, survivors blame themselves. The myriad of unresolved feelings and the profound absence of communication that the act of suicide implies deeply influence the grieving process.

To complicate matters even further, survivors of suicide may find it difficult to find the same kind of general support that other bereaved families or individuals are offered. There is a strong social stigma attached to suicide, and families may feel ostracized. Many religious teachings regard suicide as a sinful or improper act. In working through his or her grief, the survivor is required to cope with these additional burdens. In these cases, professional help and support may be necessary.

If the deceased was terminally ill and chose suicide as an alternative to what for him or her was unacceptable debilitation or unendurable pain, you may have had the opportunity to prepare for your loss (or even to share in the process of coming to terms with such a decision). This kind of suicide (sometimes called "self-deliverance") does not create the same shock as sudden death and usually results in the type of grief experienced after an anticipated death. (See chapter 5 for a discussion of self-deliverance and related issues.)

RELATIONSHIP

Obviously, the relationship between a survivor and the deceased also plays a part in determining the process of mourning. The nature and degree of perceived loss depends on the role the deceased played in our lives—how attached, how involved, or how interdependent we were.

This can be seen most clearly in the case of grief over a spouse's death. The survivor, who in large part defined his or her own identity as one-half of a couple, no longer has that role to fall back on.

Spouse

Married or partnered people grow accustomed to being regarded as one-half of a social unit. The death of one of them destroys the unit. As pointed out by Colin Murray Parkes, a pioneering psychiatrist in grief studies, bereavement requires a dramatic shift in perspective from "ours" to "mine," from "we" to "I." This compels widows and widowers to find new roles and learn how to relate to people in an entirely different way.

Gender roles, as well as pervasive cultural attitudes, account for significant differences in the grief experience of widows and widowers. Speaking very generally, men tend to recover more quickly on a social level, while they take a longer time making deep-seated emotional recoveries. Women are seen to suffer more from practical problems, financial difficulties, and loneliness, all of which can intensify or complicate the mourning process.

To find support, advice, and assistance, contact AARP's Widowed Persons Service or the National Association for Widowed People. They will be able to refer you to resources in your area. (See listings at the end of this chapter.)

Child

The death of one's child is generally regarded as one of the most devastating traumas that anyone can experience. This has not always been the case.

Death in early childhood used to be more common and, as a consequence, less dramatic an occurrence. In describing life and death in the Middle Ages, the authors of the excellent compilation *Dying: Facing the Facts* say, "The rates of infant and maternal mortality were very high, disease was rampant, nutrition and medical technology were inadequate, and everyday life was a hazardous affair."[6] Parents could expect to lose as many as half of their children in early childhood, and within the society as a whole, juvenile death was a familiar experience.

Even as recently as the nineteenth century, children died frequently. In the death-education textbook *The Last Dance,* the authors describe it this way,

> To our predecessors, the death of an infant or a child was not so uncommon. Although such deaths did not go unmourned, they were not seen as inappropriate. Today, because of the tremendous reduc-

tion in infant and child mortality, we are inclined to consider a child's death as quite unfair and inappropriate.[7]

Bereaved parents today usually suffer from an acute sense of guilt and regret, feeling in large part responsible for the death of their child—whatever the particular circumstances of that death might have been. Many feel that they have failed in the most essential responsibility of parenthood: taking care of their children and protecting them from harm. By blaming themselves, parents are attempting to regain a small degree of control over their lives, trying to make sense of the senseless. In the absence of some sort of explanation, they can feel totally powerless to protect other children they may have.

Even when an adult child dies, a parent may find it impossible to comprehend that this child could die now, when s/he had managed to protect him or her during the much more dangerous times of childhood.

A child's death can create intense anger in a parent, who may look for someone to blame. It is not uncommon for parents to blame one another, either secretly or overtly, with or without cause. The death of a child can take its toll on a parental partnership in other ways, too. Because both individuals confront this monumental loss at the same time, they usually can't offer one another the support they would normally provide in a different situation.

There are a number of organizations providing support, advice, and assistance to bereaved parents, including a membership group called The Compassionate Friends. (See listings at the end of this chapter.)

Infant
Miscarriage and stillbirth also cause grief. More and more psychiatric and medical professionals are encouraging the acknowledgment of grief in such situations and suggesting ways to help parents come to terms with the loss.

Sudden infant death syndrome (SIDS)—which kills 14,000 babies every year, most under the age of four months—generates intense grief. A SIDS death leaves a pronounced void in the lives of parents because families usually focus so much attention on caring for a baby in the months following birth. All SIDS deaths are investigated by police until the authorities are satisfied that the infant did indeed die from SIDS and not from some other circumstance. The tension and attendant suspicion created by such an investigation can be very hard on the parents and seriously complicates the normal mourning process. Because parents tend to view SIDS, perhaps more than any other cause of death, as preventable, the grief and guilt may linger for many years—even for the rest of their lives. This kind of grief may require special counseling. Contact the National SIDS Foundation for advice and support. (See listings at the end of this chapter.)

Parent
Because the death of a parent is the most common death most adults experience, we are generally expected to accept it with little difficulty. Yet the death of a parent, at any age, is a significant loss. It can symbolize the loss of unconditional love, a safe haven, or the parental home. It can bring us face-to-face with mortality for what may be the first time. It may also signal a liberation of sorts. With our parents gone, we can no longer see ourselves as children, even if only in relationship to them. In rethinking and reformulating our roles through the grieving process, we may find a new maturity that makes us feel truly adult for the first time in our lives.

In addition, if you have siblings, the death of a parent can produce profound changes in your relationships with them. For some people, a parent's death draws them closer to brothers and sisters, forming new and stronger bonds to one another. For others, however, the death—and the practical matters of making decisions for disposition and funeral services, administering a will, and perhaps arranging care for a surviving parent—can reawaken sibling rivalries and unresolved conflicts.

CHILDREN AND GRIEF

Child psychologists and other professionals generally presume that most children do have some understanding of death beginning at about age two. Often preschool children become very curious about death. Until age four or five, when they may begin to grasp the concept of linear time, most children see death as a reversible separation rather than a permanent condition. After about age five or six, children begin to develop a sense that some things are irreversible and by the preteen years have usually developed an understanding of death as a concrete biological process.

Adolescents, caught in the midst of so many other changes, can find it particularly difficult to cope with death. Teenagers may want to handle their grief on their own, but at the same time they still may depend on others—especially their parents—for comfort. The conflict between their continuing dependence and their emerging independence can make it difficult for adolescents to ask for the help they need.

The Death of a Parent

In addition to simple grief and tremendous sadness at the death of a parent, most children also experience an especially strong fear of abandonment. To defend against their growing feelings of insecurity, children may vent a lot of rage—both at the parent who has abandoned them and at the one who has survived but has been altered by grief.

Young children can experience enormous confusion about the death of a parent. They may believe they have somehow played a part in causing the death or take on responsibility for it, assuming (consciously or unconsciously) that they must have done something terribly wrong to "make" their parent leave them.

The Death of a Sibling

The death of a brother or sister will almost undoubtedly cause a great deal of insecurity in children. In some cases, it may provide them with their first real inkling that their parents cannot protect them from everything and that they, too, might die. Due to the powerful ambivalence that so often characterizes relationships between siblings, the death of a brother or sister may produce in a child a range of ambivalent emotions. The instability in a family following the death of a child may only heighten the surviving child's new sense of insecurity.

GOOD GRIEF

When psychologists talk about "resolving grief as a goal of the bereavement process," they are speaking of reaching a point where loss has been acknowledged and accepted and the survivor is able to function in the world. This isn't easy if you've lost someone you love.

Initially, you may have trouble getting through the day—or the night. Simply coping with the practical requirements of life may be a tremendous challenge. But eventually, if grief takes its course, you will be able to think of the deceased without crying or suffering unduly, to express regrets without feeling guilt, and to love others without a fear that you are betraying the deceased.

For many bereaved people, being able to remember the deceased without falling apart provides the first big sign that they are beginning to move through the process. Other signs include being able to forget the deceased for a while without feeling guilty, being able to enjoy yourself without feeling guilty, looking forward to the future, and seeing the death in perspective. In the case of the death of a spouse or partner, forming new friendships signals a turning point in recovery. Although this goal may seem impossible or even undesirable when you first begin to grieve, new friendships do signal a willingness to resume life without the deceased.

Successfully working through grief doesn't mean that you forget the deceased or that you stop missing him or her. It does mean that you can live your life in spite of your loss.

BAD GRIEF

In some cases, the progress of grief goes awry along the way. Symptoms of problems can take any of the following forms: a pronounced absence or inhibition of grief, prolonged or excessive grief, or the distortion of grief. These "atypical" behaviors prevent the bereaved from entering into a new life.

Psychiatrist Colin Parkes points out that these atypical forms do not really differ from normal grief in any of its symptoms or reactions but simply in the intensity and duration of the reactions. It's as if the mourner got stuck in one of the usual phases of grief (shock, anger, or guilt for instance), distorting, intensifying, or prolonging a typical reaction and making it chronic.

Absence of Grief
An apparent absence of the symptoms of grief does not usually indicate that the mourner doesn't feel the loss, only that s/he has delayed any reaction. Although sometimes due to the prolongation of the shock or denial reaction, absence of grief can be an act of will. The apparent lack—which prohibits resolution—may yield to either prolonged or distorted forms of mourning.

Psychologists point out that people may actively prevent themselves from grieving for any number of reasons. They may have a pronounced fear of losing control of themselves or their grief. This anxiety often stems from cultural conditioning that depicts the uncontrolled expression of emotion as "weak." Bereaved people might also stop themselves from grieving for fear that reviewing the relationship would unearth guilt or anger—feelings regarded as unacceptable toward a dead loved one. Finally, if the relationship was not recognized by the larger society, the bereaved might not feel "allowed" to mourn over it.

Excessive Grief

Excessive grief involves an unconscious unwillingness to let the deceased go. Months and even years can elapse following the death of a loved one, but excessive grievers may still maintain the characteristics of a recent bereavement. They may refuse to form new relationships. Chronic mourners cling to the deceased, almost as if they were keeping the dead alive through their prolonged grief. Some may fear that to overcome the loss would somehow betray a tacit pact with the deceased never to live a life separate from him or her. They cling to the pain of loss because it is all they have left of the loved one.

Certain types of death seem to demand protracted periods of grief in order to adapt to the loss. The death of a child, for instance, generally requires a longer period of bereavement than the death of an aged parent. Similarly, it usually takes longer to move toward acceptance of a sudden and unexpected death—especially a suicide—than it does to grieve over a death that follows an extended terminal illness. However, if symptoms appropriate in acute grief persist too long without changing, it can be a sign that the survivor needs professional help in coming to terms with the loss.

Distorted Grief

Distorted grief manifests itself primarily through self-destructive acts, obsessive thoughts of self-destruction, or extreme mental or emotional aberrations. Prolonged inattention to basic survival needs, such as eating and sleeping, or social needs, such as friendships and social activities, are symptomatic of distorted grief.

HOW TO FIND HELP

In 1917, Sigmund Freud wrote,

> It is well worth notice that, although mourning involves grave depar-
> tures from the normal attitude to life, it never occurs to us to regard
> it as a pathological condition and to refer it to medical treatment. We
> rely on its being overcome after a certain lapse of time, and we look
> upon any interference with it as useless or even harmful.[8]

While it is true that grief is a normal response to loss, it may be
that today it is more difficult to cope with that response on our own.
Often we do not have the support of a large, extended family or of
ritualized customs that maintain us throughout a lengthy mourning
period. And while the psychopathic condition of necrophobia (an
abnormal fear of death) would not be ascribed to most "normal"
people, we do, as a society, suffer from a cultural or mass necrophobia. It adversely affects us all by creating a general environment in
which a positive death experience is very difficult to achieve and grief
is an embarrassment. If we never allow ourselves to think about
death, we don't know how to deal with bereavement. Most people
need support during mourning, often beyond that available from
family and friends. Psychotherapy, counseling, or other professional
help can provide that support.

Bereavement counseling is becoming more specialized as mental
health professionals develop a better understanding of how to assist
with the grief process. In looking for a good clinician, you should
try to find one of these specialists, someone who works specifically
with grief and who has experience with the type of bereavement you
are dealing with (anticipated, sudden, or violent death, suicide,
etc.).

Another resource is a self-help support group. Filling the void left
by the vanishing extended family, peer support groups have developed to address many specialized needs, from widows and widowers
to families of suicide victims. Since members of these groups have
gone through similar experiences, they can often provide advice or
support in a more informed manner than could a relative or friend.
Chances are a self-help group exists nearby that can help you deal
with the particular circumstances of your bereavement.

RESOURCES AND SUPPORT

Books

Bereavement: A Magazine of Hope and Healing. For a free brochure, entitled "What's Good About Bereavement," contact Bereavement Publishing, 350 Gradle Drive, Carmel, IN 46032; (317) 846-9429.

Marguerite Bouvard with Evelyn Gladu. *The Path Through Grief: A Practical Guide.* Portland, Oreg.: Breitenbush Books, Inc., 1988.

Lynn Caine. *Being a Widow.* New York: William Morrow & Company, 1988.
[A book offering practical advice, including how to deal with stress and depression.]

Bob Deits. *Life After Loss: A Personal Guide Dealing with Death, Divorce, Job Change and Relocation.* Tucson, Ariz.: Fisher Books, 1988.
[Self-help for those recovering from loss.]

Robert C. DiGiulio. *Beyond Widowhood: From Bereavement to Emergence and Hope.* New York: Macmillan, Free Press, 1989.
[Guidance based on the author's own experiences, research, and interviews of how widowed persons handle the death of their spouse. Extensive annotated appendix lists sources of organized support.]

Katherine Fair Donnelly. *Recovering from the Loss of a Sibling.* New York: Dodd, Mead & Company, Gamut Books, 1988.
[Using case studies, the author examines the psychosocial problems of parents and surviving siblings. The author discusses accidental death, suicide, death after a terminal illness, murder, and death of an infant. Includes an annotated listing of support groups and suggested readings.]

Genevieve Davis Ginsburg. *To Live Again: Rebuilding Your Life After You've Become a Widow.* New York: Bantam Books, 1989.
[A practical guide for widows.]

Earl A. Grollman. *Living When a Loved One Has Died.* Boston: Beacon Press, 1987.
[A book written to help those who have experienced the death of a loved one.]

John W. James and Frank Cherry. *The Grief Recovery Handbook: A Step-by-Step Program for Moving Beyond Loss.* New York: Harper & Row, Perennial Library, 1989.

Ronald J. Knapp. *Beyond Endurance: When a Child Dies.* New York: Shocken Books, 1986.
[Written by a sociologist after interviewing 155 families. Examined are death after a catastrophic illness, sudden or unexpected death, and death by murder.]

Jill Krementz. *How It Feels When a Parent Dies.* New York: Alfred A. Knopf, Borzoi Books, 1988.
[Eighteen children retell their experiences and feelings after the death of a parent. Includes photographs. For children and adults.]

Tony Lake. *Living with Grief.* London: Sheldon Press, 1984.
[An examination of the aspects of grief following bereavement. Includes discussion of unexpected death, suicide, death of a child, and loss of a parent.]

Stephen Levine. *Healing into Life and Death.* New York: Doubleday, Anchor Press, 1989.

————. *Meetings at the Edge: Dialogues with the Grieving and the Dying, the Healing and the Healed.* New York: Doubleday, Anchor Books, 1984.

Eda LeShan. *Learning to Say Good-by: When a Parent Dies.* New York: Avon Books, 1978.
[For children in elementary or intermediate grades.]

Candy Lightner and Nancy Hathaway. *Giving Sorrow Words: How to Cope with Grief and Get On with Your Life.* New York: Warner Books, 1990.

Ruth Jean Loewinsohn. *Survival Handbook for Widows (and for Relatives and Friends Who Want to Understand).* Rev. and updated. Washington, D.C.: American Association of Retired Persons; Glenview, Ill.: Scott, Foresman and Company, AARP Books, 1987.

Christopher Lucas and Henry M. Seiden. *Silent Grief: Living in the Wake of Suicide.* New York: Bantam Books, 1990.
[This book offers practical advice and help with the psychological trauma that afflicts many survivors of suicide. Includes an appendix of support groups keyed to type of support and whether or not a fee is charged.]

Edward Myers. *When Parents Die: A Guide for Adults.* New York: Penguin Books, 1987.
[An examination of the psychological effects of losing a parent. Appendices include suggestions for further reading and a listing of additional resources.]

Nancy O'Connor. *Letting Go with Love: The Grieving Process.* New York: Bantam Books, 1989.

Colin Murray Parkes. *Bereavement: Studies of Grief in Adult Life.* 2nd ed. Harmondsworth, England: Penguin Books, 1987.
[A psychiatrist's examination of the many components and effects of bereavement.]

Lily Pincus. *Death and the Family: The Importance of Mourning.* 1976. Reprint, New York: Shocken Books, 1988.
[Explores the effects on the family of death and bereavement.]

Therese A. Rando. *Grieving: How to Go On Living When Someone You Love Dies.* Lexington, Mass.: Lexington Books, 1988.
[A comprehensive book examining grief and its resolution. Addresses different forms of death, including sudden and anticipated death and death of a spouse, parent, child, or sibling. Finding effective professional and self-help groups for assistance is also discussed. Includes sections adapted from the author's professional writings.]

Beverley Raphael. *The Anatomy of Bereavement.* New York: Basic Books, 1986.
[An examination of the phases of bereavement and how they affect various age groups.]

Lilly Singer, Margaret Sirot, and Susan Rodd. *Beyond Loss: A Practical Guide Through Grief to a Meaningful Life.* New York: E. P. Dutton, 1988.

Carol Staudacher. *Beyond Grief: A Guide for Recovering from the Death of a Loved One.* Oakland, Calif.: New Harbinger Publications, 1987.
[Includes sections on understanding and coping with grief and surviving specific types of loss, including the death of a spouse, parent, or child; suicide; murder; accidental death; and death during childhood.]

Judith Viorst. *Necessary Losses: The Loves, Illusions, Dependencies and Impossible Expectations That All of Us Have to Give Up in Order to Grow.* New York: Fawcett Crest, 1987.

Widowed Persons Service. *WPS Directory of Services for the Widowed in the United States and Canada.* Washington, D.C.: Widowed Persons Services, 1991. Available at no charge by sending a postcard to WPS, AARP (American Association of Retired Persons), 1909 K Street, NW, Washington, DC 20049.
[A directory of national, regional, and local groups helpful to widowed persons, including groups concerned with providing support to those who are grieving.]

Agencies/Service Organizations

American Association of Suicidology
2459 South Ash Street
Denver, CO 80222
(303) 692-0985
An information clearinghouse concerned with aspects of suicide, including the referral of survivors of suicide to local resources. Publishes a bibliography/resource list, available at no charge.

The Compassionate Friends
900 Jorie Boulevard
Oak Brook, IL 60521
(708) 990-0010
A self-help membership organization (with chapters nationwide) for parents who have experienced the death of a child. Local chapters have contact people, also bereaved parents, who accept phone calls on a voluntary basis. Provides free literature and also distributes books on grief and bereavement.

National Association for Uniformed Services/Society of Military Widows
5535 Hempstead Way
Springfield, VA 22151
(703) 750-1342
A lobbying organization that serves the interests of widows of active or retired servicemen.

National Sudden Infant Death Syndrome (SIDS) Foundation
10500 Little Patuxent Parkway
Suite 420
Columbia, MD 21044
1-800-221-SIDS
(301) 964-8000 (in Maryland)
This national organization, with local chapters, promotes research surrounding SIDS and also provides support to bereaved parents.

National Victim Center
307 West Seventh Street
Suite 1001
Fort Worth, TX 76102
(817) 877-3355
An advocacy and resource center. Services include referrals for emotional and legal counseling. A publications catalog is available free of charge.

Parents of Murdered Children
100 East Eighth Street, B-41
Cincinnati, OH 45202
(513) 721-5683
A national self-help organization with local chapters for family members or
friends of murdered children. Services include a newsletter, advocacy, and
counseling by telephone and by letter.

Survivors of Suicide
Suicide Prevention Center, Inc.
P.O. Box 1393
Dayton, OH 45401-1393
(513) 223-9096 Business office
(513) 223-4777 Hotline
This organization has a nationwide directory of support groups for survi-
vors of suicide. Call them for information and referrals.

THEOS Foundation (They Help Each Other Spiritually)
717 Liberty Avenue
Pittsburgh, PA 15301
(412) 471-7779
National membership organization with volunteer network of widowed
people throughout the United States and Canada. Offers help with over-
coming grief through mutual support chapters and individual outreach.
Their publications program includes *Survivors Outreach Magazine.*

Widowed Persons Service
American Association of Retired Persons (AARP)
1909 K Street, NW
Washington, DC 20049
(202) 728-4370
A program of the American Association of Retired Persons offering a wide
range of services; supports nationwide network of chapters with volunteers
offering support to widowed persons. Local chapters operate telephone
referral services and group sessions. The WPS helps organize technical
assistance to local groups. Literature is available at no charge, including a
selected annotated bibliography; the booklet "On Being Alone," which
offers practical advice for the newly widowed; and their magazine *Insights.*

Additional Resources for Finding Help Facing Death

Come lovely and soothing death,
Undulate round the world, serenely arriving, arriving,
In the day, in the night, to all, to each,
Sooner or later, delicate death.

Walt Whitman

Because death is hidden in our society, all the questions it raises are also hidden—until death itself forces us to face them. At that point we are quite alone. How do we find help with the emotional and psychological issues raised by death? Putting our external house in order is one thing; fully accepting our own impermanence is quite another.

This book addresses the practical matters death raises. It does not address those other fundamental questions hidden within each individual—the intensely personal matter of what death means to you.

Of course, many resources do exist for finding help facing death. A wealth of books approach the subject from a myriad of viewpoints, and there are a number of centers and institutes devoted to teaching, counseling, and exploring death and dying issues. Following is an introductory listing of some of them. Many of these books contain selected bibliographies and appendixes, which in turn can lead you to additional sources of support. The organizations listed throughout this book can often refer you to other assistance local in your area and appropriate for your needs. Good luck to you.

General Reading

Philippe Ariès. *The Hour of Our Death.* Translated by Helen Weaver. New York: Random House, Vintage Books, 1982.
[A scholarly examination of attitudes toward death in Western Christian cultures. This classic work spans the Middle Ages to modern times.]

_____. *Western Attitudes Toward Death: From the Middle Ages to the Present.* Translated by Patricia M. Ranum. Baltimore: Johns Hopkins University Press, 1975.
[Four brief essays by the pioneer social historian of death.]

Paul Badham and Linda Badham, eds. *Death and Immortality in the Religions of the World.* God: The Contemporary Discussion Series. New York: Paragon House, New Era Books, 1987.
[Essays examine the traditional beliefs of the African religions, Judaism, Christianity, Islam, Hinduism, and Buddhism concerning death and dying.]

Georges Bataille. *Death and Sensuality: A Study of Eroticism and the Taboo.* New York: Walker and Company, 1962.

Ernest Becker. *The Denial of Death.* New York: Macmillan, Free Press, 1973.
[A classic work exploring the effect of death denial and fear on our society and human behavior.]

E. A. Wallis Budge. *The Book of the Dead.* London: Arkana, Penguin, 1989.
[Often called The Egyptian Book of the Dead.]

David Dempsey. *The Way We Die: An Investigation of Death and Dying in America Today.* New York: McGraw-Hill Book Company, 1977.
[A classic work on death and dying. This book is currently out of print. Check with your local library or used-book store.]

Lynne Ann DeSpelder and Albert Lee Strickland. *The Last Dance: Encountering Death and Dying.* 2nd ed. Mountain View, Calif.: Mayfield Publishing Company, 1987.
[A death-education textbook that includes sections on cultural and historical perspectives and attitudes.]

Norbert Elias. *The Loneliness of the Dying.* Translated by Edmund Jephcott. Oxford and New York: Basil Blackwell, 1986.
[A philosophical exploration of some of society's taboos concerning
death and dying.]

W. Y. Evans-Wentz, ed. *The Tibetan Book of the Dead: Or the After-Death
Experiences on the Bardo Plane.* New York: Oxford University Press,
1960.

Francesca Fremantle and Chogyam Trungpa, trans. *The Tibetan Book of the
Dead: The Great Liberation Through Hearing in the Bardo.* Berkeley,
Calif.: Shambhala Publications, 1975.

E. J. Gold. *The American Book of the Dead.* Nevada City, Calif.: Gateways,
1987.

———. *The Lazy Man's Guide to Death and Dying.* Nevada City, Calif.:
IDHHB, Inc., 1983.
[Currently out of print; check with your local library or used-book
store.]

Philip Kapleau. *The Wheel of Life and Death.* New York: Doubleday, 1989.

Kenneth Kramer. *The Sacred Art of Dying, How World Religions Understand Death.* New York: Paulist Press, 1988.
[A discussion of comparative religion and death, written in a very
accessible manner.]

Robert Jay Lifton. *The Broken Connection: On Death and the Continuity
of Life.* New York: Basic Books, 1983.

Robert Jay Lifton and Eric Olson. *Living and Dying.* New York: Bantam,
1975.

Peter Prunkl and Rebecca L. Berry. *Death Week: Exploring the Dying
Process.* Series in Death Education, Aging, and Health Care. New
York: Hemisphere Publishing, 1989.
[Examines the stages and phases of death.]

Susan Sontag. *AIDS and Its Metaphors.* New York: Farrar, Straus and
Giroux, 1989.

———. *Illness as Metaphor.* New York: Farrar, Straus and Giroux, 1978.

Lewis Thomas. *The Lives of a Cell: Notes of a Biology Watcher.* New York:
Bantam Books, 1975.

Alice Walker. *To Hell with Dying.* New York: Harcourt Brace Jovanovich,
1967.
[A story for children, illustrated by Catherine Deeter.]

Hannelore Wass, Felix M. Berardo, and Robert Neimeyer, eds. *Dying: Facing the Facts.* 2nd ed. Series in Death Education, Aging, and Health Care. New York: Harper & Row, Hemisphere Publishing, 1989.
[This textbook is useful for both professionals and laypeople; includes discussion of death anxiety.]

Practical Advice

Robert Buckman. *"I Don't Know What to Say . . .": How to Help and Support Someone Who Is Dying.* Boston: Little, Brown & Company, 1989.
[Includes sections on talking and listening to the dying, the process of dying, and practical advice for caregivers.]

Earl A. Grollman. *Talking About Death: A Dialogue Between Parent and Child.* 3rd ed. Boston: Beacon Press, 1990.
[A guide for parents and children. Includes a read-along story and a comprehensive list of resources and organizations.]

Earl A. Grollman, ed. *Concerning Death: A Practical Guide for the Living.* Boston: Beacon Press, 1974.
[Essays on care of the dying; includes a discussion of what it is like to be dying.]

Elisabeth Kübler-Ross. *AIDS: The Ultimate Challenge.* New York: Macmillan, 1987.

_____. *On Children and Death.* New York: Macmillan, Collier Books, 1985.

_____. *On Death and Dying.* New York: Macmillan, Collier Books, 1982.
[The author's first and most influential book.]

_____. *Questions and Answers on Death and Dying.* New York: Macmillan, Collier Books, 1974.
[Written as a follow-up to *On Death and Dying.*]

_____. *Working It Through.* New York: Macmillan, Collier Books, 1987.
[Stories from Kübler-Ross's Workshops on Life, Death and Transition.]

_____, ed. *Death: The Final Stage of Growth.* Englewood Cliffs, N.J.: Prentice-Hall, Spectrum Books, 1975.
[A collection of essays examining death and dying from the perspective of other cultures and also from personal experience.]

Stephen Levine. *Healing into Life and Death.* New York: Doubleday, Anchor Press, 1989.

————. *Meetings at the Edge: Dialogues with the Grieving and the Dying, the Healing and the Healed.* Doubleday, Anchor Books, 1984.

————. *Who Dies? An Investigation of Conscious Living and Dying.* New York: Doubleday, 1982.

Averil Stedeford. *Facing Death: Patients, Families and Professionals.* London: Heinemann Medical Books, 1984.
[This book is written by a psychiatrist for those who work with the dying. Includes sections on the psychological responses to physical symptoms and the fears of death.]

Personal Accounts
Simone De Beauvoir. *A Very Easy Death.* Translated by Patrick O'Brian. New York: Pantheon Books, 1985.

Robert E. Kavanaugh. *Facing Death.* Baltimore: Penguin Books, 1974.

Michael Lesy. *The Forbidden Zone.* New York: Doubleday, Anchor Books, 1989.
[An exploration of contemporary death; Lesy examines the lives and places of people who deal with death on a daily basis, including a homicide detective, an undertaker, and death row inmates.]

Gilda Radner. *It's Always Something.* New York: Simon and Schuster, 1989.

Le Anne Schreiber. *Midstream: The Story of a Mother's Death and a Daughter's Renewal.* New York: Viking Penguin, 1990.

Anthologies and Bibliographies
D. J. Enright, ed. *The Oxford Book of Death.* Oxford and New York: Oxford University Press, 1987.
[Anthology of poetic texts concerned with death and dying.]

David Meltzer, ed. *Death: An Anthology of Ancient Texts, Songs, Prayers and Stories.* San Francisco: North Point Press, 1984.

Charles Panati. *Panati's Extraordinary Endings of Practically Everything and Everybody.* New York: Harper & Row, Perennial Library, 1989.
[Facts and anecdotes about endings, including death, last wills and testaments, and the death styles of the rich and famous.]

Michael A. Simpson. *Dying, Death and Grief: A Critical Bibliography.*
Pittsburgh: University of Pittsburgh Press, 1987.
[A comprehensive bibliography listing and evaluating a wide range of
death literature. Simpson's comments, criticisms, and analyses are
knowledgeable, pithy, and to the point.]

Hannelore Wass and Charles A. Corr, eds. *Childhood and Death.* Series in
Death Education, Aging, and Health Care. Washington, D.C.:
Harper & Row, Hemisphere Publishing, 1984.
[Includes sections on fears and anxieties of death and children's con-
cepts of death.]

Agencies/Service Organizations

Elisabeth Kübler-Ross Center
South Route 616
Head Waters, VA 24442
(703) 396-3441
Conducts a variety of workshops and training programs (both at the Center
and at retreats around the country) dealing with topics that include chronic
and terminal illness, AIDS, and bereavement. The book *Working It Through*
(see above) is the story of the Workshop on Life, Death and Transition.

Make Today Count
168 Panoramic
Camdenton, MO 65065
(314) 346-6644
An international organization with local chapters that provides support to
people with life-threatening illnesses.

National Hospice Organization
1901 North Moore Street
Suite 901
Arlington, VA 22209
(703) 243-5900
The predominant national organization serving as an advocacy group and
clearinghouse for information on hospices and hospice care for both health
professionals and laypeople. The NHO can make referrals to local counselors or support groups that may be of help to the dying.

St. Francis Center
5417 Sherier Place, NW
Washington, DC 20016
(202) 363-8500

A nonprofit, nonsectarian organization whose services revolve around aspects of death and dying. Their programs include the Friends Program, a group of professionally guided volunteers who provide personal and practical support to the terminally ill.

Shanti Project
525 Howard Street
San Francisco, CA 94105
(415) 777-2273
Originally begun as a volunteer support group for the terminally ill, the Shanti Project now concentrates its efforts mainly on support services to people with AIDS. They offer an extensive videotape program that instructs volunteers how to counsel people with AIDS.

Source Notes

PREFACE

1. Philippe Ariès, *Western Attitudes Toward Death* (Baltimore: Johns Hopkins University Press, 1974), p. 85.

CHAPTER 1

1. Denis Clifford, *Nolo's Simple Will Book* (Berkeley, Calif.: Nolo Press, 1988), p. 2:2.
2. Hayden Curry and Denis Clifford, *Legal Guide for Lesbian and Gay Couples,* 5th ed. (Berkeley, Calif.: Nolo Press, 1989), p. 9:24.
3. Norman F. Dacey, *How to Avoid Probate!* (New York: Collier Books, Macmillan Publishing, 1990), p. 23.
4. Theodore E. Hughes and David Klein, *A Family Guide to Wills, Funerals & Probate: How to Protect Yourself and Your Survivors* (New York: Charles Scribner's Sons, 1987), p. 63.
5. Hughes and Klein, *Wills, Funerals & Probate,* p. 80.

CHAPTER 2

1. Michael Specter, "Hot Tombs, The Last Yuppie Status Symbol," *New Republic,* 11 September 1989, p. 25.
2. Editors of Consumer Reports, *Funerals: Consumers' Last Rights: The Consumers Union Report on Conventional Funerals and Burial . . . and Some Alternatives,*

Including Cremation, Direct Cremation, Direct Burial, and Body Donation (New York: W. W. Norton, 1977), p. 16.
3. Specter, "Hot Tombs," p. 23.
4. Thomas C. Nelson, *It's Your Choice: The Practical Guide to Planning a Funeral* (Washington, D.C.: American Association of Retired Persons; Glenview, Ill.: Scott, Foresman and Company, 1983), pp. 51–52.
5. Martin A. Corry, "In the Matter of Funeral Industry Practices Trade Regulation Rule, 16 CFR Part 453" (Washington, D.C.: American Association of Retired Persons, 1989), p. 139.
6. Judi Culbertson and Tom Randall, *Permanent Parisians: An Illustrated Guide to the Cemeteries of Paris* (Chelsea, Vt.: Chelsea Green Publishing, 1986), p. 3.
7. Theodore E. Hughes and David Klein, *A Family Guide to Wills, Funerals, & Probate* (New York: Charles Scribner's Sons, 1987), p. 89.
8. Continental Association of Funeral and Memorial Societies, "Facts About Cremation" (Bethesda, Md.: CAFMS).
9. Nelson, *It's Your Choice*, p. 16.
10. Mark Dowie, *"We Have a Donor": The Bold New World of Organ Transplanting* (New York: St. Martin's Press, 1988), p. 43.
11. Joel Swerdlow, *Matching Needs, Saving Lives, Building a Comprehensive Network for Transplantation and Biomedical Research* (Washington, D.C.: Annenberg Washington Program, 1989), p. 33.
12. David Owen, "Rest in Pieces," *Harper's,* June 1983, p. 74.
13. Ibid., p. 73.
14. D. G. Mandelbaum, "Social Uses of Funeral Rites," in H. Feifel, ed., *The Meaning of Death* (New York: McGraw-Hill, 1959), p. 189. Quoted in Therese A. Rando, *Grief, Dying, and Death: Clinical Interventions for Caregivers* (Champaign, Ill.: Research Press Company, 1984), p. 173.
15. Therese A. Rando, *Grief, Dying and Death: Clinical Interventions for Caregivers* (Champaign, Ill.: Research Press Company, 1984), p. 176.
16. Drawn from Ernest Morgan, *Dealing Creatively with Death: A Manual of Death Education and Simple Burial* (Burnsville, N.C.: Celo Press, 1984), pp. 68–70.
17. List drawn from Robin Micheli, "Paying for the Big Chill," *Money,* December 1988, p. 144.
18. *Federal Register* (31 May 1988), vol. 53, no. 104, p. 19864.
19. Hughes and Klein, *Wills, Funerals, & Probate*, p. 138.
20. Allison Engel and Margaret Engel, "The L.L. Been Catalogue," *Esquire,* November 1990, p. 154.
21. Micheli, "Paying for the Big Chill," p. 146.
22. Nelson, *It's Your Choice*, p. 62.

CHAPTER 3

1. Thomas A. Raffin, M.D., Joel N. Shurkin, and Wharton Sinkler III, M.D., *Intensive Care: Facing the Critical Choices* (New York: W. H. Freeman, 1989), p. 183.
2. Concern for Dying, *The Living Will and Other Advance Directives: A Legal Guide to Medical Treatment Decisions* (New York: Concern for Dying, 1986), p. 4.

3. Society for the Right to Die, "You and Your Living Will" (New York: Society for the Right to Die, 1990).
4. Society for the Right to Die, "What You Should Know About Medical Durable Power of Attorney" (New York: Society for the Right to Die, 1990).
5. Thomas Scully, M.D., and Celia Scully, *Making Medical Decisions: How to Make Difficult Medical and Ethical Decisions for Yourself and Your Family* (New York: Simon & Schuster, Fireside Books, 1989), pp. 114–18.
6. List drawn from the *Handbook of Living Will Laws* (New York: Society for the Right to Die, 1987), p. 15.
7. *Cruzan v. Director, Missouri Department of Health,* Supreme Court of the United States [110 S. Ct. 2841 (1990)].
8. New York State Department of Health, "Do Not Resuscitate Orders: A Guide for Patients and Families," pamphlet.
9. Mary Kay Blakely, "Coma: Stories from the Edge of Death," *Life,* July 1989, p. 80.
10. Melvin Konner, M.D., "The Loss of Self," *New York Times Magazine,* 25 June 1989, p. 42.
11. Barry Shapiro, M.D., letter to the editor, *New York Times Magazine,* 23 October 1988.

CHAPTER 4

1. Ruth Macklin, *Mortal Choices: Ethical Dilemmas in Modern Medicine* (Boston: Houghton Mifflin, 1987), p. 61.
2. Thomas A. Raffin, Joel N. Shurkin, and Wharton Sinkler III, *Intensive Care, Facing the Critical Choices* (New York: W. H. Freeman, 1989), pp. 17–18.
3. List quoted from Thomas Scully, M.D., and Celia Scully, *Making Medical Decisions: How to Make Difficult Medical and Ethical Decisions for Yourself and Your Family* (New York: Simon & Schuster, Fireside Books, 1989), p. 275.
4. List drawn from Scully and Scully, *Making Medical Decisions,* p. 276.
5. Macklin, *Mortal Choices,* p. 58.
6. Raffin, Shurkin, and Sinkler, *Intensive Care,* p. 142.
7. "Standards and Guidelines for Cardiopulmonary Resuscitation (CPR) and Emergency Cardiac Care (ECC), *Journal of the American Medical Association* 244 (1980): 453, quoted in George J. Annas, *The Rights of Patients: The Basic ACLU Guide to Patient Rights,* 2nd ed., revised, American Civil Liberties Handbooks (Carbondale, Ill.: Southern Illinois University Press, 1989), p. 214.
8. List drawn from Scully and Scully, *Making Medical Decisions,* p. 120.
9. Elisabeth Rosenthal, "Crowding Causes Agonizing Crisis in Intensive Care," *New York Times,* 22 August 1989, p. C1.
10. Raffin, Shurkin, and Sinkler, *Intensive Care,* p. 138.
11. Scully and Scully, *Making Medical Decisions,* p. 278.
12. In the matter of Claire C. Conroy, Supreme Court of New Jersey, A-108, decided 17 January 1985, quoted in Macklin, *Mortal Decisions,* p. 79.
13. Derek Humphry and Ann Wickett, *The Right to Die* (New York: Harper & Row, 1987), p. 129.

14. Concern for Dying, *Living Will,* pp. 24–27; see also: David Hendin, *Death as a Fact of Life* (New York: W. W. Norton & Co., 1984), p. 86; Colen, *Living Will,* p. 13.

15. *New England Journal of Medicine* 310 (26 April 1984).

16. S. Bedell and T. Delbanco, "Choices About CPR in the Hospital: When Do Physicians Talk with Patients?" *New England Journal of Medicine* 310 (26 April 1984), cited in American Association for Retired Persons, *A Matter of Choice: Planning Ahead for Health Care Decisions* (Washington, D.C.: AARP, 1986), p. 5.

17. Scully and Scully, *Making Medical Decisions,* p. 264.

18. List drawn from Scully and Scully, *Making Medical Decisions,* p. 265.

19. *Otis R. Bowen, Secretary of Health and Human Services, Petitioner v. American Medical Association et al.,* Supreme Court of the United States, No. 84-1529 (B2750-B2804), 1986.

CHAPTER 5

1. *The Random House Dictionary of the English Language,* 2nd ed. unabridged, s.v. "bioethics."

2. Arthur Caplan quoted in Thomas Scully and Celia Scully, *Making Medical Decisions: How to Make Difficult Medical and Ethical Decisions for Yourself and Your Family* (New York: Simon & Schuster, Fireside Books, 1989), p. 19.

3. The Hastings Center, "Portrait of an Organization Filling a Need," pamphlet.

4. Scully and Scully, *Making Medical Decisions,* pp. 277–78.

5. "Report of the Medical Consultants on the Diagnosis of Death to the President's Commission for the Study of Ethical Problems in Medicine and Biomedical and Behavioral Research," 1981, p. 2. Quoted in Robert Veatch, *Death, Dying, and the Biological Revolution: Our Last Quest for Responsibility,* rev. ed. (New Haven: Yale University Press, 1989), p. 52.

6. Lewis Thomas, *The Lives of a Cell: Notes of a Biology Watcher* (New York: Bantam, 1974), p. 58.

7. Daniel Callahan, "Can We Return Death to Disease?" *Hastings Center Report* 19, supplement (January/February 1989): 4.

8. Lynne DeSpelder and Albert Lee Strickland, *The Last Dance: Encountering Death and Dying,* 2nd ed. (Mountain View, Calif.: Mayfield Publishing, 1987), p. 414.

9. Judge Edward H. Johnson, Re: Larry James McAfee as reported in Peter Applebome, "Judge Rules Quadriplegic Can Be Allowed to End Life," *New York Times,* 7 September 1989, p. A16.

10. Robert M. Veatch, *Death, Dying, and the Biological Revolution: Our Last Quest for Responsibility* (New Haven: Yale University Press, 1989), p. 106.

11. List drawn from Pieter Admiraal, "Justifiable Active Euthanasia in the Netherlands," in *Euthanasia: The Moral Issues,* eds. Robert M. Baird and Stuart E. Rosenbaum (Buffalo: Prometheus Books, 1989), p. 125.

12. Ibid., p. 126.

13. A. A. Scitovsky, and A. M. Capron, "Medical Care at the End of Life: The Interaction of Economics and Ethics," *Annual Review of Public Health* 7

(1986): 59–75; Anne A. Scitovsky, "The High Cost of Dying: What Do the Data Show?" *Milbank Memorial Fund Quarterly/Health and Society* 62 (1984): 591–608; James Lubitz and Ronald Prihoda, "The Use and Costs of Medicare Services in the Last 2 Years of Life," *Health Care Financing Review* 5 (Spring 1984): 117–31.

14. Victor Fuchs quoted in Daniel Callahan, "Limiting Health Care for the Old," *Nation,* 15/22 August 1987, p. 125.

15. Selma Abramowitz, "Pain, as a Matter of Policy," *New York Times,* 24 October 1989, p. A27.

CHAPTER 6

1. William J. Winslade and Judith Wilson Ross, *Choosing Life or Death: A Guide for Patients, Families, and Professionals* (New York: Macmillan, Free Press, 1986), pp. 66–67.
2. Jeanne Quint Benoliel, "Institutional Dying: A Convergence of Cultural Values, Technology and Social Organization," in *Dying: Facing the Facts,* eds. Hannelore Wass, Felix M. Berardo, and Robert A. Neimeyer (Washington, D.C.: Harper & Row, Hemisphere Publishing, 1988), p. 168.
3. Charles E. Rosenberg, *The Care of Strangers: The Rise of America's Hospital System* (New York: Basic Books, 1987), p. 10.
4. Christine M. Mumma and Jeanne Quint Benoliel, "Care, Cure, and Hospital Dying Trajectories," *Omega* 15 (1984–85): 275–88; cited in Jack B. Kamerman, *Death in the Midst of Life: Social & Cultural Influences on Death, Grief and Mourning* (Englewood Cliffs, N.J.: Prentice-Hall, 1987), p. 46.
5. Thomas P. Hackett and Avery D. Weisman, "Reactions to the Imminence of Death," in *The Threat of Impending Disaster: Contributions to the Psychology of Stress,* eds. George H. Grosser, Henry Wechsler, and Milton Greenblatt (Cambridge, Mass.: MIT Press, 1964); cited in Kamerman, *Death in the Midst of Life.*
6. Margaret Gold, "Life Support: Families Speak About Hospital, Hospice and Home Care for the Fatally Ill," Summary Report (New York Institute for Consumer Policy Research, Consumers Union Foundation, 1983), p. 11.
7. Winslade and Ross, *Choosing Life or Death,* p. 80.
8. Thomas Scully and Celia Scully, *Making Medical Decisions: How to Make Difficult Medical and Ethical Decisions for Yourself and Your Family* (New York: Simon & Schuster, Fireside Books, 1989), p. 264.
9. G. Hess, "Health Care Needs Inherent in Emergency Services—Can They Be Met?" *Nursing Clinics of North America* 5 (1970): 243–49; quoted in Benoliel, "Institutional Dying" in *Dying: Facing the Facts,* eds. Hannelore Wass, Felix M. Berardo, and Robert Neimeyer (Washington, D.C.: Harper & Row, Hemisphere Publishing, 1988), p. 173.
10. Joseph M. Darby, M.D., Keith Stein, M.D., Ake Grenvik, M.D., and Susan A. Stuart, R.N., "Approach to Management of the Heartbeating 'Brain Dead' Organ Donor," *Journal of the American Medical Association* 261 (21 April 1989): 2222–28.
11. Mark Dowie, *"We Have a Donor": The Bold New World of Organ Transplanting* (New York: St. Martin's Press, 1988), p. 145.

12. John A. Robertson, *The Rights of the Critically Ill* (New York: Bantam Books, 1983), p. 126.
13. Dowie, *"We Have a Donor,"* p. 150.
14. Benoliel, "Institutional Dying," in *Dying: Facing the Facts,* eds. Wass, Berardo, and Neimeyer, p. 170.
15. Mark A. Sager et al., "Changes in the Location of Death After Passage of Medicare's Prospective Payment System," *New England Journal of Medicine* 320 (16 February 1989): 433–39.
16. Robert N. Brown with Legal Counsel for the Elderly, *The Rights of Older Persons,* 2nd ed., completely revised and up-to-date, American Civil Liberties Union Handbooks (Carbondale, Ill.: Southern Illinois University Press, 1989), p. 289.
17. Jean Crichton, *Age Care Sourcebook: A Resource Guide for the Aging and Their Families* (New York: Simon & Schuster, Fireside Books, 1987), pp. 229–30.
18. Lynne Ann DeSpelder and Albert Lee Strickland, *The Last Dance, Encountering Death and Dying,* 2nd ed. (Mountain View, Calif.: Mayfield Publishing, 1987), p. 121.
19. Tamar Lewin, "Widespread Abuses," *New York Times,* 27 February 1990, p. A20.
20. List drawn from Little, Deborah Whiting, *Home Care for the Dying* (New York: Doubleday, Dial Press, 1985).
21. Ida M. Martinson et al., "Home Care for Children Dying of Cancer," *Research in Nursing and Health* 9 (March 1986): 11; Sandra R. Edwardson, "The Choice Between Hospital and Home Care for Terminally Ill Children," *Nursing Research* 32 (January/February 1983): 29–34.
22. David Adams, "Helping the Dying Child," in *Childhood and Death,* eds. Hannelore Wass and Charles A. Corr (Washington, D.C.: Hemisphere Publishing, 1984), p. 110.
23. Scully and Scully, *Making Medical Decisions,* p. 257.
24. National Consumers League, *A Consumer Guide to Home Health Care* (Washington, D.C.: National Consumers League, 1985), p. 4.
25. National Association for Home Care statistics compiled in 1988, quoted in Linda Puig, "Health Care Comes Home for Savings," *Business & Health,* November 1989, p. 12.
26. Ernest Morgan, *Dealing Creatively with Death: A Manual of Death Education and Simple Burial* (Burnsville, N.C.: Celo Press, 1984), p. 106.

CHAPTER 7

1. National Consumers League, *A Consumer Guide to Hospice Care* (Washington, D.C.: National Consumers League, 1986), pp. 3–4.
2. Vincent Mor, David S. Greer, and Robert Kastenbaum, "The Hospice Experiment: An Alternative in Terminal Care," in *The Hospice Experiment,* eds. Mor, Greer, and Kastenbaum (Baltimore, Md.: Johns Hopkins University Press, 1988), p. 9.
3. National Hospice Organization, "The Basics of Hospice" (Arlington, Va.: National Hospice Organization, 1988), pamphlet.

4. Glen W. Davidson, *The Hospice, Development and Administration* (New York: Hemisphere Publishing, 1985), p. 3.
5. Mor, Greer, and Kastenbaum, in *The Hospice Experiment*, p. 10.
6. Anne Munley, *The Hospice Alternative, A New Context for Death and Dying* (New York: Basic Books, Inc., 1983), p. 20.
7. Cicely Saunders, "Control of Pain in Terminal Cancer," *Nursing Times* 72 (1 July 1976): 13, quoted in Munley, *Hospice Alternative*, p. 20.
8. Harry van Bommel, *Choices: For People Who Have a Terminal Illness, Their Families, and Their Caregivers* (Toronto: NC Press, 1986), p. 83.
9. Ibid.
10. Sandol Stoddard, *The Hospice Movement: A Better Way of Caring for the Dying* (New York: Stein and Day, 1978), p. 48.
11. National Hospice Organization. "Meeting the Challenge for a Special Kind of Caring: Standards of a Hospice Program of Care Recommended by the National Hospice Organization" (Arlington, Va.: National Hospice Organization), p. 3.
12. National Consumers League, *Consumer Guide to Hospice Care*, p. 6.
13. Glen W. Davidson, "Hospice Care for the Dying," in *Dying: Facing the Facts*, eds. Hannelore Wass, Felix M. Berardo, and Robert Neimeyer (Washington, D.C.: Harper & Row, Hemisphere Publishing, 1988), p. 190.
14. This list is taken from National Consumers League, *Consumer Guide to Hospice Care*, p. 8.
15. Ibid., p. 3.
16. From the literature of Children's Hospice International.
17. "Corporations Establishing Hospice Benefit," *NHO Hospice News* (National Hospice Organization), June/July 1987, p. 2.

CHAPTER 8

1. Lynne Ann DeSpelder and Albert Lee Strickland, *The Last Dance: Encountering Death and Dying* (Mountain View, Calif.: Mayfield Publishing Company, 1987), p. 184.
2. List quoted from Ernest Morgan, *Dealing Creatively with Death: A Manual of Death Education and Simple Burial*, 10th ed., rev. and expanded (Burnsville, N.C.: Celo Press, 1984), p. 44.
3. Lawrence K. Altman, "Sharp Drop in Autopsies Stirs Fears that Quality of Care May Also Fall." *New York Times*, 21 July 1988.

CHAPTER 9

1. Theodore E. Hughes and David A. Klein, *A Family Guide to Wills, Funerals, & Probate* (New York: Charles Scribner's Sons, 1987), p. 4.
2. Denis Clifford, *Plan Your Estate: Wills, Probate Avoidance, Trusts & Taxes* (Berkeley, Calif.: Nolo Press, 1989), p. 19/4.
3. Hughes and Klein, *Wills, Funerals, & Probate*, p. 166.
4. Clifford, *Plan Your Estate*, p. 7/3.

5. Kay Ostberg, *Probate, Settling an Estate: A Step-By-Step Guide* (New York: Random House, 1990), pp. 39–40.
6. Hughes and Klein, *Wills, Funerals, & Probate,* p. 204.

CHAPTER 10

1. "Bereavement and Grief, Part II," *Harvard Medical School Mental Health Letter,* vol. 3, no. 10 (April 1987), p. 2.
2. "Bereavement and Grief, Part I," *Harvard Medical School Mental Health Letter,* vol. 3, no. 9 (March 1987), p. 2.
3. Therese A. Rando, *Grieving: How to Go On Living When Someone You Love Dies* (Lexington, Mass.: Lexington Books, 1988), p. 94.
4. Ibid., p. 90.
5. Ibid., p. 108.
6. Hannelore Wass, Felix M. Berardo, Robert A. Neimeyer, *Dying: Facing the Facts* (New York: Hemisphere Publishing Co., Harper & Row, 1988), p. 201.
7. Lynne Ann DeSpelder and Albert Lee Strickland, *The Last Dance, Encountering Death and Dying* (Mountain View, Calif.: Mayfield Publishing Co., 1988), p. 236.
8. Sigmund Freud, "Mourning and Melancholia," Standard Edition of *The Complete Psychological Works of Sigmund Freud,* vol. 14 (London: Hogarth Press, 1957), p. 244.

Bibliography

Abts, Henry W., III. *The Living Trust: The Fail-Proof Way to Pass Along Your Estate to Your Heirs Without Lawyers, Courts, or the Probate System.* Chicago: Contemporary Books; Markham, Ont.: Beaverbooks, Ltd., 1989.

Ajemian, Ina, and Balfour Mount, eds. *The R.V.H. Manual on Palliative/ Hospice Care: A Resource Book.* Salem, N.H.: Ayer, 1980.

Alderman, Linda. *Why Did Daddy Die?: Helping Children Cope with the Loss of a Parent.* New York: Pocket Books, 1989.

Alexander, George J. *Writing a Living Will: Using a Durable Power-of-Attorney.* New York: Praeger, 1988.

Alsop, Stuart. *Stay of Execution: A Sort of Memoir.* New York: Lippincott, 1973.

American Association of Retired Persons. *A Matter of Choice: Planning Ahead for Health Care Decisions.* Planning for Difficult Times Series. Washington, D.C.: AARP, n.d.

_____. *Tomorrow's Choices: Preparing Now for Future Legal, Financial, and Health Care Decisions.* Planning for Difficult Times Series. Washington, D.C.: AARP, 1988.

Anderson, Ray S. *Theology, Death and Dying.* Oxford, England: Basil Blackwell, 1986.

Annas, George J. *The Rights of Patients: The Basic ACLU Guide to Patients'*

Rights. 2nd ed., completely revised and up-to-date. American Civil Liberties Union Handbooks. Carbondale, Ill.: Southern University Press, 1989.

Anosike, Benji O. *How to Do Your Own Probate and Estate Settlement Without a Lawyer.* New York: Do-It-Yourself Legal Publishers, 1984.

Appel, Jens C., and F. Bruce Gentry. *The Complete Will Kit.* New York: John Wiley & Sons, 1990.

Ariès, Philippe. *The Hour of Our Death.* Translated by Helen Weaver. New York: Random House, Vintage Books, 1982.

———. *Western Attitudes Toward Death: From the Middle Ages to the Present.* Translated by Patricia M. Ranum. Baltimore, Md.: Johns Hopkins University Press, 1975.

Arya, Pandit Usharbudh. *Meditation and the Art of Dying.* Honesdale, Penn.: Himalayan International Institute of Yoga Science and Philosophy, 1979.

Ashley, Paul P., updated by Jennifer L. Olanie. *You and Your Will: The Planning and Management of Your Estate.* Rev. and updated ed. New York: New American Library, Mentor Books, 1985.

Association for the Care of Children's Health. *Your Child with Special Needs at Home and in the Community.* Washington, D.C.: Association for the Care of Children's Health, 1989.

Austin, Louis. *The Living Trust Alternative.* Kansas City, Mo.: Hudspeth Publishing Company, 1988.

Badham, Paul, and Linda Badham, eds. *Death and Immortality in the Religions of the World.* God: The Contemporary Discussion Series. New York: Paragon House, New Era Books, 1987.

Baird, Robert M., and Stuart E. Rosenbaum, eds. *Euthanasia: The Moral Issues.* Contemporary Issues in Philosophy series. Buffalo: Prometheus Books, 1989.

Bataille, Georges. *Death and Sensuality: A Study of Eroticism and the Taboo.* New York: Walker and Company, 1962.

Baulch, Evelyn M. *Extended Health Care at Home: A Complete and Practical Guide.* Berkeley, Calif.: Celestial Arts, 1989.

Bausell, R. Barker, Michael A. Rooney, and Charles B. Inlander. *How to Evaluate and Select a Nursing Home.* People's Medical Society Books. Reading, Mass.: Addison-Wesley Publishing, 1988.

Becker, Ernest. *The Denial of Death.* New York: Macmillan, Free Press, 1973.

Bedell, S., and T. Delbanco, "Choices About CPR in the Hospital: When Do Physicians Talk with Patients?" *New England Journal of Medicine* 310 (26 April 1984).

Bender, Martin S. *Everyone Needs a Will.* Holbrook, Mass.: Bob Adams, Inc., 1990.

Benoliel, Jeanne Quint, ed. *Death Education for the Professional.* Series in Death Education, Aging, and Health Care. Washington, D.C.: Hemisphere Publishing, 1982.

Bereavement: A Magazine of Hope and Healing. Carmel, Ind.: Bereavement Publishing.

Biggs, Don, with Stephen L. Bluestone and Jerry M. Dale. *How to Avoid Lawyers: Step-by-Step Guide to Being Your Own Lawyer in Almost Every Situation.* New York: Garland, 1985.

Body, Mind and Spirit magazine. *The New Age Catalogue: Access to Information and Sources.* New York: Doubleday, Dolphin Books, 1988.

Bouvard, Marguerite, in collaboration with Evelyn Gladu. *The Path Through Grief: A Practical Guide.* Portland, Oreg.: Breitenbush Books, Inc., 1988.

Bove, Alexander, Jr. *The Complete Book of Wills & Estates.* New York: Henry Holt and Co.; Markham, Ont.: Fitzhenry & Whiteside Limited, 1989.

Brosterman, Robert, and Thomas Brosterman. *The Complete Estate Planning Guide.* Rev. ed. New York: New American Library, Mentor Books, 1987.

Brown, Robert N., with Legal Counsel for the Elderly. *The Rights of Older Persons.* 2nd ed. Completely revised and up-to-date. American Civil Liberties Union Handbooks. Carbondale, Ill.: Southern University Press, 1989.

Buckingham, Robert W. *Care of the Dying Child: A Practical Guide for Those Who Help Others.* New and expanded edition of *A Special Kind of Love.* Continuum Counseling Series. New York: Continuum, 1989.

Buckman, Robert. *"I Don't Know What to Say . . .": How to Help and Support Someone Who Is Dying.* Boston: Little, Brown & Company, 1989.

Caine, Lynn. *Being a Widow.* New York: William Morrow & Company, 1988.

_____. *Lifelines.* New York: William Morrow & Company, 1977.

Callahan, Daniel. *Setting Limits: Medical Goals in an Aging Society.* New York: Simon & Schuster, Touchstone Books, 1988.

_____. *What Kind of Life: The Limits of Medical Progress.* New York: Simon & Schuster, 1990.

Callari, Elizabeth S. *A Gentle Death: Personal Caregiving to the Terminally Ill.* Greensborough, N.C.: Tudor Publishers, 1987.

Carlson, Lisa. *Caring for Your Own Dead.* Hinesburg, Vt.: Upper Access Publishers, 1987.

Carper, Jean. *Health Care U.S.A.* New York: Prentice Hall, 1987.

Chaney, Earlyne. *The Mystery of Death and Dying: Initiation at the Moment of Death.* York Beach, Me.: Samuel Weiser, 1988.

Chase, Deborah. *Dying at Home with Hospice.* St. Louis, Mo.: C. V. Mosley, 1986.

Chesser, Barbara Russell. *Because You Care: Practical Ideas for Helping Those Who Grieve.* Waco, Tex.: Word Books, 1987.

Clifford, Denis. *Plan Your Estate: Wills, Probate Avoidance, Trusts & Taxes.* Berkeley, Calif.: Nolo Press, 1989.

———. *Simple Will Book: How to Prepare a Legally Valid Will.* Berkeley, Calif.: Nolo Press, 1990.

———. *The Power of Attorney Book.* 2nd ed. Berkeley, Calif.: Nolo Press, 1990.

Clifford, Terry. *Tibetan Buddhist Medicine and Psychiatry: The Diamond Healing.* York Beach, Me.: Samuel Weiser, 1984.

Colen, B. D. *Hard Choices: Mixed Blessings of Modern Medical Technology.* New York: G. P. Putnam's Sons, 1986.

———. *The Essential Guide to a Living Will.* New York: Pharos Books, 1987.

Concern for Dying. *The Living Will and Other Advance Directives: A Legal Guide to Medical Treatment Decisions.* New York: Concern for Dying, 1986.

Consumer Law Foundation. *The Complete Legal Kit.* Philadelphia: Running Press, 1988.

Consumer Reports. *Funerals: Consumers' Last Rights: The Consumers Union Report on Conventional Funerals and Burial . . . and Some Alternatives, Including Cremation, Direct Cremation, Direct Burial, and Body Donation.* New York: W. W. Norton, 1977.

Copperman, Harriet. *Dying at Home.* New York: Wiley, 1984.

Council of Better Business Bureaus and National HomeCaring Council. *All About Home Care: A Consumer's Guide.* 2nd ed. Arlington, Va.: Council of Better Business Bureaus; New York: National HomeCaring Council, 1983.

Crenshaw, David A. *Bereavement: Counseling the Grieving Throughout the Life Cycle.* New York: Continuum, 1990.

Crichton, Jean. *The Age Care Sourcebook: A Resource Guide for the Aging and Their Families.* New York: Simon & Schuster, Fireside Books, 1987.

Crumbley, D. Lawrence, and Edward E. Millam. *Keys to Estate Planning and Trusts.* Barron's Business Keys Series. New York: Barron's, 1989.

Culbertson, Judi, and Tom Randall. *Permanent Parisans: An Illustrated Guide to the Cemeteries of Paris.* Chelsea, Vt.: Chelsea Green Publishing, 1986.

Curry, Hayden, and Denis Clifford. *A Legal Guide for Lesbian and Gay Couples.* 5th ed. Berkeley, Calif.: Nolo Press, 1989.

Dacey, Norman F. *How to Avoid Probate!* 1990 rev. ed. New York: Macmillan, Collier Books, 1990.

Daly, Eugene J. *Thy Will Be Done: A Guide to Wills, Taxation, and Estate Planning for Older Persons.* Buffalo, N.Y.: Prometheus Books, 1990.

Davidson, Glen W. *The Hospice: Development and Administration,* 2nd ed. New York: Hemisphere Publishing, 1985.

Davies, Phyllis. *Grief: Climb Toward Understanding: Self-Help When You Are Struggling.* New York: Carol Communications, Lyle Stuart Books, 1988.

De Beauvoir, Simone. *A Very Easy Death.* Translated by Patrick O'Brian. New York: Pantheon Books, 1985.

Degner, Lesley F., and Janet I. Beaton. *Life-Death Decisions in Health Care.* Series in Death Education, Aging, and Health Care. New York: Taylor & Francis Group, Hemisphere Publishing, 1987.

Deits, Bob. *Life After Loss: A Personal Guide Dealing with Death, Divorce, Job Change and Relocation.* Tucson, Ariz.: Fisher Books, 1988.

Dempsey, David. *The Way We Die: An Investigation of Death and Dying in America Today.* New York: McGraw-Hill Book Company, 1977.

DeSpelder, Lynne Ann, and Albert Lee Strickland. *The Last Dance: Encountering Death and Dying.* 2nd ed. Mountain View, Calif.: Mayfield Publishing Company, 1987.

Diagram Group. *The Brain: A User's Manual.* New and expanded ed. New York: G. P. Putnam's Sons, Perigree, 1987.

DiGiulio, Robert C. *Beyond Widowhood: From Bereavement to Emergence and Hope.* New York: Macmillan, Free Press, 1989.

Donnelly, Katherine Fair. *Recovering from the Loss of a Sibling.* New York: Dodd, Mead & Company, Gamut Books, 1988.

Doress, Paula Brown, Diana Laskin Siegal, and the Midlife and Older Women Book Project. *Ourselves, Growing Older: Women Aging with Knowledge and Power.* New York: Simon & Schuster, Touchstone Books, 1987.

Dowie, Mark. *"We Have a Donor": The Bold New World of Organ Transplanting.* New York: St. Martin's Press, 1988.

Draznin, Yaffa. *How to Prepare for Death: A Practical Guide.* New York: Hawthorn Books, 1976.

Duda, Deborah. *Coming Home: A Guide to Dying at Home with Dignity.* New York: Aurora Press, 1987.

Dychtwald, Ken, and Joe Flower. *Age Wave: The Challenges and Opportunities of an Aging America.* Los Angeles, Calif.: Jeremy Tarcher, 1989.

Easwaran, Eknath. *Dialogue with Death: The Spiritual Psychology of the Katha Upanishad.* Petaluma, Calif.: Nilgiri Press, 1987.

Edinberg, Mark A. *Talking with Your Aging Parents.* Boston: Shambala, 1987.

Edwardson, Sandra R. "The Choice Between Hospital and Home Care for Terminally Ill Children." *Nursing Research* 32 (January/February 1983):29–34.

Elias, Norbert. *The Loneliness of the Dying.* Translated by Edmund Jephcott. Oxford and New York: Basil Blackwell, 1985.

Elias, Stephen. *Legal Research: How to Find and Understand the Law.* 2nd ed. Berkeley, Calif.: Nolo Press, 1986.

Engram, Sara. *Mortal Matters: When a Loved One Dies.* Kansas City, Mo.: Andrews and McMeel, 1990.

Enright, D. J., ed. *The Oxford Book of Death.* New York: Oxford University Press, 1987.

Equicor. *1987 Hospital Daily Service Charges: An Annual Report.* Nashville, Tenn.: Equicor, 1987.

Evans-Wentz, W. Y., comp. and ed. *The Tibetan Book of the Dead: Or the After-Death Experiences on the Bardo Plane.* 3rd ed. New York: Oxford University Press, 1960.

Fleisher, Elan. *Unpleasant Ways to Die.* New York: St. Martin's Press, 1989.

Flint, Margaret M. *A Consumer's Guide to Nursing Home Care in New York State.* New York: Friends and Relatives of Institutionalized Aged, 1987.

Foehner, Charlotte, and Carol Cozart. *The Widow's Handbook: A Guide for Living.* Golden, Colo.: Fulcrum, 1989.

Foos-Graber, Anya. *Deathing: An Intelligent Alternative for the Final Moments of Life.* York Beach, Me.: Nicolas-Hays, Inc., 1989.

Forbes, Malcolm. *They Went That-a-Way.* New York: Ballantine Books, 1988.

Frantz, Thomas T. *When Your Child Has a Life-Threatening Illness.* Rev. ed. Washington, D.C.: Association for the Care of Children's Health; The Candlelighters Childhood Cancer Foundation, 1988. Available from the Association, 3615 Wisconsin Avenue, NW, Washington, DC 20016; (202) 244-1801.

Fremantle, Francesca, and Chogyam Trungpa, trans. *The Tibetan Book of the Dead: The Great Liberation Through Hearing in the Bardo.* Berkeley, Calif.: Shambhala, 1975.

Frist, William, M.D. *Transplant: A Heart Surgeon's Account of the Life-and-Death Dramas of the New Medicine.* New York: Atlantic Monthly Press, 1989.

Gatov, Elizabeth Smith. *Widows in the Dark: Rescuing Your Financial Position.* New York: Warner Books, 1986.

Gaylin, Willard, and Ruth Macklin, eds. *Who Speaks for the Child?: The Problems of Proxy Consent.* New York: Plenum, 1982.

Gervais, Karen Grandstrand. *Redefining Death.* New Haven: Yale University Press, 1986.

Ginsburg, Genevieve Davis. *To Live Again: Rebuilding Your Life After You've Become a Widow.* New York: Bantam Books, 1989.

Gold, E. J. *The American Book of the Dead.* Nevada City, Calif.: Gateways/ IDHHB, Inc., 1987.

_____. *The Lazy Man's Guide to Death and Dying.* Nevada City, Calif.: IDHHB, Inc., 1983.

Gold, Margaret. *Life Support: Families Speak About Hospital, Hospice and Home Care for the Fatally Ill.* Mount Vernon, N.Y.: Institute for Consumer Policy Research, 1983.

Goleman, Daniel. *Vital Lies, Simple Truths: The Psychology of Self-Deception.* New York: Simon & Schuster, 1985.

Gonda, Thomas Andrew, and John Edward. *Graceful Dying: A Practical Approach to Terminal Care.* Menlo Park, Calif.: Addison-Wesley, 1983.

Gonda, Thomas Andrew, and John Ruark. *Dying Dignified: The Health Professional's Guide to Care.* Reading, Mass.: Addison-Wesley, 1984.

Granta 27 (Summer 1989).

Grof, Stanislav, and Christina Grof. *Beyond Death: The Gates of Consciousness.* London: Thames and Hudson, 1980.

Grollman, Earl A. *Living When a Loved One Has Died.* Boston: Beacon Press, 1977.

_____. *Suicide: Prevention, Intervention, Postintervention.* 2nd ed. Rev. and expanded. Boston: Beacon Press, 1988.

_____. *Talking About Death: A Dialogue Between Parent and Child.* Boston: Beacon Press, 1990.

_____. ed. *Concerning Death: A Practical Guide for the Living.* Boston: Beacon Press, 1974.

Grosz, Anton. *Letters to a Dying Friend, What Comes Next.* Wheaton, Ill.: The Theosophical Publishing House, 1989.

Halpern, James. *Helping Your Aging Parents: A Practical Guide for Adult Children.* New York: Fawcett Crest, 1988.

Hardt, Dale V. *Death: The Final Frontier.* Englewood Cliffs, N.J.: Prentice-Hall, 1979.

Hastings Center Report. Briarcliff, N.Y.: The Hastings Center.

Health Care Financing Administration. *Hospice Benefits Under Medicare.* Washington, D.C.: Government Printing Office, 1989.

Hendin, David. *Death as a Fact of Life.* New York: W. W. Norton & Co., 1984.

Hopkins, Jeffrey, and Lati Rinbochay. *Death, Intermediate State and Rebirth in Tibetan Buddhism.* Ithaca, N.Y.: Snow Lion Publications, 1985.

Horne, Jo. *The Nursing Home: A Guide for Families.* Washington, D.C.: American Association of Retired Persons; Glenview, Ill.: Scott, Foresman and Co., 1989.

How to Make a Will, How to Use a Trust. 5th ed. Dobbs Ferry, N.Y.: Oceana Publications, 1986.

Hughes, Theodore E., and David Klein. *A Family Guide to Wills, Funerals, & Estate Planning: How to Protect Yourself and Your Survivors.* New York: Charles Scribner's Sons, 1987.

Humphry, Derek. *Let Me Die Before I Wake: Hemlock's Book of Self-Deliverance for the Dying.* 5th ed. Eugene, Oreg.: Hemlock Society; distributed by Grove Press, 1986.

———. *The Right to Die: Understanding Euthanasia.* New York: Harper and Row, Perennial Library; Toronto: Fitzhenry & Whiteside Limited, 1987.

———, with Ann Wickett. *Jean's Way.* New York: Harper & Row, Perennial Library, 1986.

James, John W., and Frank Cherry. *The Grief Recovery Handbook: A Step-by-Step Program for Moving Beyond Loss.* New York: Harper & Row, Perennial Library, 1988.

Joint Commission on the Accreditation of Hospitals. *The Nature, Characteristics, and Processes of Hospice Care in the United States.* vol. 2., *Service Delivery.* Chicago: Joint Commission on Accreditation of Hospitals.

Kamerman, Jack B. *Death in the Midst of Life: Social and Cultural Influences on Death, Grief and Mourning.* Englewood Cliffs, N.J.: Prentice-Hall, 1988.

Kapleau, Philip. *The Wheel of Life: A Practical and Spiritual Guide.* New York: Doubleday, 1989.

———. *The Wheel of Life and Death.* New York: Doubleday, 1989.

Kaufman, Howard H., M.D., ed. *Pediatric Brain Death and Organ/Tissue Retrieval: Medical, Ethical, and Legal Aspects.* New York: Plenum Medical Book Co., 1989.

Kavenaugh, Robert E., *Facing Death.* Baltimore, Md.: Penguin Books, 1974.

Knapp, Ronald J. *Beyond Endurance: When a Child Dies.* New York: Schocken Books, 1986.

Kothari, Manu L., and Lopa A. Mehta. *Death: A New Perspective on the Phenomena of Disease and Dying.* London: Marion Boyars Publishers, 1986.

Kramer, Kenneth. *The Sacred Art of Dying: How World Religions Understand Death.* New York: Paulist Press, 1988.

Krementz, Jill. *How It Feels When a Parent Dies.* New York: Alfred A. Knopf, Borzoi Books, 1988.

Kübler-Ross, Elisabeth. *AIDS: The Ultimate Challenge.* New York: Macmillan, Collier, 1989.

———. *Living with Death and Dying.* New York: Macmillan, Collier Books, 1982.

———. *On Children and Death.* New York: Macmillan, Collier Books, 1985.

———. *On Death and Dying.* New York: Macmillan, Collier Books, 1982.

———. *Questions and Answers on Death and Dying.* New York: Macmillan, Collier Books, 1974.

———. *Working It Through.* New York: Macmillan, Collier Books, 1987.

_____, ed. *Death: The Final Stage of Growth*. Englewood Cliffs, N.J.: Prentice-Hall, Spectrum Books, 1975.

Kushner, Harold S. *When Bad Things Happen to Good People*. New York: Schocken Books, 1981.

Lake, Tony. *Living with Grief*. London: Sheldon Press, 1984.

Lama Lodo. *Bardo Teachings: The Way of Death and Rebirth*. Ithaca, N.Y.: Snow Lion Publications, 1987.

Lamb, David. *Death, Brain Death and Ethics*. London: Croom Helm, 1988.

Lande, David S. "Explaining Legal Fees for Probate." *New York State Bar Journal*, February 1988, pp. 40–44.

Larsen, David C. *Who Gets It When You Go? A Guide for Planning Your Will, Protecting Your Family's Financial Future, Minimizing Inheritance Taxes and Avoiding Probate*. New York: Random House, 1982.

_____. *You Can't Take It with You: A Step-by-Step Personalized Approach to Your Will to Avoid Probate and Estate Taxes*. New York: Random House, Vintage Books, 1988.

Legal Counsel for the Elderly. *Decision-Making, Incapacity and the Elderly: A Protective Services Manual*. Washington, D.C.: Legal Counsel for the Elderly, 1987; supplement, 1989.

LeShan, Eda. *Learning to Say Good-by: When a Parent Dies*. New York: Avon Books, 1978.

Lester, Toni P. *How to Settle an Estate or Prepare Your Will*. New York: Putnam, Perigee Books, 1988.

Lesy, Michael. *The Forbidden Zone*. Doubleday, Anchor Books, 1989.

Levine, Stephen. *Healing into Life and Death*. New York: Doubleday, Anchor Books, 1987.

_____. *Meetings at the Edge: Dialogues with the Grieving and the Dying, the Healing and the Healed*. Doubleday, Anchor Books, 1984.

_____. *Who Dies? An Investigation of Conscious Living and Conscious Dying*. New York: Doubleday, 1982.

Leviton, Daniel, ed. *Horrendous Death, Health, and Well-Being*. New York: Hemisphere Publishing Co., 1991.

Lifton, Robert Jay. *The Broken Connection: On Death and the Continuity of Life*. New York: Basic Books, 1983.

_____, and Eric Olson. *Living and Dying*. New York: Bantam Books, 1975.

Lightner, Candy, and Nancy Hathaway. *Giving Sorrow Words: How to Cope with Grief and Get On with Your Life*. New York: Warner Books, Inc., 1990.

Little, Deborah Whiting. *Home Care for the Dying: A Reassuring, Comprehensive Guide to Physical and Emotional Care*. New York: Doubleday, Dial Press, 1985.

Loewinsohn, Ruth Jean. *Survival Handbook for Widows (and for Relatives and Friends Who Want to Understand)*. Rev. and updated. Washington, D.C.: American Association of Retired Persons; Glenview, Ill.: Scott, Foresman and Company, AARP Books, 1984.

Lubitz, James, and Ronald Prihoda. "The Use and Costs of Medicare Services in the Last Two Years of Life." *Health Care Financing Review* 5 (Spring 1984):117–31.

Lukas, Christopher, and Henry M. Seiden. *Silent Grief: Living in the Wake of Suicide*. New York: Bantam Books, 1990.

Lyon, Jeff. *Playing God in the Nursery*. New York: W. W. Norton, 1985.

Macklin, Ruth. *Mortal Choices: Ethical Dilemmas in Modern Medicine*. Boston: Houghton Mifflin, 1987.

Martelli, Leonard J., with Fran D. Peltz and William Messina. *When Someone You Know Has AIDS: A Practical Guide*. New York: Crown, 1987.

Martinson, Ida M., et al. "Home Care for Children Dying of Cancer." *Research in Nursing and Health* 9 (March 1986):11.

Maxwell, Katie. *No Lifetime Guarantee: Dealing with the Details of Death*. Crozet, Va.: Betterway Publications, 1988.

McDannell, Colleen, and Bernhard Lang. *Heaven: A History*. New Haven: Yale University Press, 1988.

Meltzer, David, ed. *Death: An Anthology of Ancient Texts, Songs, Prayers and Stories*. San Francisco, Calif.: North Point Press, 1984.

Memorial Society Fund. *Helping the Elderly Make Choices About Funeral & Memorial Planning*. Washington, D.C.: The Memorial Society Fund, 1988.

Merck Manual of Diagnosis and Therapy, The. 15th ed. Rahway, N.J.: Merck & Co., Merck Sharp & Dohme Research Laboratories, 1987.

Micheli, Robin. "Paying for the Big Chill." *Money*, December 1988, 147.

Miller, Albert J., and Michael James Acri. *Death: A Bibliographical Guide*. Metuchen, N.J.: Scarecrow Press, 1977.

Mitford, Jessica. *The American Way of Death*. New York: Fawcett Crest, 1963.

Moldow, D. Gay, and Ida M. Martinson. *Home Care for Seriously Ill Children: A Manual for Parents*. 2nd ed. Arlington, Va.: Children's Hospice International, 1984.

Moody, Raymond A., Jr. *Life After Life*. New York: Bantam Books, 1978.
———. *Reflections on Life After Life*. New York: Bantam Books, 1977.

Mor, Vincent, David S. Greer, and Robert Kastenbaum, eds. *The Hospice Experiment*. Johns Hopkins Series in Contemporary Medicine and Public Health. Baltimore, Md.: Johns Hopkins University Press, 1988.

Morgan, Ernest. *Dealing Creatively with Death: A Manual of Death Education and Simple Burial*. 11th ed., revised and expanded. Edited by Jennifer Morgan. Burnsville, N.C.: Celo Press, 1988.

Muktananda. *Does Death Really Exist?* South Fallsburg, N.Y.: SYDA Foundation, 1983.

Mullin, Glenn H. *Death and Dying: The Tibetan Tradition.* Boston: Arkana, 1986.

Munley, Anne. *The Hospice Alternative: A New Context for Death and Dying.* New York: Basic Books, 1983.

_____. Cynthia S. Powers, and John B. Williamson. "Humanizing Nursing Home Environments: The Relevance of Hospice Principles." *International Journal of Aging and Human Development* 15 (1982):263–84.

Myers, Edward. *When Parents Die: A Guide for Adults.* New York: Penguin Books, 1987.

Nassif, Janet Zhun. *The Home Health Care Solution: A Complete Consumer Guide.* New York: Harper & Row, Perennial Library, 1985.

National Center for Education in Maternal and Child Health. *A Guide to Resources in Perinatal Bereavement.* Washington, D.C.: NCEMCH, 1988.

_____. *Reaching Out: A Directory of National Organizations Related to Maternal and Child Health.* Washington, D.C.: NCEMCH, 1989.

National Consumers League. *A Consumer Guide to Home Health Care.* Washington, D.C.: National Consumers League, 1986.

_____. *A Consumer Guide to Hospice Care.* Washington, D.C.: National Consumers League, 1986.

Nelson, Thomas C. *It's Your Choice: The Practical Guide to Planning a Funeral.* Washington, D.C.: American Association of Retired Persons; Glenview, Ill.: Scott, Foresman and Co., AARP Books, 1983.

Newman, Stephen A. "Will Power." *New York,* 23 March 1987, p. 75.

New York Academy of Medicine. *Autopsy Manual with Guidelines for Organ and Tissue Donations.* 5th ed. New York: New York Academy of Medicine, 1988.

New York State Department of Health. *Do Not Resuscitate Orders: A Guide for Patients and Families.* New York: New York State Department of Health, 1989.

Nissley, Julia. *How to Probate an Estate.* California ed. Berkeley, Calif.: Nolo Press, 1988.

Office of Technology Assessment Task Force. *Life-Sustaining Technologies and the Elderly.* Philadelphia: J. B. Lippincott; Science Information Center, 1987.

Omega: Journal of Death and Dying. Amityville, N.Y.: Baywood Publishing Co., Inc.

Ostberg, Kay, in association with HALT. *Probate, Settling an Estate: A Step-by-Step Guide.* New York: Random House, 1990.

Panati, Charles. *Panati's Extraordinary Endings of Practically Everything and Everybody.* New York: Harper & Row, Perennial Library, 1989.

Parkes, Colin Murray. *Bereavement: Studies of Grief in Adult Life*. 2nd ed. Harmondsworth, England: Penguin Books, 1987.

Perry, Gail, and Jill Perry, eds. *A Rumor of Angels*. New York: Ballantine Books, 1989.

Petersen, Sheila. *"A Special Way to Care": A Guide for Neighbors, Friends and Community in Their Efforts to Provide Financial and Emotional Support for Terminally Ill and Catastrophically Ill Children*. Croton Falls, N.Y.: Friends of Karen, 1988.

Petterle, Elmo A. *Legacy of Love: How to Make Life Easier for the Ones You Leave Behind*. Bolinas, Calif.: Shelter Publications, 1986.

Phipps, William E. *Cremation Concerns*. Springfield, Ill.: Charles C Thomas, Publisher, 1989.

Pincus, Lily. *Death and the Family: The Importance of Mourning*. 1976. Reprint. London: Faber and Faber, 1988.

Plotnick, Charles K., and Stephen R. Leimberg. *The Executor's Manual: Everything You Need to Know to Handle an Estate*. New York: Doubleday, 1986.

President's Commission for the Study of Ethical Problems in Medicine and Biomedical and Behavioral Research. *Deciding to Forgo Life-Sustaining Treatment: A Report on the Ethical, Medical, and Legal Issues in Treatment Decisions*. Washington, D.C.: Government Printing Office, 1983; reprint, New York: Concern for Dying, 1983.

Prunkl, Peter R., and Rebecca L. Berry. *Death Week: Exploring the Dying Process*. Series in Death Education, Aging, and Health Care. New York: Taylor & Francis Group, Hemisphere Publishing, 1989.

Radner, Gilda. *It's Always Something*. New York: Simon and Schuster, 1989.

Raffin, Thomas A., M.D., Joel N. Shurkin, and Wharton Sinkler III, M.D. *Intensive Care: Facing the Critical Choices*. New York: W. H. Freeman, 1989.

Rando, Therese A. *Grief, Dying, and Death: Clinical Interventions for Caregivers*. Champaign, Ill.: Research Press, 1984.

———. *Grieving: How to Go On Living When Someone You Love Dies*. Lexington, Mass.: Lexington Books, 1988.

Raphael, Beverley. *The Anatomy of Bereavement*. New York: Basic Books, 1983.

Regan, John, J.S.D., with Legal Counsel for the Elderly. *Your Legal Rights in Later Life*. Washington, D.C.: American Association of Retired Persons; Glenview, Ill.: Scott, Foresman and Company, 1989.

Roberson, Cliff. *Avoiding Probate: Tamper-Proof Estate Planning*. Blue Ridge Summit, Penn.: Tab Books, Liberty House, 1989.

Robertson, John A. *The Rights of the Critically Ill*. Rev. ed. American Civil Liberties Union Handbooks, New York: Bantam Books, 1983.

Robin, Eugene D., M.D. *Matters of Life and Death: Risk vs. Benefits of Medical Care.* New York: W. H. Freeman, 1984.

Robinson, Rita. *Survivors of Suicide.* Santa Monica, Calif.: IBS Press, 1989.

Rofes, Eric E., and the Unit at Fayerweather Street School. *The Kids' Book About Death and Dying.* Boston: Little, Brown and Company, 1985.

Rollin, Betty. *Last Wish.* New York: Warner Books, 1986.

Rosenbaum, Ernest H., and Isadora R. Rosenbaum, eds. *"Going Home": A Home-Care Program.* Palo Alto, Calif.: Bull Publishing, 1980.

Rosenberg, Charles E. *The Care of Strangers: The Rise of America's Hospital System.* New York: Basic Books, 1987.

Sager, Mark A., et al. "Changes in the Location of Death After Passage of Medicare's Prospective Payment System." *New England Journal of Medicine* 320 (16 February 1989):433–39.

Saunders, Cicely, and Mary Baines. *Living with Dying: The Management of Terminal Disease.* 2nd ed. Oxford and New York: Oxford University Press, 1989.

Schneidman, Edwin. *Voices of Death: Letters, Diaries, and Other Personal Documents from People Facing Death That Provide Comforting Guidance for Each of Us.* New York: Bantam Books, 1982.

Schreiber, Le Anne. *Midstream.* New York: Viking, 1990.

Schwartz, Robert J. *Write Your Own Will.* Rev. ed. New York: Macmillan, Collier Books, 1986.

Scitovsky, Anne A. "The High Cost of Dying: What Do the Data Show?" *Milbank Memorial Fund Quarterly/Health and Society* 62 (1984):591–608.

———, and A. M. Capron. "Medical Care at the End of Life: The Interaction of Economics and Ethics." *Annual Review of Public Health* 7 (1986):59–75.

Scully, Thomas, M.D., and Celia Scully. *Making Medical Decisions: How to Make Difficult Medical and Ethical Choices for Yourself and Your Family;* originally published as *Playing God: The New World of Medical Choices.* New York: Simon & Schuster, Fireside Books, 1989.

Sheehy, Patrick Francis, M.D. *On Dying with Dignity.* New York: Pinnacle Books, 1981.

Shelp, Earl E. *Born to Die? Deciding the Fate of Critically Ill Newborns.* New York: Free Press, 1986.

Silverstone, Barbara, and Helen Kandel Hyman. *You and Your Aging Parent: A Family Guide to Emotional, Physical, & Financial Problems.* 3rd ed. New York: Pantheon Books, 1989.

Simpson, Michael A. *Dying, Death, and Grief: A Critical Bibliography.* Pittsburgh, Penn.: University of Pittsburgh Press, 1987.

Singer, Lilly, Margaret Sirot, and Susan Rodd. *Beyond Loss: A Practical Guide Through Grief to a Meaningful Life.* New York: E. P. Dutton, 1988.

Siverd, Bonnie. *Count Your Change: A Woman's Guide to Sudden Financial Change.* New York: Arbor House, 1983.

Sloane, Irving J. *The Right to Die: Legal and Ethical Problems.* Legal Almanac Series, no. 90. New York: Oceana Publications, 1988.

Society for the Right to Die. *Handbook of Living Will Laws.* 1987 ed. New York: Society for the Right to Die, 1987.

Soled, Alex J. *The Essential Guide to Wills, Estates, Trusts, and Death Taxes.* Updated and expanded ed. Washington, D.C.: American Association of Retired Persons; Glenview, Ill.: Scott, Foresman and Co., AARP Books, 1988.

Sontag, Susan. *AIDS and Its Metaphors.* New York: Farrar, Straus & Giroux, 1989.

―――. *Illness as Metaphor.* New York: Farrar, Straus & Giroux, 1978.

Specter, Michael. "Hot Tombs, The Last Yuppie Status Symbol." *New Republic,* 11 September 1989, p. 25.

Spiegel, Allen D. *Home Health Care: Home Birthing to Terminal Care.* Owings Mills, Md.: National Health Publishing, 1983.

Spilling, Roy, ed. *Terminal Care at Home.* General Practice Series, no. 10. Oxford and New York: Oxford University Press, 1986.

Sri Chinmoy. *Death and Reincarnation.* New York: Agni Press, 1974.

Starr, Paul. *The Social Transformation of American Medicine.* New York: Basic Books, 1982.

Staudacher, Carol. *Beyond Grief: A Guide for Recovering from the Death of a Loved One.* Oakland, Calif.: New Harbinger Publications, 1987.

Stedeford, Averil. *Facing Death: Patients, Families and Professionals.* London: Heinemann Medical Books, 1984.

Stillion, Judith M., Eugene E. McDowell, and Jacque H. May. *Suicide Across the Life Span: Premature Exits.* Series in Death Education, Aging, and Health Care. New York: Hemisphere, 1989.

Stock, Barbara R. *It's Easy to Avoid Probate.* Updated ed. Orlando, Fla.: Linch Publishing, 1985.

Stoddard, Sandol. *The Hospice Movement: A Better Way of Caring for the Dying.* Briarcliff Manor, N.Y.: Stein and Day, 1978.

Swerdlow, Joel L. *Matching Needs, Saving Lives: Building a Comprehensive Network for Transplantation and Biomedical Research: A Report on Policy Options.* Washington, D.C.: Annenberg Washington Program, 1989.

Thomas, Lewis. *The Lives of a Cell: Notes of a Biology Watcher.* New York: Bantam Books, 1975.

Upson, Norma S. *When Someone You Love Is Dying.* New York: Simon & Schuster, Fireside Books, 1986.

Van Bommel, Harry. *Choices: For People Who Have a Terminal Illness, Their Families and Caregivers.* Toronto: NC Press Limited, 1986; distributed in U.S. by Seven Hills Book Distributors.

Veatch, Robert M. *Death, Dying and the Biological Revolution: Our Last Quest for Responsibility.* Rev. ed. New Haven: Yale University Press, 1989.

Viorst, Judith. *Necessary Losses: The Loves, Illusions, Dependencies and Impossible Expectations That All of Us Have to Give Up in Order to Grow.* New York: Fawcett Gold Medal, 1987.

Walker, Alice. *To Hell with Dying.* New York: Harcourt Brace Jovanovich, 1988.

Walton, Douglas N. *Ethics of Withdrawal of Life-Support Systems: Case Studies in Decision Making in Intensive Care.* New York: Praeger, 1987, text ed.

Wanzer, Sidney H., et al. "The Physician's Responsibility Toward Hopelessly Ill Patients." *New England Journal of Medicine* 320 (30 March 1989):844.

Wass, Hannelore, Felix M. Berardo, and Robert Neimeyer, eds. *Dying: Facing the Facts.* 2nd ed. Series in Death Education, Aging, and Health Care. Washington, D.C.: Harper & Row, Hemisphere Publishing, 1988.

Wass, Hannelore, and Charles A. Corr. *Childhood and Death.* Series in Death Education, Aging, and Health Care. Washington, D.C.: Harper & Row, Hemisphere Publishing, 1984.

Wass, Hannelore, Charles A. Corr, Richard A. Pacholski, and Cameron S. Forfar. *Death Education II: An Annotated Resource Guide.* Series in Death Education, Aging, and Health Care. Washington, D.C.: Harper & Row, Hemisphere Publishing, 1985.

Watts, Tim J. *The Funeral Industry: Regulating the Disposition of the Dead.* Public Administration Series, no. P-2454. Monticello, Ill.: Vance Bibliographies, 1988.

Weir, Robert F. *Abating Treatment with Critically Ill Patients: Ethical Limits to the Medical Prolongation of Life.* Oxford and New York: Oxford University Press, 1989.

————, ed. *Ethical Issues in Death and Dying.* 2nd ed. New York: Columbia University Press, 1986.

Whitaker, Agnes, ed. *All in the End Is Harvest: An Anthology for Those Who Grieve.* London: Darton, Longman & Todd, 1988.

White, Paula. *Home Care of the Hospice Patient: An Information/Instructional Booklet for Caregivers in the Home.* Norwalk, Conn.: Purdue Frederick Company, 1986.

Widowed Persons Service. *WPS Directory of Services for the Widowed in the United States and Canada.* 1988–89 ed. Washington, D.C.: Widowed Persons Services, 1988.

Willson, Martin. *Rebirth and the Western Buddhist.* London: Wisdom Publications, 1987.

Winslade, William J., and Judith Wilson Ross. *Choosing Life or Death: A*

Guide for Patients, Families, and Professionals. New York: Macmillan, Free Press, 1986.

Zimecki, Michael. "Filling Out the Last Form, The Bureaucrat at Death's Door." *Harper's,* October 1988, p. 50.

Zimmerman, Jack M., M.D. *Hospice: Complete Care for the Terminally Ill.* 2nd ed. Baltimore, Md.: Urban and Schwartzberg, 1986.

Index

Buckman, Robert, 24
Burial, 37–44, 203, 209–10
  aboveground, 40–41, 44, 210
  of ashes, 46–47, 212
  buying a plot for, 38–40
  coffins and caskets for, 41–42
  committal service before, 61
  cost of, 44
  direct, 49
  grave liner or vault for, 40, 44, 209
  headstones and statuary for, 42–43, 210
  home, 41, 223
  transporting body long distance for, 215–16

Callahan, Daniel, 129
Caplan, Arthur, 124–25
Cardiopulmonary resuscitation (CPR), 88–89, 106–7
Carlson, Lisa, 56, 64, 221
Caskets, 41–42, 44, 207–8
Cellular death, 127
Cemetery plot, 38–40, 44, 209–10
  burying ashes in, 46
Children
  grief after death of, 264–65
  grieving by, 266–67
  guardian for, 6, 239–40
  home care for, 163
  hospice for, 188–89
  hospital care for, 146–47
  life-support cessation for, 114–16
Children's Hospice International (CHI), 180, 189
Clifford, Denis, 9–11, 13, 85, 242–43
Clinical death, 127
Codicils, 19
  revoking, 20
Coffins, *see* Caskets
College of American Pathologists, 214
Columbaria, 47
Coma, 104, 114, 126

Commemoration, 32–36, 59–72, 217–19
  memorial societies and, 68–69
  See also Funerals
Committal services, 61, 203, 217, 218
Compassionate Friends, 265
Computer software for will, 21
Concern for Dying, 86–87, 90, 112
Connecticut Hospice, Inc., 179
Consumer Reports, 33, 64, 70
Consumers Union, 35
Continental Association of Funeral and Memorial Societies (CAFMS), 48–49, 53, 68–70
Credit cards, 251
  insurance on, 248
Cremation, 45–47, 203, 210–12
  committal service before, 61
  direct, 48–49
Cremation Association of North America (CANA), 34
Crichton, Jean, 157, 160
Cruzan, Nancy, 79
Cryonics, 56–59
Cryonics Institute, 56
Culbertson, Judi, 42–43
Curry, Hayden, 85

Dacey, Norman F., 16
Dailey, Ann Armstrong, 188–89
Davidson, Glen W., 186
Death, determination of, 125–27
Death benefits, 236, 246–50
Death certificates, 233–35
  funeral directors and, 236
Death notices, 231–32
Debts of estate, 244, 245, 251
Delta Airlines, 216
DeSpelder, Lynne, 158
Determination of death, 125–27
Direct disposition, 47–49, 203, 204
Disposition, 32–59, 202–5
  anatomical gifts and, 49–54
  burial, 37–44, 209–10
  cremation, 45–47, 210–12

for children, 114–16
dealing with uncertainty about, 118
Do Not Resuscitate order and, 106–7
ethics committees and, 111–12
laws on, 112–14
and monetary costs of treatment, 80–81, 116–17
ordinary and extraordinary measures, 109–10
patient's wishes and, 105–6
settings and circumstances of, 103–4
standard procedures and, 108–9
who makes decision on, 102–3
Lightner, Candy, 64, 218
Living Bank, The, 53
Living will, 19, 81, 82, 85–86, 102
laws on, 84
revocation of, 87
See also Advance directives
Long-distance transporting of body, 215–16

Mandelbaum, D. G., 59, 60
Martelli, Leonard J., 24
Mausoleum, 40–41, 44, 210
Maxwell, Katie, 233, 249
Mechanical breathing, 89
Medicaid, 117, 160, 167, 180, 189–91
Medical costs
for dying, 133–35
for home care, 167–68
for hospice programs, 189–91
for hospital care, 154–55
life-support cessation and, 80–81, 116–17
for nursing home care, 159–61
Medical durable power of attorney, *see* Durable power of attorney
Medic Alert, 53
Medicare, 116–17, 155, 160, 167, 180, 189–91
Memorial Cremation Society, 48
Memorial parks, 210
Memorial services, 61, 63–64, 203, 205, 217, 218
Memorial societies, 68–69, 204–5

Memorial Society Association of Canada (MSAC), 68
Mercy killing, 130
Miscarriage, grief after, 265
Mitford, Jessica, 39, 65, 68
Monroe, Marilyn, 44
Monuments, 42–43, 210
Mor, Vincent, 178
Morgan, Ernest, 60–61, 64, 167–68, 203, 218, 223, 250
Mortgage insurance, 248
Mortuaries, 205
Mummification, 59
Munley, Anne, 181

Nassif, Janet Zhun, 164–65
National Academy of Sciences, 107
National Association for Home Care, 167
National Association of Widowed People, 264
National Citizens' Coalition for Nursing Home Reform, 160–61
National Consumers League, 165
National Council on Death and Dying, 86
National Funeral Directors Association (NFDA), 34, 55
National Hospice Organization (NHO), 165, 177, 179, 180, 184, 191
National Institute for Jewish Hospice, 180
National Kidney Foundation, 53
National League for Nursing, 165
National SIDS Foundation, 266
Nelson, Thomas C., 40
Neonatal intensive care, 115–16
Neptune Society, 48, 69, 204
New England Journal of Medicine, 155
Newspaper announcements and obituaries, 231–32
Next of kin, 5
Notification, 230–33
by funeral directors, 235–36
Nursing homes, 156–61
advance directives and, 158–59